My Ancillary Life

A Chess Game

By Whip Rawlings

*I*t was April 11th 2004,

I returned to Indianapolis Indiana to retrieve some clothes from my daughter's house that I left there during my last trip. I made a point to visit my oldest sister and my father. My sister Sherry was plagued by lupus, a crippling decease and my father was a sickly man with one foot in the grave, he survived two triple heart bypass surgeries and a stroke.

I have not seen or talked to him in five years, and this was the first time I purposely sat down to have a meaningful conversation with him during my life time. I felt a need to have closure even if it meant I had to forgive him. My father was uneducated and ignorant. I guess his ignorance and low self-esteem kept him from progressing beyond the sixth grade, he didn't care about anything or anyone around him, not even himself. His physical health was rapidly deteriorating as a result of no physical activity and his unhealthy eating habits. He had every aging physiological failure known to man, diabetes, high blood pressure, congestive heart failure, and other aging ailments not yet discovered. My Father grew up in a lower social economic class, and the only positive role models he had was farmers or general laborers, he felt that being a gangster was his only way out of poverty.

My father was a short, stocky, strong man. His shoulders favor that of a football player and his thighs were big like a professional wrestler. By the time he was 50 he had just about wither down to nothing, his broad shoulders sagged down like wet sponges. His muscular thighs were that of shaved chicken legs. His cast-iron frame was just a weaker shell of the person he once was. His eating habits were very poor, his daily meal consisted of pig feet and a bowl of cornflakes with extra sugar. His eating habits was pushing him towards a grave quick, fast and in a hurry. I did not know if I would get another chance to hear him say

"I'm sorry for not being a father to you."

I knew I had to see him before I returned to Sacramento. I asked my mother if she knew my father's address and phone number. She abruptly sprang from her chair and dashed up the stairs to her bedroom, where she dug through a stack of miscellaneous papers, she returned one minute later and handed me his address. I jumped into my rental car then drove west on 10th St. across the once grand metal bridge that stood over White River.

I pulled slowly up to the front of the house, I sat in the car and pondered about what I was going to say to him and how I was going to approach the situation. Violent visions ran rapidly through my mind. I had thoughts of kicking in the door, bum rushing him, forcing him to the floor, forcing him to apologize for disappearing for 18 years of my childhood. I wanted to make him pay for being an absentee father, I didn't want money, I needed a coup de grace. I spent many years in the military and was trained how to hurt and kill people but it wasn't in my heart to hurt anyone, even someone who purposely abandoned me during my greatest time of need during the most impressionable time of my life. But the thought of attacking him was inescapable in my mind.

After running the thought of extirpating him back and forth through my mind for several more minutes, I stepped out of my car assured. I walked up his driveway then towards the side door entrance. As I approached the door I noticed my father walking past the door, taking short choppy steps as though he just had another stroke. He looked very weak and disheveled, with an unwashed T-shirt, homemade cutoff shorts and a worn out pair of slippers.

He slowly walked as he dragged his feet carrying his dishes to the sink, this was the moment I'd held in my murky subconscious for 42 years, and this is the moment I rehearsed in waking hours of my restless nights. I slowly walked up to door, prowling like a tiger about to pounce on fresh meat, I snatched the screen door open and quickly stepped into the kitchen catching him completely off guard. I looked at him with a stern look and said.

"What's my name?"

He replied "Mikey".

I was totally amazed, even in his weak condition, for the first time in 30 years he had gotten my name right. He usually called me Denton, my brothers name and I spent the first 30 years of my life correcting him.

The fact that he actually got my name right for the first time in the history of my life helped to deflate the anger I was ready to unleash on him. "I need to talk to you about something, about my childhood and what I went through because you decided not to be a part of my life," Instead I sat patiently waiting to hear those words (I'm sorry son) but he never uttered a word, he didn't even provide an explanation for his being an absentee parent.

He could barely talk or acknowledge anything I said, the stroke left his voice impaired, and his once strong cast iron frame was now just a shell of a man I once knew. I told my father of the hard times I had growing up without his financial and physical support. How I used card board to line the bottom of my shoes to keep snow from entering the holes on the soles of my shoes. And how I kept his birthday card I couldn't send to him because I never knew where he lived. Tears fell from his eyes as I recounted my economical dilemmas enhanced by his absence. But I soon realized that his tears were from his sickness and not from listening to my past cries for fatherly love.

I explained to my father I was only three years old when he was arrested. I described everything he wore as he sat in the back of the police car handcuffed. He wore a London fog trench coat and a black fedora hat. I was only a toddler but the incident was so emotionally traumatic it burnt an impression in my mind that I would carry the rest of my life. "Come on, I want to show you something" he said, As he lead me into his bedroom I realized that his life has come to this, a rented room with torn curtains, a broken down bed, shoved in the corner without a frame, lying squarely on the floor, an empty safe where he kept his life possessions. A watch of little value, a seven diamond cluster ring and a news articles of himself in the back seat of a police car being arrested after an unsuccessful bank heist.   My father was sixty-seven years old and his only claim to fame was a foiled Bank robbery.

I don't expect or want anything from him other an apology and a chance to forgive him. He played his best hand in life and by doing so he played himself. After waiting forty-four years hearing my father say, "Son, I am sorry" was no longer necessary, his life circumstance apologized for his uncaring, thoughtless, selfish behavior. Although I am not extremely pleased with the downward spiral of my father's life. I wish he had been more an auspicious part of my life. Our two hour bonding session had come to an abrupt end but before I left I asked for a hug, this would be my first hug from my father in forty four years, and then I said,

"Dad I forgive you for what happened in our past".

At that very moment I felt the tension in my shoulders loosen, my shoulders slumped down to a relaxed position, it felt as if 100 pounds of hate, that had been haunting my soul for more then 40 years, released and I instantly felt revised. I closed this chapter of hate in my life, and opened a chapter of forgiveness for my dad. I returned to my mother's house and sat on the front porch recounting my pass childhood experiences.

I was born on a cold windy December morning in 1959 at 4 AM. It was the year of the pig, the temperature high for the year was 50° and the low was 39°. Sam the rhesus monkey was launched into space from Wallops Island Virginia. The Barbie doll goes on sale, debut 8 million sold. The first weather satellite was launched. US president Dwight Eisenhower signed Hawaii in the statehood. The Dalai Lama fled China and was granted political asylum in India. Cuba invaded Panama. Benjamin O. Davis Jr became the first black Major General in the US Air Force. America's new 49 star flag honoring Alaska statehood unfurled. The Lincoln Memorial design on the US penny went into circulation. The total snowfall for the year was 5.20 inches.

I was blessed with a long-term memory that stretches back more than 55 years. In 1962 my mother repetitiously dressed me in a blue sailor suit. I can recall when my brother Dale died in 1962, and a year later my little sister was born in 1963. I can recall my grandfather's tall lanky 6'3 thinner then a rail frame. His head was covered with grey straight hair and the smell of his pipe reeked throughout the house. I recall the times I watched him shave with a straight razor and the day he killed his Rooster with an axe because the Rooster chased my sister around the yard and pecked her on the leg. I was born into the world of life without a compass. I landed on my destination of being born a mischievous kid, thrust down the river of a life of excitement and uncertainty without a paddle.

My mother always said I was different from the rest of my siblings. That I wasn't afraid to try new things and I enjoyed life to the fullest. By the time I arrived on the scene my mother had already given birth to five other children. She was a young 23-year-old girl, with a husband who couldn't seem to get his life together. My father was a hard worker I guess, sometimes I think the pressure of having another child was too much for him to contemplate. My mother was six months pregnant with me the day she decided to laid around the house and have a little time to herself.

She laid idling on the bed reading a newspaper and out of nowhere my father came flying through the air diving on the bed barely missing my mother's stomach. She rolled quickly out of his way before he could splash down on top of her. I would have been sent back to the ages if my mother hadn't roll over to one side preventing him from landing forcefully on her stomach ending my embryonic life. Although I don't have many good memories of my father or my early child hood, I was a very conscious child early in my life. Conscious enough to remember the first few years of my life seemed cold and empty.

I believe a difficult childhood makes for a really conscious child.

I must have been overly conscious, I remember everything, I remembered my mother often dressing me up in a blue sailor suit because she thought it was cute. I could remember my father and mother not being at home very often. I don't remember my father picking me up or talking to me or hugging me. I only remember how distant I was from him, how cold and disengaged I was from the father son relationship. My father was far from being Andy Griffin, and my family is far from being a middle class nuclear family. Any one of my siblings could testify to how very little hugs or affection we received, mostly because I was the sixth child and got lost somewhere in the shuffle.

We were a family of six with one on the way. We had little money and our clothes and meals were statements of poverty not yet written. My life took off as if it was a pre-written story. The early drama I experience helped aide in the development of my long term memory. I was three and a half years of age when my first official accident occurred. What I mean by official, the incident was officially recorded as a medical and legal document. My mother was out shopping late one evening, I wasn't sure of her where abouts but that didn't deter me from taking full advantage of her absence, so I took the liberty of using her bed as a trampoline to play cowboys and Indians. My sisters didn't seem to care what I did as long as I didn't interrupt their routine of watching their favor programs on one of the three TV channels. Aluminum foil wrapped around the antenna and wire stretching to the window trying to pick up a reception.

"Another cowboy and Indian movie" I thought to myself, It seemed to me the Cowboys always win in the movies and since I had 1% Chippewa Indian blood in me I was sure to make the Indians win this battle.

I began franticly jumping up and down on the bed while my siblings desperately tried to watch TV. Sherry would reach back and slap me on the leg as many times as it took to get me to quit jumping up and down, they stopped watching TV long enough to quiet me down by placing their hands over my mouth. Soon they over powered me by sitting on my back and my legs. I pretended I was hurt for a second and being the soft hearted girls that they are they felt empathy for me and quickly jumped off my back and freed my legs. I laid on the bed idle for several minutes, but as soon as they were back watching their program, I returned to my jumping exhibition.

I decided an Indian ccouldn't possibly fight Cowboys without a weapon so I leaped from the bed losing my footing and almost knocking the TV off the cart. I ran to the kitchen, scrambled through a few drawers and grabbed my weapon of choice. I looked admiringly at a fork and said.

"Those Cowboys are in for it now".

Back to the bedroom I ran, crawling over my sisters to get back to the imaginary battlefield. I was submerge deep into my fighting scene when I jumped too high in the air. My feet must have been 5 feet above the bed. I began falling uncontrollably. As I landed, I totally missed the bed thereby landing on the floor.

The metal points on the fork were sticking straight in the air and drove their way deep into my right eyebrow stopping only after the entire fork was embedded in my head. As I laid motionless on the floor, my oldest sister Sherry said.

"Ha ha, see what you get".

She wasn't yet aware of the trouble I was in. She thought I had just fell off the bed and bumped my head but I lay lifeless, pools of blood begin to run from my forehead profusely until the blood touch my sister Tinana's finger. Tinana screamed.

"Mikey is bleeding"

Sherry jumped to her feet screaming and crying for someone to call for help, Sherry's panic caused my other sisters to panic. It was total chaos, my face was saturated with blood, and I could see feet running back and forth while blood slowly blurred my vision.

Sherry kneeled down beside me trying her best to comfort me by patting me on the back and crying out loud.

"Someone please get help!"

I could no longer see past the blood streaming down my face but I could feel the uncertainly and the fear coming from my sisters pulsating hand gripping my arm. I began to slowly go into an unconscious state of mind, and eventually I blacked out. I was awakened by pressure being placed on my forehead by a tall white men wearing a white uniform with broad shoulders. He tried desperately to remove the fork from my head. The more he pulled on the fork, the more I kicked, yelled and screamed bloody hell for him to stop pulling. After three minutes of trying to remove the fork he couldn't take it anymore, he gave into my whining and screaming.

He said, "Lets go, they will have to remove the fork at the hospital".

Placing me on the guerney they pushed me down the steps toward the ambulance. He reassured me as I was shoved into an old ambulance that resembled a funeral hearse. I was taken to Wishard Memorial Hospital replace my mother gave birth to me and it just so happens the hospital was less than three miles from my grandparents house. The siren screamed as the red lights illuminated the ground 10 feet in front and 5 feet on either side causing cars to move to one side of the road just for me. I arrived at the hospital in a delirious state. I was rushed immediately into the operating room then strapped down on the table. A heavyset African-American woman pushed a silver tray next to my bed, displaying small gold hooks and syringes filled with a liquid substance, capped off with long dual needles.

I couldn't believe what my eyes were seeing. The needles were as long as my arm. I recognized the hooks from my uncle George's bait and tackle box but I had no clue as to why the needles were there.   A tall white gentleman wearing a long white coat stretching down to his knees entered the room.   He gently palpated the orbital rim of my eye, I screamed bloody hell as he touched and applied pressure with his oversized fingers. I screamed and kicked until my mother and father were summoned into the operating room. My mother did her best trying to hold my arms and my father held my legs down until they tightened up the loosely fitting bed straps over my legs.

 The doctor removed one of the long needles filled with a clear liquid substance from the cart. He didn't hesitate shoving the needle right into my eyebrow. I was so traumatized by the event I squirmed free from under the bed straps then slapped the needle from the doctor's hand.

"Hold his legs and arms down tight!" the doctor yelled.

He repositioned and re-insert the needle. Just as I was fading asleep a grey square shaped cloth that resembles the cover of a 45 record with a hole in the middle was placed over my eye partially blocking my view of the tray on the left side of the bed filled with needles, hooks and thread. I just knew this wasn't for me, someone must have left it there by accident or forgot it and they would be back soon to claim it.

That never happened, once again the man in the white coat approached the left side of my bed holding the needle in the air, tiny drops of fluid leaked for the tip and that was the last thing I remember before going to sleep.   My mother was standing beside my hospital bed when I awoke; tears pierced her eyes as she looked at me shaking her head in disbelief. My father sat in the corner with his lips poked out and a swollen face as though he had been in a fight. The car ride home was anything but joyous. I sat in the front seat of the passenger side of the car wrapped in my mother's arms, my father was silent the entire trip, but if looks could kill, his look were so hard and so cold my sensitive side took over and I began to cry. After I arrived home my sisters were glad to see me, it was not long before they begin teasing me and making jokes about my accident. Time passed and I watch my family regroup and return to our drama free lifestyle.

Three weeks had passed since the fork accident, my life returned to some sense of normalcy, boring mornings, watching my brothers and sisters get ready for school. My sister Sherry skipped school that morning because she was fighting the flu. Any other day my feisty behavior would be more than Sherry could handle, but due to the medication I was taking it left me groggy and off balance, cutting my energy level in half, making me a dull normal child. The house was empty and cold as though no one had ever lived there, with every step I could hear my footsteps echo down the empty hallway. Suddenly there was a loud bang at the back door. I wasn't allowed to answer the door, so I yelled for my big sister Sherry. The banging on the door intensified.

Sherry griped, moaned, groaned and complained as she climbed from her bed, placing her feet on the cold hardwood floor, she made her way to the kitchen door. I peaked around the corner and I could see the fear in Sherry's eyes as she slowly approached the backdoor. As I stood there I observe a tall white male wearing a blue suit with many Silver buttons lined down the front of his jacket flanked by a metal badge on his chest and hat.

He instructed Sherry to open the door, she nodded her head no.

She said, "I'm not allowed to open the door for strangers".

The police then instructed her to back away from the door, just as she moved away from the door. I ran toward the door dragging a chair behind me. I placed the chair at the door trying to get a view of what was going on, just as the policeman was about to crash through the door, he looked up and saw me peeking through window.

He came to a screeching halt smacking his shoulder against the frame of the door then yelling.

"Pull that kid out of the way".

Just as Sherry reached up and grabbed me by the arm, pulling me from the chair the door exploded as if a bomb had gone off. Glass and broken wood flew past my freshly bandage eye. I broke free from my sister's grip and ran upstairs to search for my weapon. I made a quick search underneath the bed where I last saw my fork; the fork was nowhere to be found. So, I opened my dresser drawer, digging frantically under a combination of mixed socks. I didn't find my fork but I found something more powerful. Something that will give me total control over the entire situation. I found my Superman ring at the bottom of a half eaten bag of Chesty potato chips.

I was in luck. I knew I could power up by placing the ring on my finger and holding it high in the air. I could fight these villains. So I hid behind the door waiting for the first sign of a blue suit lined with silver buttons. I could hear heavy footsteps approaching at a rapid pace from a distance in the hallway. By this time I was fully powered up and ready to save the day, as I've seen so many times on Batman and Robin. As the officer turned the corner. I sprung from behind the door grabbing onto the officer's leg. I tried lifting him in the air. Surprisingly, my feet began to take flight as though I was actually flying. By the time I was in mid-flight, I realized I was being held by the back of my shirt in midair. The officer looked at me while gasping for air. His gun was in his left hand with his finger wrapped around the trigger.

He stumbled and fell back against the wall still holding me in midair. He had a look in his eyes that was very familiar, it was the same look my father had given me only a week earlier while in the hospital. The officer lowered me to my feet and said.

"Don't ever do that again, you could've gotten hurt".

But once again I broke free from his clutches and sprinted down the wooden steps, dashing towards the front door. I could see my sister's and my mother standing on the front porch, the men in the blue suit walked quickly past me out to his car with one red light flashing on the top of the car as it turned in a circle. There was someone sitting restlessly in the backseat of the police car with their hands bound behind them. I wanted to get a closer look, because maybe it was one of the villains I fight every day after I power up with my Superman ring.

I scurried closer to the car for a better view of the villain. The person became more recognizable the closer I got. He slowly turned his head towards me then stared straight into my eyes. I stumbled back and fell in the snow, my heart was beating like a rabbit being chased by a fox. It was my father! Still wearing the same trench coat and fedora hat he was wearing as he left for work this morning. I didn't understand, so I reach for the door handle of the car and pulled the door until it was slightly ajar. Before I knew it I was flung to the ground.

My mother yelled out frantically from the porch.

"Keep your damn hands off my son!"

My hand hit the ground so hard it shattered my plastic Superman ring. I was powerless. I didn't know what else to do. The officer slammed the door shut yelling.

" Stay away from the car and move back!"

I didn't know what else do I reached around my mother to get one more look. I stood so close to the car with my face pressed against the glass until it began to fog up, I drew a smiling face on the window just before the car drove off. My mother and I stood there watching the patrol car as it turned the corner, and within seconds my father disappeared and I would not see him for another three years.

My father was on his way to prison for robbing a bank. This bright ideal of my father and his brothers left my mother alone to take care of six children, with one bun in the oven. My mother was unemployed prior to my father's incarceration. He left her penniless, powerless and unable to pay the rent.

Three weeks had passed and we found ourselves facing a new challenge. 'Rent' was due and our support system was on his way to a federal prison for three to six years. Our furniture was tossed out onto the snow covered front yard and the doors were locked behind us. Tiana and I bundle up together trying to stay warm on a slightly damped snow covered couch. I was only three and a half years of age but I was no stranger to recognizing pain and uncertainty on my mother's face, she wanted to cry but she fought back her tears sparing us any discomfort and freeing us from worry.

$\mathcal{V}$alley Avenue

We moved less than a half mile down the street to my fathers grandmother's double. A cozy little green double with a concrete wall separating the front porchs. There was one small problem, a tall strange looking black man was going from window to window looking inside our house. I've never seen this fool before and I had no way of defending myself. My Superman ring was broke and my weapon I used to fight the Cowboys with was placed out of my reach. This strange man wore a Dockers men's ear flap hat, also known as Elmer FUD hat, he also wore a checkered hunting jacket and black rubber snow boots that he never buckled up. Mother told us he's no one to fear, this is your uncle Robbie. Robbie was tall and slim, with huge lips flopping around like two uncooked pieces of baloney. Lips that only a mother could love. My father never spoke of Robbie because Robbie was mentally challenged which made him a source of embarrassment for my father.

I don't recall too much about this house other than it had huge sunflowers and Venus fly traps as tall as my grandfather in the backyard. I wasted no time testing the reflexes of the fly traps. I poked and prodded until my grandmother told me that the fly traps could eat me whenever they wanted too. I don't know if I believed what she said was true or not. What I did know is I didn't have my power ring and I wasn't going to test that theory until I could power up again. Robbie was mentally challenged, but, I felt safe around him; he patrolled inside and outside the house several times a day, including late into the night. I would catch him peeking through my bedroom window scaring us half to death. After several weeks we got use his antics and he just became another part of the landscape. He was very tender hearted and sensitive but very strong inside. He reminded me of the man that saved the little boy and girl in the movie To Kill a Mocking-bird. He was a reclusive person. He never spoke, he only observed from a distance and acted as a protector of the house. I could tell that he loved us, although being mentally undeveloped he was unable to express his emotions clearly. The months hurried by, the spring turned into summer the summer to fall, time wasn't waiting for anyone neither was my unborn baby-sitter Denise, because she was pushing hard and overly eager to enter the New racially charging world.

$\mathcal{S}$cheffield Street

My mother was very fortunate in some aspects of her life. She had a macro support system including two living parents and five sisters. Her parents didn't have much mon-ey, the only help she would get from her parents was their much needed love and the succor she needed for the moment. During her visit to the hospital they offered to tend to our needs while she delivered my little sister. We packed our bags and piled into my aunt's 1963 Buick Oldsmobile.

The car was brand-new, and despite having an adult son whom lived independent of her household, nevertheless she felt compelled to have plastic perfectly tailored to the car seats. We were fortunate that the ride was less than 20 minutes, because on a hot day you could dehydrate if you rode more than 30 minutes inside of that sauna on wheels. My grandparents lived in a small white turn-of-the-century clapboard house with Ionic style design on the front. The small Ft 800.² home didn't even have a bathroom. The toilet was located in the backyard just like in the western movies, and we took baths in a large metal tub placed in the center of the kitchen floor. I loved my grandparents but I could only deal with them three hours at a time, not for an entire week. We've never stayed with them in the past and they weren't aware of my physical shortcomings once I fell into a deep sleep.

They've never experienced the nocturnal monster (bed wetting) in their house and I didn't know how they would react once they saw the nocturnal monster occupy forbidden territory. The house was so small there was no escaping my grandparents not finding out about the nocturnal monster. The house was cramped with only two bedrooms, a front room, kitchen and a cellar in the kitchen floor. The house totally creeped me out. I could feel the presence of the prior tenants from the 1800s walking around the house in their ghostly figures. The wooden floors squeaked for no reason at all as if someone walked constantly around the house. The coterie of my family sat around the kitchen table filling the house with laughter as I sequesteed myself in the frontroom staring at the bowl of orange slice candy that permeated my every thought.

There were five of us, including my cousin Tommy and his mother, who also resided in the small house. My grandparents didn't seem to mind us moving in with them temporarily, at least they never spoke badly of us living with them out loud.   I tried to be as inconspicuous as possible, staying out of their way, trying   not to make our stay there any more difficult than it was, because I didn't want anything else bad to happen to my mother.

She has been through enough, putting up with my fathers antics and his laissez faire approach to raising kids. Her face was flushed from pain and fear but at the same time, I could see determination in her eyes. Although her parents were only able to provide minimal financial support, she wasn't alone. Her sister Dorothy provided transportation whenever she could and Dorothy's husband George occasionally dropped by to deliver a box of day-old donuts from his job at a local bakery. He often made himself feel good when he threw a hand full of coins in the air and watched us scramble around the floor gathering his loose change.

I couldn't have imagine how my mother felt, nor could I imagine the uncertainty she was feeling. How could my father make this unilateral decision without considering his children? How could he leave us in dire straits? There was a huge question hovering over my head, an empty void that I had to find someway to fill. How was she going to make it without the support of another income, without the strength of our father? How long would it take, before we wore out our welcome at our grandparent's house. While my brothers and sisters played in the front yard with our cousins I sat on the porch staring down the street in anticipation of my mother turning the corner any minute.

There I waited day in and day out. Once again I was distracted by the large glass candy bowl filled with orange slices that set centered on the front room table taunting me from a distance. The top was made of a thin metal that made a pinging sound anytime someone try to remove the top. This kept me occupied for hours on end, but once I realize I couldn't remove the candy from the bowl without getting caught, I went back onto the front porch and watched for my mother. I was hoping she would turn the corner any minute, just seeing her would make everything all right in my mind. We just lost our father, now our mother is missing in action.

I knew she was having a baby but I thought a huge bird would deliver it to our house. So I searched the sky with my eyes, looking for a huge stork with a baby hanging from its beak.

"Why are you looking at the sky for boy". My grandmother said.

"I'm looking for my little sister, isn't she going to be delivered by a large stork" I said.

With a puzzled look on my face my grandmother kissed me on the forehead, laughing to herself she walked back in the house.

I love my grandparents, especially my grandmother because she made the best baloney sandwiches on the planet. She took her time when she smeared the sandwich spread on the bread and delicately placed a piece of cheese with an unfamiliar taste right between the mayonnaise and the baloney. Then she cut the sandwich in two triangular pieces and wrapped it in wax paper. But I missed my mom because I depended on her for everything, and besides my grandmother wasn't a part of my microsystem, someone I'd depended on for life not just for an occasional great tasting bologna sandwich.

I went to bed wondering where my mother was and how she was doing. I could barely eat my dinner or hold a single thought in my head. Although I visited my grandparents many times, I still was not use to sleeping in a strange bed. The rules of their house were much different them my own home. We all had to take baths, one at a time, in a steel bathtub placed in the center of kitchen, my grandmother boiled pot after pot of hot water. It was a tedious and a never ending process. I sat quietly in the front room watching my sister's file in and out of the kitchen. While my grandmother was busy bathing my sisters I was hatching a plot to relieve her candy dish of several orange slices staring me smack in the face. I couldn't believe it. A house full of people, and I was the only one in the front room. I leaned over the coffee table and smelled the aroma of the orange slices piercing my nose.

I slowly removed the metal top from the glass candy dish, the disk let out a loud pinging sound that went unheard because of all the noise coming from the kitchen, so I removed three orange slices from the dish, wrapped them in tissue and stuffed them deep in my pants pocket. Finally after three hours of waiting to take a bath I was called into the kitchen by my grandmother.

"Take off your clothes and get into the tub" she said,

While standing by the stove boiling water. The water was so hot I thought she was trying to boil lobster.

"Don't just look at the water get in" she said,

By the end of my bath I was exhausted, the hot water put me at ease, the bed was comfortable, in fact it was the softest bed I have ever slept on. Because I was the last one to take a bath and get in the bed I had to climb over my brothers and sisters and squeeze in the middle of the bed in a very dangerous spot. If the nocturnal monster showed his ugly face there will be no escaping that disaster.

By the time I made it to bed, my brothers and sisters had all fallen asleep, sleeping head to toe in a large queen size bed. This gave me ample opportunity to devour my ill-gotten gains. I laid in the bed nibbling away at my orange slices, listening to the 100-year-old house settled for the night. These were very uncertain times and even at a young age I detested not having control over my life. However; the orange slice candy did provide a sense of comfort. I tried my best to stay awake, even holding my eyelids open up with my fingers, but the sandman got the best of me. The next morning I was awoken by panic and screaming, my sister Tiana screamed bloody hell.

"Mikey wet the bed!".

I was just as surprised as she was, I didn't know where or how the urine got their but nevertheless it was there. The nocturnal monster had paid me a visit, and I didn't even know where it came from or how to get rid of it. I just knew I was in trouble.

My grandfather was very irritated at the fact that I wet his bed and wanted to whip me with his razor strap. My grandfather was a tall, slim, fair skinned man with fine silk grey hair that displayed his Cherokee Indian heritage and his Irish roots. He was 6'3' tall, he stood towering over me with his razor strap in his right hand. I was afraid because I did not have my power ring, surprisingly my grandmother came to the rescue. She snatched the strap from him and told him to sit down. I was so ashamed and for once the brass spunky kid was nestling in a corner not wanting to show his face.

I was too embarrassed to sit at the kitchen table with everyone else so I sat in the front room and listened to the laughter echoing from the kitchen table and my sister Sherry praising the huge cornflake she found in her bowl of cereal. From this point on I was scared to death to fall asleep in their house. I tried my best not to drink water throughout the day, especially at night. This was a cardinal time in my life. I was living in some-one's house other than my own home, with strange rules and traditional family meetings at the dinner table that didn't exist in my own home. I loved my grandparents, but I didn't know them, I felt disenfranchised and out of place.

My cousin Tommy lived with my grandparents and they treated him like royalty. He had carte blanche, he could go anywhere in the Ft 800.^{2} house without limitations, including the cellar. He got to eat as much cake and candy as he wanted without anyone questioning him. I was reduced to admiring the cake from a distance but somehow I was going to have my way with that caramel cake sitting on the kitchen table freshly frosted. The cake didn't stand a chance as long as I was within a mile of it, my whole day was consumed with having a taste.

As usual after breakfast everyone ventured outside to play in the back yard. I patrolled around outside of the house, occasionally peaking in the kitchen at the caramel cake through the rusty screen fixed over the window on the side of house. My grandmother and aunt sat on the front porch having an idol conversation about church members and past buyers on the street. My siblings were preoccupied with my cousin, playing dodgeball in the back yard. This gave me the perfect opportunity to creep into the house and relieve my grandmother's cake of some of its frosting.

I looked in all directions making sure the coast was clear, then I ran my finger along the bottom of the cake trying not to be detected. I scooped up about an inch of frosting. I couldn't believe it, I was successful just like the Joker on the Batman show. I thought to myself, staring at the inch of frosting smothering my finger, the Joker would be proud of me. Just as I was about to devour the evidence. A leather strap came flying out of no where and slapped me on my butt. I was so shocked I grabbed the seat of my pants smearing icing all of my pockets." Now get your butt outside" my grandfather said, as he rolled the strap around his hand. I couldn't believe it, I almost got away with the perfect crime.

After eating dinner that evening we all sat at the kitchen table and watched as my grandmother slice the caramel cake, placing it on wax paper and handing each of us a slice. Before she could give me a piece of cake my grandfather divulged our little secret.

"Mikey had enough cake for the night" he said.

"What do you mean by that"? My grandmother asked.

My grandfather just look at me out of the corner of his eye, he took a deep breath then walked out of the kitchen.

I set at the table with tears in my eyes, watching my sisters and brother pork down their caramel cake and wash it down with a tall glass of milk. Denton purposely demonstrated how good the cake taste, by savoring every bite, as he smiled at me, and chuckling to himself then ran off into the back yard to chase Lightning bugs. Everyone else finished their cake and adjourned to the front room to watch the Ed Sullivan show. I sat idle at the kitchen table in total disappointment. Just before my tears could hit the tablecloth, my grandmother slid a huge slice of caramel cake right under my nose, twice the size of my brother and sister's cakes, with a tall glass of refreshing milk to wash it all down.

I smiled as she rubbed her fingers in my curly hair, then adjourned to the front room. It took me twice the amount of time to eat my cake as it took the others. I rubbed my belly and smiled at Denton standing outside the kitchen door staring through the glass at my huge slice of cake. I was afraid to sit at the table much longer by myself, I could see the dark green spooky house next door from the kitchen window and it gave me the creeps. The Knox family lived next door to my grandmother. They were very elderly and seemed to be twice the age of my grandparents as if they had come from the 1850s during slavery.

Mr. Knox would walk down the street with his cane in hand, he seemed to be well over a hundred but at the same time he was ambulatory. I waited till he got near the edge of the fence, then I ran from behind the bushes and barked as though I was a large dog. He playfully turned to me and said.

"I'm going to cut your ear off."

Tiana and I loved scaring Mr. Knox. It wasn't until the week before our departure that we discovered he was our great-grandfather on our father's side of the family. All of a sudden I was no longer scared of him and his wife or their dark house. I even made it my business to go over and have a casual conversation with them on their front porch. I wasn't emotionally connected to them, it was just nice to see the other side of my family.

Andy

After my mother was back on her feet we moved into our own two bedroom house located on Hillside Street. The house had a chicken coop, a barn, and a garage. The new addition to the family had arrived which meant I could push someone around. Before Denise was three she and my brother Denton went to live with my grandparents. Tiana became my best friend until she started school the following year in 1963. I was left alone with my mother and her boyfriend Andy.

Andy was not a handsome man, in fact he look like he was fresh off the boat from Africa, but he was a hard worker, a 'Hustler'. I believe that's what my mother liked about him. I found them both extremely boring to spend my day with. I rode in the back seat of his pink 1950 Buick while he handed me a large half eaten France's big boy hamburger. The sandwich was too big for me to fit in my mouth but it tasted delicious as

I nibble around the edges.

I enjoyed that hamburger but I had things I wanted to do, such as climb on the garage and walk on the railroad tracks or play inside the big empty abandoned school with rotting floorboards that sat on top of the hill behind our house. It was once believed that John Dillinger and his gang used the school for their hideout. Other than spending time with my mother and her boyfriend, I spent small periods of my time with my dog Frisky, playing in the back yard until we were both exhausted. We leaned against the back of the house. I rubbed her belly while eating a grocery bag full of green apples. I ate apple after apple until I was blue in the face.

Spending the entire morning with my mother made the day long and boring. I would find myself gazing out the window at the end of the block, hoping Tiana would soon turn the corner. She was my best friend and I could not wait to see her and here tales of her day in school. Tiana and I would spend most of our time fighting one another or making mud pies, either way we were happy just playing together. She was the bigger kid and a little crazy so I did all I could to avoid fighting with her. Tiana had a violent temper, she would often get mad and throw uncontrollable fits if things didn't go her way.

Summertime had arrived which meant Denton was packing his bags and heading back home once again. We played together well, as long as I did what he said and stayed away from him and his friends. Denton and his friends were very creative when it came to finding things to do. They pushed a large truck tire to the top of the hill. Once they stopped, they began whispering to one another, all the sudden they looked in my direction.

"Climb in" Denton said.

Once I climbed inside the tire, he shoved the tire down the steep hill right into the cross traffic. A car came to a screeching halt but not before slamming into the tire knocking me inside the tire a block and a half down the street. Denton laughed as he picked the tire up.

" You'll be okay, don't go home crying to mama like a baby" he said. While rolling the tire back up the hill.

" You wanted to hang with the big boys remember".

I made no bones about it, I Just followed him back up the hill for another run. The police arrived just as we reached the top of the hill, we dropped the tires then ran in different directions. I was the smallest, but I wasn't the slowest. Buggy was three years older than I but he was as big as a house and couldn't keep up with the rest of the group, so he just hid in the garage.

Once the police officers were out of view we thought it will be fun to climb on the stack of old tires placed along side of the garage. We invented another game called para-troopers, climbing up the tires and onto the garage, then jumping off the garage onto the stack of tires. Buggy was as slow as molasses. I could climb up on the garage, jump down, then climb back up before he could jump off the garage. I grew very impatient with his morbidly obese body. He stood at the edge of the garage teetering, trying to build up courage to jump. I couldn't take anymore, so I shoved him off the garage head first onto the tires. He slowly dragged himself from the tires holding his side, crying as if he had been hit by a freight train. Instantly he was enraged.

"I'm going to kill you" he said, holding his side chasing me around the yard.

He tried to catch me but I was just too fast. I eventually ran into the house leaving him by the garage in tears. The day turned into night, allowing the crickets to make music and the lightning bugs to beautify the night with their yellow lights. I could hear rocks bouncing off the side of the house.

" Oh boy I thought, a rock battle".

I sprang to my feet and ran right in the middle of the battle. I didn't care which side I was on, so I began throwing rocks in both directions. I didn't care who I hit or if I got hit, I just wanted to throw rocks. I wasn't good at hiding but I was good at throwing. I stuck my head around the corner to peek at my aggressors, within seconds a huge rock busted me right in the middle of my forehead. I hit the ground like a sack of potatoes, dust flying in the air as I laid on the ground lifelessly.

"I think your brother is hurt, Denton" Buddy said. As he chuckled to himself.

"That's what you get punk for pushing me off the garage".

The rock battle stopped mid stream to allow my brother to drag me into the house.
Once again I lay in the hospital with my mother sitting beside the bed waiting for me to wake up. Two weeks later I was back outside, full steam ahead, playing freeze tag in the backyard. It was getting late in the hour around 8 o'clock at night. It was so dark along the grass cover path between our houses I couldn't see my hands in front my face. Buggy jumped from the bushes scaring me half to death, I took off running like a

bat out of hell, all of a sudden I tripped and fell face down on a large brick. I didn't feel any pain, so I didn't think anything was wrong. I got up and staggered my way into the house. Tiana looked up and started yelling.

"Mikey got blood all over his face".

My mother came running from the bathroom,

" Boy you need stitches again, call Dorothy to see if she can give me a ride to the hospital".

Within two weeks time I was a bloody mess, two accidents in two weeks. My mother thought I was accident prone, and she do not buy a house near a river because she knew it would be too much temptation for me to handle.

Another year went by and I still was denied entrance in the public school. Since my birthday was in December I was forced to wait until the following year. Life wasn't all bad, after school Tiana and I picked green apples from the tree behind our garage. We'd spend hours picking bags of apples. Tiana stopped eating when she got full, I kept eating until all the apples were gone, pouring salt on top of the apples with every bite. Within three hours of eating all the green apples I had a violent reaction. I began choking on my tongue, my mother wasn't even a nurse yet but she knew what to do. She put a spoon down my throat to hold my tongue in place, allowing me to breath while transporting me to the hospital. I was put to sleep while my stomach was being pumped. I awakened to black Charcoal residue around my mouth and a bad after taste.

" Damn, I have to keep my eye on you every second" my mother said.

After the last incident she appointed my older sister 'Sherry' as my personal babysitter. I I didn't recognize her authority and never listened to anything she said. She was a pushover. Tiana and I ran around the house like wild heathens, eating all the peanut butter and jelly we could find. Sherry did her best to control us, we only quieted down when she threatened to tell our mother of our unruly and mischievous behavior. The only time I was quiet was when Tiana was in school. The rest of the day we were both hell raisers.

Tiana went to school everyday leaving a huge blank spot in my day. I was always in search of something to do. I was quickly out growing riding around in the backseat of Andy's car. I needed to be in school and Tiana wasted no time telling me horror stories about kindergarten and how scary school was. She even pointed out how big the needles were that went into our arm because every student was required to get a vaccination shot. Tiana had always been an agitator and she was proving it to the last minute. The fall has once again emerged for the fourth time in my young life. Colorful leaves lie lifelessly on the ground. Trick-or-treaters kick their way through the piles of leaves stacked in the front yard. Turkeys roasting in the oven for Thanksgiving and Christmas was just a blink of an eye away. For the first time in my life I was made to feel special on December 4. Andy called me into the bedroom, he lit four candles and had me practice blowing them out. He escorted me to the kitchen table where a large cake with my name printed right in the middle. 'Happy birthday Mikey'.

I felt so loved I almost cried. I blew the candles out and rip the box away from around my Long ranger cowboy pistols. He even gave me a horse. A horse head on a stick, that I rode around in circles kicking up dust driving my siblings crazy. Denting got so mad he grabbed the horse and tossed it into the oncoming traffic on the street. I didn't even break stride or look in any direction as I ran head first into the street chasing down my horse. Cars and trucks came to a screeching halt, smoke coming from the wheels as rubber gripped the pavment. My mother and siblings screaming from the front porch as I stood in the middle of the street wiping the dirt from my horse. I took my time mounting my horse in the traffic, then off into the sunset I rode. My birthday was just a tidbit If what Christmas would be like.

This Christmas would be much different then any other Christmas I've ever had. With my father nesting in prison, Andy took full charge of the household. He purchase two sets of bunk beds stacked three high, he pay the bills and purchased food. I thought he was a nice guy but it was all put into perspective the night he and my mother were entertaining guests. I was summonsed to go into the bedroom to get an ashtray. I was only four years old, a typical kid. Once I stepped into the bedroom and saw all those toys stacked on the bed, every square foot of the bed was covered from the foot of the bed to the headboard, up to the ceiling. It was as if I had just walked into a toy factory. I couldn't help but to examine them and before I knew it 10 minutes had gone by. Andy stepped in the bathroom.

" Were you playing with these toys boy?" Andy said.
 No, I said, I'm just trying to find an ashtray"

I stood there with a cap gun in my hand trying to explain myself. But Andy wasn't buying my excuse. He pulled the belt from around his waist, grabbing my right arm he swung his belt. I jumped in the air and he missed. I had his rhythm down perfect, every time he swung the belt I jumped in the air causing him to miss. But all of a sudden he got smart, he pretended as though he was going to swing the belt, I jumped, he waited for me to land on the ground then swatted me with the belt. I ran into the bedroom and climbed over the railing of my baby bed. I was four years old still sleeping in an infants crib because my sisters feared the nocturnal monster. Each morning my sister Marcia lifted me from the bed and placed me on the floor. Everyone had their own bed except for me. I slept where I can fit in. A few months prior I was sleeping with my mother in her bed but once Andy moved into the house I was hastily exported to my siblings bedroom.

My days were long and mentally exhausting, because I was a four-year-old with nothing to do. However; my turn did come for attending school and I was going to make sure that my mother was going to be there each and every day with me. I never been away from my mother for more than a week at a time but if I was away from her more than a week at a time I had my grandparents as a support system in her absence.

I gladly walked to school with my mother and siblings. My mother gladly escorted me to my kindergarten class and set attentively by the teacher's desk (Mrs. Collie). The classroom was filled with children that appeared to be my age. Most of the children seem to have been groomed for the first day of school, they played idly at their small round tables and appeared to be having fun. The atmosphere seemed pleasant and I couldn't wait to get started.

I sat on the floor in front of Ms. Collie's desk drawing on a blank piece of paper she handed me. As she talked to my mother, I neatly removed one crayon at a time from the box and systematically replaced it when I was done using the Crayon. Occasionally I'd stopped drawing and gazed in my mother's direction trying to get a glimpse of her. Each time I looked up my mother had moved to a different part of the room seemingly closer to the door, then eventually out of the classroom.

It was my first time being away from her, and I fell instantly to pieces, kicking, screaming, and ripping the paper in half and throwing crayons across the room, the teacher's desk was the biggest target within reach and I wasted no time in expressing my artistic ability. I hastily drew pictures on her desk, mostly scribbling unrecognizable lines as though I was a great artist, one step from cutting my ear off. I heard a little girl say.

" Look at him Mrs. Collie, he's drawing on your desk".

Not bound by any corporal punishment laws Ms. Collie snatched me up by the rear of my pants, slapping me on my butt, then scorned me for acting like a three-year-old. She ripped a large brown piece of paper from the roller hanging from the wall, tossing it on the floor in front of her desk and forced me to set in the middle of the paper, once Ms. Collie walked back towards her desk, I violently shoved the paper from under my legs and began drawing on the floor.

Ms. Collie became outraged. She exploded out of her chair, snatched me from the floor and hastily escorted me to the corner of the room where I stood for more than an hour facing the wall until it was time to take a nap.

This type of discipline was new to me. I couldn't understand why I obeyed her the first time she punished me, normally it would take me six or seven times before I got the message. Mrs. Collie ordered me to retrieve my sleeping pad from the corner and lie down. I slumped sedately toward the ground managing to avoid hitting my well bruised fanny on the linoleum floor. After an hour long nap we were given milk and gram crackers. My first year in school went by fast, I soon discoverTiana was telling the truth about getting shots and the endless stack of needles located on a cart to the right of the entryway to the nurse office. Everyone did got shots, the line stretched around the corner and down the steps. We lined up outside the nurses office, one kid more scared than the other. I could here kids screaming and crying, then walking out of the nurse's office holding their arm weeping with a little speck of blood showing through the bandage. The closer I got to the door the more anxious I got.

The line shrinked one person at a time, and finally I was next in line to go in the nurse's office. A large nurse stepped outside the door wearing white shoes, white hat and white dress. She reminded me of the ushers at my grandmother's church. She stood over me looking down, grinning like a chesire cat on Alice in Wonderland. Her huge white hand reached out to grab my arm. The back of her hand was so hairy I thought I was being grabbed by a grizzly bear, so I took off running down the hallway.

" Catch him!" she yelled.

As I scurried down the hallway and up the double wide stair case. No one could catch me, because I was running for my life. I was so fast, my sister Marica was brought from her classroom to the nurse's office to help catch me. She told me to calm down as she stood by the nurse's office blocking the door to ensure that I got my shots. Once the door opened I hesitantly walked inside the nurse's office. The walls were lined with white wood and glass cabinets, there was a metal cart full of syringes and the room smelled of alcohol, a familiar stench I recognized from my past visits to the hospitals.

I was in familiar surroundings, but this time the needles were a little longer. Cotton balls and several bottles of a clear solution were lined up on the table. The nurse raised the needle high in the air and shoved it into the bottle of clear solution.

"This is not going to hurt, your just going to feel a little pinch" she said.

Then she wiped my arm with a wet cotton ball. I yelled and screamed bloody hell.

" It's just a cotton ball little boy, see it's just a cotton ball".The nurse said.

I calmed down for a split second right before she shoved the 12 inch needle in my arm.

$\mathcal{A}$ marriage of convenience

Time passed and I adjusted to school life well. I no longer missed my mother's presence or longed for the long boring rides in the back of Andy's car. I was under a new environment, a new system that measured and challenged my behaviors, whether they were positive or negative. The school system taught me, for every action there is a reaction. The year had passed, I was now in the first grade, the kids where more advanced in reading, math and social skills. I seem to have been doing okay, not like Tiana, who repeated kindergarten due to her outlandish behavior. I passed kindergarten the first time around and happily took my place amongst my fellow kindergarten graduates in the first grade.

My social skills were soon put to the test when a love letter was passed to me by one of the prettiest girls in the class. I was so shocked that she noticed me, I sat there with the unfolded letter in my hand. I took a deep breath and slowly slid it on the desk and quietly unfolded the letter as it clung to my sweaty palms. In the letter, she asked if I would marry Stella Glass and she would marry the another boy in the class. I hastily replied.

"I want to marry you, let him marry Stellar Glass".

I folded the letter, then scanned the classroom for the whereabouts of my teacher. I leaned forward to pass the note back to the pretty girl. As luck would have it, my teacher was in my blind spot and before I knew it the teacher was quick to grab my hand pulling me to the front of the classroom, holding my arm high in the air displaying the letter for the entire class to see. She called the other three note passers to the front of the class, then marched all of us to the principal's office. We sat in the hallway awaiting for our day of execution.

The principal's office was the forbidden zone; because anytime you were summoned to such a high office it would mean you would have to face the (Pedal), a long wooden board used to discipline students by giving them three whacks on their bottoms if they became disruptive. The heavy wooden door to the principal's office opened, I could barely move as I stared at the 250 lb. men who occupy the entire frame of the doorway.

He lined us up in front of his desk, after looking us over; he reached over to his book shelve and removed a big black book. The words were to advanced for me to comprehend. I although I recognize the book, it was the same book my grandmother carrie to church every Sunday.

(The principal) "Stela Glass lock arms together with Michael and you other two kids do the same".

He began reading from the book which he had pulled from his shelf, I didn't understand what he was doing or the reason that he was reading out of that book. Stela was smiling as if she understood every word the principle was saying.   It all came together when he said.

"I now pronounce you man and wife".

Blood rushed to my head, tears began streaming down my face. Stella grabbed my arm smiling while lying her head on my shoulder keeping me from breaking free of our pseudo bond.

Here I was married to the most unattractive girl, not just in the class but in the entire school, her bifocal glasses and her uncombed hair threw me into a frantic plea for my freedom.

(Mikey) "I promised to never pass another note as long as I live if you would release me from this marriage".

The principle and the teacher could barely contain themselves from laughing out loud, he held the book in front of his face and the teacher turned towards the wall to muffle her mouth with her hand to keep from laughing out loud.

The principal agreed to annul this marriage as long as we all agreed not to pass any more notes in school. This was a lesson I would never forget, I can't remember the last time I passed a note in or out of school. The day passed fast, it was a Friday and life was good, I was free of wife and single again.

Once that school bell sounded I was off to the Christian center were the fun began. Just as I entered the door my sister Sherry pulled me to the side and whispered in my ear.

"Daddy's home from prison".

I dropped my creative basket and ran for home as though I had won a candy raffle. My mother and Andy were standing on the sidewalk. Andy handed her something then walked away. I was so excited I bounced onto the front porch as if I was on a springboard, just as I stretched my hand for the door knob, my mother grabbed my wrist and said,

"Wait a minute Mikey".

She pushed the door all the way open, something was obstructing the door from opening completely.

"Come from behind the door Raymond". She said.

My father stepped from behind the door with a knife in his hand.

(Father) "I'm going to cut you up".

I stood there waiting for my mother to run. Had she ran I wouldn't have been far behind her, but she didn't run? She stood her ground, she invited him to come forward with his knife and he obliged her. He came toward her knife in hand, I felt powerless, and I thought surely she was going to die.

Once he got within 12 feet she pulled a small gun from her trench coat and dropped it down to her side. He stopped dead in his tracks.

(Mom) "What did you say you were going to do 'nother Fucker?"

(Father)" wait a minute Phyllis".

She fired once at his feet, he jumped and moved closer, she shot the gun two more times at his feet then yelled.

"Dance motherfucker". The next shoot was in his leg.

(Father yelling) "Phyllis, Phyllis, Phyllis"!

As he fell to the floor with both hands clutching his leg, blood pouring between his fingers and onto his London fall trench coat, he begged her not to shoot him again. I backed into a corner watching from a distance as the drama unfolded. Once again the police had come to our house, and once again my father was returned to prison to complete his prison time for violating his parole.

Now I was truly a displaced child in a dysfunctional home torn between the love for my two parents. I feared for the life of my father, and the safety of my mother. The police arrived before my father could walk away, they handcuffed him as I watched them escort him into an ambulance and drive away. Once again I stared at my father leaving with my face pressed against the front room window. Tears pierced my eyes and flowed freely down my badly worn winter coat. I could since It would be a long time before I would see or hear from him again.

These were confusing and frustrating times. I wanted nothing more than to escape this roller coaster ride of emotion and uncertainty. Months sailed by and I hadn't hear from my father sense he had gone back to prison for attempted assault with a deadly weapon. Andy departed and he took his new bunkbeds with him. I guess I could say I don't blame him. He didn't want to put up with the baby daddy drama.

The Christmas of 1965 would be the harshest Christmas, so I thought. We had nothing in the house that resemble the holiday spirit. Fortunate for my mother someone knew about her dilemma they were courteous enough to place her name in a basket at someone's church. I was young but I could feel the emptiness in the house, the absence of Andy's spirit, especially his spirit of giving. There was a knock at the door, and I did exactly as I was instructed not to do.

I opened the door and allow three strangers to walk in our house. A tall white male and two white females. They said they were from a church and they were given our name to sponsor for Christmas. They dragged in a huge Christmas tree, the tree was so tall it scraped the ceiling and had to be taken back outside and cut to the correct size. We pop popcorn, made ornaments and put it on thread and wrapped it around the Christmas tree. We sang Christmas carols, and baked cookies and prepared a Christmas dinner fit or a King. They gave us plastic toy blocks as Christmas gifts, and dolls for my sisters. It wasn't anything expensive or extravagant but somehow the Christmas spirit was upon us and we were happier then we ever have been doing this holiday season.

My mother had moved onto a new life and a new relationship. She try her hand at the prospect of dating someone from another race. Too young well-dressed white man appeared at our front door, looking dapper, wearing white dress shirts, ties and trench coats. One of the young man came bearing ice cream cones for all of us. It wasn't meant for the young white gentleman to see us but my auntie thought it best that she bring them over to meet my mothers children, seeing how she only had one child. I guess she wanted to discourage the young man from dating my mother and it worked.

We never saw them again. I guess the thought of dating a woman with seven kids was too much for him so he opted out. However, I must say he delivers swell ice cream.

Rayford was still running around the streets at 10 years old and I was still the only male member of my family consistently at home during sleeping hours. Rayford spent a lot of time chasing girls, even at a very young age he stayed out until the waking hours of the next morning. I thought my big brother could beat anyone and wasn't afraid of anything, little did I know he was afraid of a bully that lived several blocks from us. The bully was a young kid that had family problems. He decided to act out his dysfunctional family ways on his friends and anyone within reach. Unfortunate for my brother he was chosen by this kid to act out his frustrations. My brother didn't want to fight and just walked away but the kid push the envelope forcing the fight. Finally he crossed the line grabbing my brother by the arm ripping his shirt. Rayford lit into him like a match to gasoline. He returned home later that afternoon looking as though he just been through a tornado. Buttons were ripped off his shirt, blood dripping slightly from his nose. He gave as good as he got and discovered the boy wasn't as tough as he thought he was, as a matter of fact he won the fight very easily. The boy never bothered Rayford again, the bully maintained his distance the remainder of the year.

$\mathcal{D}$elaware Street- out of sight, out of mind

A few months later, into my life walks Bryce 5ft '5' inches tall and 157 lbs, slanted eyes as though he was of the Chinese descent. His temperament was hard to grasp. I stayed away from him as much as possible because I knew if anything were to happen between us it wouldn't be good. Spring was forging straight ahead pushing flowers out of the ground for our appreciation, filling the air with frequently fresh scents for the new year. Snow was slow to melt and remanence of slush line the sewers waiting for their final farewell and hello to the 50° weather welcoming spring time.

The closer summer got the more I noticed boxes stacked in corners throughout the house.   Easter was here and my sisters begin preparing for a traditional trip to our grandmother's church. The Saturday before Easter we paid a visit to my auntie Dorothy's house, a small two bedroom house on the West side of town. My sister wanted her ears pierced, but there was no extra money around the house for such luxury items. Marica always admired Dorothy's earrings, and was fascinated by the fact the Dorothy Pierced her owners ears. Marcia ask my mother if it was okay to allow Dorothy to piercing her ears.

 "They're your ears" my mother said.

Dorothy agreed and before 12 noon we are on our way to her house. I loved visiting my aunties house. She always had a coffee cake sitting on the kitchen table and her house always smelled fresh and clean. The only annoyance wasn't two ankle biting dogs that seemed to never shut up. My uncle George was always in the garage pretending like he was fixing his cars but his real reason for being in the garage was to have a couple of beers without his wife's interference.

The ear piercing process began. Dorothy removed a needle from her sewing kit and placed it on the stove burner. Marcia's eyes grew big with fright as the needle turned burning hot red. I sat at the kitchen table waiting for the incident to unfold, but occasionally I was distracted by the coffee cake sitting on the kitchen counter. My auntie removed a block of ice from the refrigerator, wrapped it in a towel and sat it on the table next to my sister.

"Bend your head to the side" she said, while removing the red hot needle from the stove.

I couldn't help but laugh, while Marcia sat at the table tapping her feet frantically. As the needle got close to her ear she began to lose all control. As the sizzling red hot needle passed her eyes, she screamed.

"Wait!".

"What's wrong". Dorothy said.

(Marcia) "Your not going to put that in my ear are you?".

"No silly, I have to cool it off with ice, but I had to sterilize it with the fire". Dorothy said.

I began laughing so hard Dorothy gave me a piece of coffee cake just to shut my mouth. She stuck the needle through Marcia's ears with a piece of thread on the end.

"Hand me those scissors Mikey"

I picked up the scissors and handed them to her point first. Dorothy screamed and yelled.

"Turn them around! Turn them around and hand me the other end".

I didn't know what all the drama was about but I did as she requested. I turned the scissors around and handed them to her with the point facing me. Tiana was next in line to have her ears pierced, or should I say roasted like two marshmallows. Marcia cried her way into the front room holding toilet paper to her ears. Tiana followed Marcia into the front room not wanting any part of Dorothy's homemade stove top ear piercing, done for free method. Tiana rushed into the front room, eyes bugging out of her head.

"Okay Tiana, it's your turn." Dorothy said.

While sterilizing two needles on the kitchen stove. Tiana ran onto the front porch ignoring Dorothy's requests to come to the kitchen.

"I'll get my ears pierced next time", Tiana said.

Shaking her head no. Dorothy was extremely disappointed she didn't get to Pierce Tiana's ears. I ventured into the back yard to talk to my uncle George and laughed as he secretly removed beers from the small refrigerator in his garage. My auntie loves her husband and didn't want him to drink, jeopardizing his health but he was bound to have a beer unknown by his wife.

I got a kick out of being around the odd couple. Dorothy was a very light, fair skinned woman. She beautifully resembled Lena Horne. She was a high strung, hypochondriac, who loved her husband so much she thought other women crave him as well. George was a 5 foot five, slightly overweight man, with bug eyes. He often moved at a turtle's pace, wearing a fisherman's hat and deck shoes as though he were going onto a boat. I didn't spend much time at their house because there was nothing to do other then play with their dogs or sit idly by and watch my uncle work on his car. If we stayed long enough we were forced to hear Dorothy's rendition of some up notches 1950s song on her newly purchased organ. For its time, the organ was very elaborate. Having several buttons that could alter sound and create different musical instruments.

I sat slumped lifelessly on her couch saturated with plastic covering slowly dehydrating as she belted out lyrics to a song I did not understand. Then came the church music and out door I went, running down the street as though I was running from a haunted house. I Stopped by Mr. Sneed's candy stor,e grabbed two packs of Now and Later's, then hopped onto my grandmothers porch, where I sat rocking back and forth in her red metal non-rocking chairs. I slid two Now & Laters into my mouth before barely getting them out of the wrapper. The juices from the banana and grape Now & Laters flowed freely as I watched lightning bugs light up the front yard by the thousands, bumblebees settled in for the night inside of huge some flowers tucked in the far reaches of the corner of the yard held up by a wire attached to the fence pole. Worms dug their way deep into the ground hiding under my grandmother's tomato patch, trying to escape the hands of feisty kids and fishermen waiting for the sun to rise.

For once in my life I had a moment of silence, looking over the tall vegetable garden that slightly obscured my view of the church across the street. I wonder about my life, and where I would be 10 years from this time. I wonder who would still be in my life 10 years from now and what role would they play. This was my mental quiet place, a place that I went all by myself. The aroma of freshly cooked greens and ham sitting on the stove. A vanilla cake smothered with chocolate icing. A candy dish full of candy that no one was allowed to touch, five red chairs lined up on the front porch, a backyard with a functioning water pump from the 1940s era and a metal tub hanging on the outside of the house displaying the changing world.

Every Easter Sunday like clock work we went to church escorted by our grandmother. I didn't mind attending church once a year only if I went with my grandmother. I knew right after church I could look forward to playing in her backyard and ending our day with a piece of cake wrapped in wax paper. The church was hot, with an antiquated cooling system. Nonfunctioning swamp coolers sat in the windows, the only fans the church had were the hand fans donated by the local funeral parlor. The first two rows were filled with old men appearing to be near death. The entire congregation appeared to have been born in the 1800s.

The preacher screamed a incomprehensible message from the pool pit of fire and brimstone as he waved his handkerchief in the air. The old women waved back praised God as I slipped into heat exhaustion. My freshly pressed green suit jacket fell to the floor. The wooden pews were just about getting the best of me, so I threw my hand in the air requesting a bathroom break. Tiana and I had the same idea and we stood outside long enough to get a breath of fresh air. Just as we were having fun running around outside the church, one of the ushers grabbed us by the shirt escorting us back to our seat.

" One more hour and this nightmare will be over with". I thought to myself, flipping my . 20 cent around in the palm of my hand with visions of great Now & Laters dancing in my head.

Once I was released from church I ran straight to Mr. Sneeze's Candy store and purchased four packs of Now & Laters. The temperature heated up all across the sleepy town over the course of the next two months. After a long frostbitten winter the summer crept its way in. The sun shone brilliantly through my window. The summer had arrived, and once again in my peripatetic childhood we move into a really quiet secluded neighborhood on 30th & Delaware Street. The neighborhood was much different from our prior address and the house was three times the size. It was a three bedroom house with an attic and a basement. Toys were scattered throughout the attic and in the toy box in the living room. It was as if the prior renters knew I was coming. A pair of pearl white ice skates caught my attention. I quickly put them on and ran up and down the street trying to skate.

"Those are for ice you idiot" said the boy next door.

"I know what there for, just leave me alone", I said, taking off the skates and running in the house.

Sam finally met my mother's request, he placed us in a nice home, in a nice neighborhood. After all these years he still managed to be our landlord. The neighborhood was composed of a mixed race of people, meaning there were both black and white people who lived on this street. The long drawn out civil rights movement was at its height, and European Americans were moving out of the inner-city and into the suburbs away from the onslaught of blacks moving into the inner-city.

Although most of the white people were retired, or over sixty years old, the African Americans were young vigorous people in their early 30s. The neighborhood was quiet and clean, most of the homes had three stories, either with a basement or an attic. Sometimes the homes had a basement and an attic and a two car garage. The Blocks were long and wide and seem to disappear at the top of the hill. I didn't hastate to cruse the new neighborhood looking at the big homes with large front porches and huge back yards.

I was even capable of making a couple of friends directly across the street from my house. Frankie, Joe and I became friends immediately. There was also a cute little girl that lived next door, she was at least a year younger than I. Her brother detested the fact Lisa and I spent so much time together, I was only seven years old and Lisa was only 5 1/2 but for some strange reason he felt we were doing more than just making mud pies. Every time we played in the backyard he would encroach on our fun.

"Go home, you're too old to play with her" he said. Shoving me toward the back fence.

"Don't touch me again" I said.

While standing my ground. He pushed me one more time, I had an immediate reaction. I grabbed a switch from the boysenberry tree then slapped him across the face with it.

"Oh shit" he said, clutching his face.

Tears formed in his eyes, He was 13 years old and a much bigger kid then I. He out-weighed me by 60 pounds. He would have no trouble throwing me around the yard if he chose to, but he decided to punch me in the nose then shove me out of his yard. My nose began bleeding profusely as I searched the ground for a rock to strike him with. Before long my "white buddy El" tennis shoes were covered with blood. I was so pre-oc-cupied with my tennis shoes being ruined by the bloodstains. I rushed upstairs to the bathroom and soaked them in the bathtub in ice cold water before the blood could set in. Over the course of time he came to realize I would continue to play with his sister, and I came to realize making mud pies wasn't worth getting a bloody nose every week, so I spent my free time across the street at Joe's and Frank's house.

.

Moving to a new location was always fun, but there was one small problem, Bryce followed us into our new home and adopted a lotus-eater life style, because he didn't have the discipline to reconciled his income with his bills. He never spoke or said anything to me until that fateful hour late one evening.

I was sitting idly gazing out my bedroom window when approached by Rayford carrying an unopened bar of soap he just purchased from the variety store earlier in the day. He cut the box away from the soap using a small carving knife, with his artistic ability he was able to carve his initials very artistically into the soap. He handed me the bar of soap and asked if I would like to do the same. Smelling from ear to ear, I was glad to oblige him. I began carving my initials in large letters.

Rayford said. "wow! let me see that man, it's really good I'm going to go show mama".

Rayford grabbed the soap and ran downstairs like his pants on were on fire. I don't believe it, he tricked me, now mom is going to yell and scream at me. But that wasn't the case. Bryce had to prove he was the head of the house. I turned around and there I saw a silhouette of his 5 foot tall frame in the door eclipsing the light entering the bedroom from the hallway. He stood there posturing with his machismo attitude. He was short in stature but his muscular frame took up the entire structure of the door.

(Bryce) "Take them off"

(Mikey) "Take what off?"

(Bryce) "Your pants and underwear".

I thought to myself. " This fool must be crazy".

I froze like a mannequin in a Macy's store window. I didn't know what to do or make of what I thought I heard or whether I understood him. He repeated it again.

(Bryce) "Take off all of your clothes, you're going to get a whipping for playing with and wasting soap.

I couldn't believe it, this man must have lost his mind, he's going to beat me with that razor strap for such a small infraction. I hesitantly drop my pants down to my ankles.

(Bryce), "Take everything off including your underwear."

I began shaking uncontrollably like leaves on a tree as I braced myself, he lifted his razor strap high in the air scraping the light fixture on the ceiling. He blazingly swung the big leather strap, hitting the back of my legs and my butt, cutting deeply into my flesh as though I was a runaway slave. Once the beating begin my brother Rayford sat in the kitchen clutching the kitchen table, realizing he made a mistake as I screamed bloody hell while the razor strap dug deep into my seven-year-old virgin flesh, leaving three-inch web marks across my back, legs and my butt. I fell on the bed shaking and crying in disbelief. I collapsed on the bed and cried myself into a twilight sleep.

I didn't know what just happened but if this was what my life was going to be like until my mother dumped this idiot, I wasn't going to stick around for maltreatment and getting beat half to death for minor infractions. I took my sister's scarf and placed my best T-shirt and a clean pair of underwear in the scarf, tied it around a stick and off I went down the street. My sisters stood in the doorway crying, my mother said.

"Let him go he'll be back."

I was determined to be on my own. I knew I could cut grass in the summer and shovel snow in the winter and I would be okay. I walked briskly down the street to my friend Peanut's apartment building where I stayed for two hours playing football on an electric football board. I sat passively and allowed Peanut's to cheat. Every time his players carried the ball, Peanuts turned the vibration up on the football machine just enough so that his players could sail smoothly across the football field. But once it was my team turn to carry the football, he would turned the machine up really high so that my players will fall over on the football field allowing him to retrieve the ball. I stayed and played as long as I could, until it was time for them to eat dinner.

Their mother asked that I come back after they finished eating their dinner. I walked slowly to the door looking back over my shoulders waiting for an invitation to stay for dinner. I can't help to wonder why she didn't invited me to stay for dinner, so I walked up and down the hallway for 35 minutes until they were done eating dinner then back to the football board where peanut cheated his way to another victory. Sooner or later the overwhelming smell of leftover meatloaf, mashed potatoes and gravy became too much. I found myself subliminally walking out of the apartment and down the stairs to the dim lit streets.

I could see my little gray house resting quietly in the middle of the block but I was determined not to go home. 8 o'clock was approaching fast, I knew I had to be somewhere, part of my social recognition training said that when the street lights flickered on, I had to be in front of the house and once the lights were totally on, I had to be in the house. Somehow this training stayed with me. So I stared down 30th St. and Talbot where the bully live.

I knew that leaving wasn't an option, so I headed back towards my home just in time for my mother to step out on the front porch and yeah.

"Boy get in this house".

I reluctantly sashayed into the living room then I was escorted to the kitchen table for a large bowl of Lima beans and one squarely cut slice of unsweetened cornbread. I hated Lima beans I would rather starve than eat those big half cooked, hard to swallow horse pills. I sat at the kitchen table never touching the beans and fell asleep in the chair. I awakened to find myself tucked securely in my bed. It was always a battle when we had black-eyed peas or Lima beans. My sister Tiana was the driving force causing me to rebel against eating Lima beans. She was quite the agitator, she didn't help the situation any. She always told me that black-eyed peas were eyes of dead people and they stared at me while I tried to eat them from the bowl. I was horrified at the thought, and wouldn't go within 10 feet of a bowl of black-eyed peas. She often played pranks on me and threatened to beat me up if I didn't comply to her wishes. Tiana was a rapscallion, everywhere she went she brought disarray with her.

Within the last three months my mother seemed very rushed. I didn't understand why until I discovered she was in nursing school and I couldn't have been more proud of her, because she was working and attending school simultaneously. We were on welfare, receiving food stamps for the time being while she went to night school. The welfare system didn't allow her to go to school and receive general assistance. Fortunately one of the welfare supervisor recognized the potential in my mother and she allowed her to attended college and work to support her seven children while receiving a small amount of food stamps. I watched my mother leave early in the mornings and return late at night. She would fix our lunch for the next day of school and place it in the refrigerator.

She ironed our clothes and laid them neatly on the couch. She would stack quarters, dimes and nickels on the kitchen counter for my elder brothers and sisters bus fare and lunch. This was just part of her daily routine, her face carried a scorned expression. I sat quietly on her bed and watched as she pressed out a stack of freshly dried clothes, sprinkling water from a loosely capped bottle of water over the clothes as she pressed and squeezed the wrinkles out of our pants.

It was that time of year again: the bitter wet and cold weather that challenged her character as she treads through the snow, books in hand, walking down the middle of the unsnow plowed streets. I watched her until she turned the corner or I could not see her any more, this became routine for me and I never missed a beat. For the next 9 months I would run to the front bedroom to watch her leave, and then I would run down stairs to put on a freshly ironed shirt and pair of pants hurrying to get dressed for school. Every morning I would venture across the street to Frank's house so that we could walk to school together. His mother thought I had beautiful hair, but I needed to comb it. She slowly approached me with a comb behind her back.

" You have such pretty hair, can I comb your hair?" she said.

As she raised the comb in the air. I violently shook my head no as I ran and ducked under their kitchen table. Every morning it was the same thing, she wanted to comb my hair and I retreated under the kitchen table.

School #60 William Bell was an antiquated school as if it was a throwback from the 1940s construction error. Little to no remolding had been done to the school, the bathroom urinals stretched down to the floor and a large metal fountain with a floor paddle that we press to wash our hands encompassed most of the bathroom. The main entrance into the school was a big double door with one single door on each end of the building. The school was a hand-me-down from the middle class white's that moved out of the neighborhood, who left the school district for suburban living, leaving the school in need of much repair. The old black chalkboards and the lift top desk were outdated, so was the public school systems policies on corporal punishment. A long wooden pedle was the only form of discipline and if the principal got creative he would drill holes in the pedle to increase the speed of the swing and provide suction on impact.

The head principal was named Mr. Lackey, a short 5 foot tall 350 pound man with at least a 54 inch waistband. He couldn't run and he didn't have to, he just remembered our faces then summoned us down to the principals office. During our lunch period, teachers stood in each corner of the cafeteria, monitoring our activity and to ensure that no one left the cafeteria before the bell rang.

During the end of the lunch period we lined up at the cafeteria door in anticipation of recess. We pushed back-and-forth against the cafeteria doors refusing to obey the demands of the teachers yelling.

"Back away from the doors!"

One teacher rushed upstairs to the principals office. Within seconds someone yelled

"Here comes, Mr. Lackey!"

Mr. Lackey, walking as fast as his 350 pound body would allow. Once he got close to the cafeteria doors, he ripped his belt from around his waist, dragging his 54' inch belt on the floor, he yelled out.

"Get back! Get back!"

Uncontrollably swinging his belt.

"Get back! Get back! Get back!".

He yelled, as he charged forward swinging violently at our heads. The young female teachers stood back smiling at Mr. Lackey admiringly as if he had accomplished a great feat. When in reality all he did was bully a bunch of kids.

All the kids fell back in the cafeteria scrambling for their seats. Within seconds Mr. Lackey had total control of the cafeteria. He walked up and down the cafeteria, belt dangling from his hand dragging along the cafeteria floor.

"Now don't get out of your chairs until I tell you to".

Latching his belt back around his waist, struggling to find the belt loops, he patrolled up and down the middle row of tables with a mean and sinister look on his face. No one dared to move a muscle.

The recess bell rang, but we remain silently in our seats, minutes later we were lined against a wall in an orderly fashion, then escorted to the playground for 30 minutes of outdoor activity. The playground was virtually free of exercise equipment with one basketball rim and all the running space we can tolerate. There were no organized activities or foot races, we ran around loosely on the playground while the more mature boys leaned against the fence posturing, trying to look cool in front of the young girls. I couldn't run too far, jump and play too hard because my shoes were in total disrepair. My socks hung freely from the bottom of my shoes, the asphalt ripped holes in the toes of my socks. The bottom of my shoes had holes the size of a quarter. If I forgot to line my shoes with cardboard my socks would eventually stick embarrassingly out of the bottom of my shoes.

I thought having tattered clothing was normal, it just meant that little boys were rough, seeing how I can't remember consistently having nice shoes or clothes. I understood my mother was doing the best she could, because she never had any financial help from my father. She often took us shopping the month before school began. She allowed us to choose our clothes for the school year then place them on layaway.

I was happy for the moment dreaming about the first day of school and being all dressed up in my new clothes. But it never came into fruition. The clothing I selected was substantially reduced to two pairs of pants and two shirts. All the other kids seemed to be dress for success for the first day of school. The smell of new jeans and patent leather shoes was as common on the first day of school as the old black chalkboards and substitute teachers that wouldn't last more then the first part of the year.

School #60 was only a little more than a mile away from my house, but the winter months proved to be challenging. I had to line the sole of my shoes with cardboard to prevent the snow from dampening my socks. I couldn't feel the cold air that chapped my lips or froze my partially exposed toes because I was having too much fun diving in the snow and throwing snowballs. By the time I got to school my clothes were completely saturated. I didn't even noticed the snow that had made its way through the holes on the bottom of my badly worn sneakers that were held together by cardboard to line the inside and tape across the front lips of my shoes. This invention was handed down to me by my older brother Rayford. Like me he had to be creative with shoe and clothes repair. Denton didn't have this problem, my mother made sure he had adequate clothing, and shoes because he lived in the presence of my grandparents.

The winters were unforgiving, and was even colder when we couldn't afford oil for the furnace. The huge three bedroom house was difficult to heat and we often found ourselves huddled in the kitchen in front of the stove, wrapped in blankets trying stay warm. Sooner or later I had to adjourn to my bed where the ice covered the windows, seeping its way inside the window frame rendering a perfectly frosted circle decorating the inside of the window and making a statement," winter has arrived".

The cold pockets of air rushed through the bathroom purposely missing the empty space my brother once occupied. The absence of my brother Rayford left the bedroom even more cold and uncomfortable. Most of the time I was scared half to death, lying in the bed staring at the attic door. I stared at the door so long, psychologically the door knob begin to turn and I would flee downstairs in a rage trying to escape the ghost that traveled to the dark crevices of the unoccupied spaces in our house.

My sisters slept comfortably through the night, because they had one another and they were always at home. My sister Sherry was known to patrol downstairs around the kitchen and living room, ensuring the doors were locked before settling down for the night. She was considered an unofficial security guard and a second mother to all of us. She had a guitar she didn't play, and a bicycle she seldom rode. She was a collector of things, kind of a young hoarder but her intentions was to reap the benefits overtime by keeping her possessions in perfect condition and allowing them to age into antiques. The idea of possessing an antique guitar went out the window as quick as the thought came into her head.

One day Sherry and Rayford were having an argument over a bet that Rayford couldn't drink an entire bottle of hot sauce. Rayford drank the entire bottle of hot sauce, but had a violent reaction afterwards. He ran through the house drinking bucket after bucket of water. The water couldn't come out of the tap fast enough, his mouth was on fire. Sherry laughed so hard tears ran down her face.

Rayford followed behind her wanting Sherry to pay him for the bet. She laughed and laughed as he followed her up and down the steps trying to requisition his pay.

"Stop following me, I'm not paying you anything." She said.

The more she laughed he became very agitated. Rayford without thinking shoved her towards the steps. She tumbled a few feet, and before he could react, she grabbed her guitar and bashed him over the head with it, then fled up the stairs. Rayford staggered around the living room trying to free himself from the guitar strings. Sherry locked herself in the bedroom and didn't come out until late in the evening. Rayford eventually calmed down and disappeared into the streets from which he came.

Spring was always a pleasant time of the year, fresh grass birthing in the front yard, while the final signs of winter flushed their ways down the sewers. Christmas was over and all the holiday sweets were gone. My sweet tooth was in high gear and my pockets were beginning to feel the effects of juvenile poverty. My entrepreneur spirit shifted into high gear. I began to think of ways I could earn money by cutting grass or picking up trash in people's yards. I didn't own a lawn mower so that idea was short-lived, it was just another obstacle in front of me and the candy store.

$\mathcal{J}$ohn

While waiting for another idea to pop into my head I sat down on the green plush grass of one of the big houses, five minutes into my thinking, the sun was suddenly eclipsed by a large shallow blocking the sun rays and interrupting my casual tanning session. I tilted my head backward and elevated my eyes in the direction of the human eclipse. There he was, a six-foot tall graying white man with a kind face and a gentle voice.

He said, "Where do you lived?"

I replied. "Across the alley from you".

Then I asked.

'Would you like your grass cut?" In a high tone overly anxious voice.

(John) "Do you have a lawn mower"?

(Mikey) "No",

(John) "How will you cut my grass if you don't have a lawn mower?"

(Mikey) "With your lawn mower".

He then stuck out his over encompassing hand (John) "My name is John".

I shook his hand, his fingers were so large and long, he reminded me of the giant I once saw at the state fair grounds. John's hand smothered my seven-year-old hand as it sunk into his palm.

(Mikey) "My name is Michael but my brothers and sisters call me Mikey".

I followed him to his back yard and was surprised at how well the lawn was maintained. The lawnmower was shoved in a corner of his well organized garage, covered with spider webs and rust invading the wheels and blades.

I was confused at how he could possibly maintain his yard so well with a dilapidated, antiquated lawn mower with a single big rusted blade in the middle, flanked by one tire on each side. The yard was really big so I charged $3.00 to cut the front and two dollars to cut the back. I began my auspicious chore cutting the grass at 10: am, and I finished cutting the grass by 2pm that afternoon.   I was totally exhausted, my shirt was cover with sweat and the palms of my hands were painfully red. As I slumped to the ground I realized that the lawn mower was older than it appeared, the blade was dull and duck tape was holding the handles together.

John came back outside; his face was red from laughing as if he had been watching the Red Skeleton show. Instead, he had watched me painfully cutting the grass the whole time. He invited me into his house to celebrate the completion of my first job. As I entered his house I was amazed at the volume of books that lined his book shelf and how clean and unlived in his house looked.

I cruised from one room to another amazed at how perfectly the boarders of the walls were trimmed with dark thick wood matching the wooden floors and bookshelves. The walls were spotless and the furniture untouched as though no child had ever occupied the space. Hundreds of books sat undisturbed and perfectly placed in volume order on the book shelfs.

I was only a child but I could see that these were law books. I was just in eyeshot of John, staring as he opened a wood grain cigar box. I stood quietly behind him as he took out a stack of one dollar bills. My eyes bulged as I thought to myself, "That must be $20 in cash, he must be rich". John paid me four dollars and some orange slices from his candy dish. I took my new found wealth home and sat admiringly in front my four sisters and counted my earnings 10 times, in 10 different ways. My siblings were surely jealous of my new wealth. I didn't know allot about money, all I knew was that Now & Laters cost five cents a pack and I could get 20 packs for one dollar, nothing else mattered. After counting my four dollars over and over I ran one block to the penny store ready to turn my pot of gold into a pot of candy.

A man that has a 1000 friends has not one friend to spare, a man that has one enemy will meet him everywhere.

As I turned the corner a boy leaped from behind the bushes, and grabbed me by my shirt, with his fist raised high in the air.

(Bully) "give me all your money".

I was nervous, and he could see the fear in my eyes. Up to this point in my life my brother Denton was the only one to make me willfully submit to him, but I knew that my brother would not cause me any harm and if he did I could call out to my mother for help. This kid was twice my size and had a mean look in his eyes.

(Mikey) "This money belongs to my mother, I was sent to the store to get some milk".

Another boy approached as the bully clenched my shirt, he couldn't have been more than six years old.

(Enron) "Leave him alone stinky man, let him go" The boy let me pass.

(Bully) " There is a toll charge for crossing this side of the street".

I was distraught even though that wasn't my first time facing bullies, but I always had the backing of friends or my brothers. Unfortunately this time my support system had collapsed. Rayford was always chasing girls and Denton lived with my grandparents on the West side of town. The corner of 30th and Delaware and cutting between houses was the shortest route to the store and there was no way of avoiding running into my would be assailant again.

I was forced to use an alternate route, walking between houses then dashing down the alley to the store, little difference did that make, the bully hung around the corner at his cousins house directly across the street from the store. If I was to have any peace I knew I would have to fight guy. As my luck would have it my mother unknowingly demanded increasingly that I go to the store and buy butter and evaporated milk, that she forgot to get it at the grocery store the day before. I ran to the corner of 30th and Delaware St, peaked around the corner, to my amazement there was no bully.

I successfully ran these black ops three times before the bully got a glimpse of me. As I scurried across the alley and got partially over the fence, an annoying yell came out of nowhere.

(Bully) "You owe me a day's toll punk, I'm going to get you next time".

While scrambling over the fence my pants leg got caught, I struggled and pulled as the bully ran closer. I took a deep breath and pulled one final time ripping a hole in the knee of my pants. I was free! I ran so fast, being so excited, I was running free of motion, swinging my arms back-and-forth not even noticing the small paper bag began ripping in shreds. The butter and milk flung in the air landing in the puddles of rainwater on street.

The bully ran to the fence, kicking the fence and screaming.

" That's the last time you're going to get away from me, next time you're going to pay double."

I stayed inside the house for the next three days rehearsing fighting scenes after watching the Green hornet. I practiced day in and day out in my bedroom, training myself for the day I was to face the bully again. My cash flow of $4-$5 every two weeks had come to a sudden halt. I had been without candy for four days and I was beginning to have withdrawals. Visions of grape, watermelon, banana, lemon, and chocolate Now & Laters were dancing in my head.

So I ventured backed out in the world of entrepreneurial ship. My first stop was at a huge home that had slave quarters in the back of the home and an oversized yard. The house sat one house from the top of the hill of 31st and Pennsylvania Street. The yard was so big I thought for sure I was on a plantation. The grass was so green and rich and beautiful, I was going blind from seeing and smelling what I thought were acres of grass. I was like a deer caught in the headlights, total burnout was set in place. The thought of cutting this grass made me sick to my stomach. But my desire for candy was even greater than my desire not to cut the yard. Up-and-down back-and-forth across the yard. The grass was so rich my white sneakers had turned green in color. The lawn mower choked every few feet from the thick richness of the lawn.

After a long day of cutting the over-sized yard, I sat on the curve drinking from the water hose that stretched from the mansion down to the sidewalk. It was the best tasting water I had ever tasted at that moment, but something was still amiss. I needed my sugar fix. I had to have my Now & Laters, and for celebratory purposes I was going to buy hostess cupcakes with white filling in the middle. The last thing on my list of cavity makers was a pack of chocolate Now & Later's.

The word on the street was that there were no chocolate Now & Laters on the market anymore. I had to have them. By 1 o'clock I journeyed down the street to the store, I was too tired to take shortcuts, or to allow anything to diverge me from the thoughts of chocolate Now & Laters that swirled around my head like marbles in the ping-pong machine. I knew I wouldn't have a clear thought in my head until I could taste the soothing chocolate flavored of Now & Laters flowing freely throughout my mouth.

I walked in the variety store, slapped one dollar bill on the counter and demanded 20 packs of chocolate Now & Laters. I didn't even allow the cashier to bag the Now & Laters, I shoved nineteen packs in my pocket, dismantling one pack and shoving all eight pieces in my mouth at the same time. The juices flowed freely as I walked out of the store in candy heaven, but as fate would have it, the bully showed up, fist in air.

(Bully) "Where's my toll Punk!".

He ran across the street stopping me in my tracks, but I was too tired to listen to his hyperbole and wasn't about to surrender my earnings. So I jumped into my boxing pose, energized by the chocolate sugar juices. I wasn't willing to share or surrender, not one Now & Later.

I was in Now & Later heaven. For a brief second I lost myself and yelled.

"I ain't giving you nothing!"

The bully ran back to the other side of the street.

(Bully) " I will fix you!".

I never had another problem from him and didn't see him again for two years. I went on that year making friends with one other kid that live two houses down from my home. He was much younger than I, at least three years younger, but I found him to be very nice and pleasant to be around. We ran and frolicked around as kids do, diving in the grass and running through the rain bare footed. As fate would have it my usual luck would show it's ugly face.

*A*n apple a day won't keep the doctors away

The torrential rains came to a sudden halt leaving puddles and puddles of water flooding in the streets, nearly creeping its way to my front door. Being Mikey, I couldn't help but roll my jeans up and jump into the ankle high water. My sisters stood on the porch watching as I ran up and down the street like Salmon swimming upstream. Suddenly there was a pricking sensation on the bottom of my foot. I noticed a trail of blood stretching at least a half block behind me.

I drag my foot slowly through the water, limping my way home. With every step I was in agonizing pain. A half broken pop bottle had lodged deep into the center of my foot. Maybe it was a sign from God I thought. The half broken pop bottle happened to have held my favorite drink on the planet. It was a grape Nehi grape soda. I squeeze my foot trying to stop the bleeding and within seconds the palms of my hands were filled with blood. Tiana's undiagnosed hypersensitivity was activated by her trigger for chaos. She began screaming bloody hell, causing everyone else in the house to panic, propelling Sherry to my rescue.

Sherry laid me on the couch and wrapped a towel around my foot, but this time before she could call an ambulance my mother walked through the door.

(Mother) "What the hell did you do now Boy"? "Dammit he needs stitches!" she said.

And within an hour I was lying on the backseat of my auntie's Buick slowly dehydrating from her plastic seat covers. Quickly I was snatched from the car and placed on a gurney. I stared at the ceilings and the white hospital walls as I was shoved into an operating room. This time the room had big silver blinding lights staring me in the face.

A young white man came into the room and begin pressing hard on the bottom of my foot.

"Lie still" he said, I have to palpate to see if there's more glass. Every time he touched my foot I screamed and kicked bloody hell.

"It's just a cotton ball" he said, rubbing it on the bottom of my foot.

The alcohol burned and stung like a pack of bumblebees. He raised a needle in the air, fluid dripping from its tip, I jumped off the bed and hobble down the hallway on one foot, and suddenly I was picked up by a large black man resembling the character on the Mr. clean bottle. He aggressively pinned me to the bed. I was frozen like a popsicle, too afraid to move. I could barely breathe with his 250 pound body lying across my small, 50 pound frame.

The doctor shoved the long needle in the bottom of my foot three times before grabbing a hook and threading it with 3-0 silk to sew the gashing whole on my foot. I spent the next two weeks getting piggy back rides from my sister Marica. Before I could return to school my mother decided she needed to remove the stitches from my foot. I never saw the bottom my foot and didn't know there were so many stitches to be removed. I thought if she waited long enough the stitches would fall out by themselves. There I was once again screaming and kicking bloody hell. Removing the stitches didn't really hurt, I just associated the metal tweezers with the 6 inch needle at the bottom of my foot. The following Monday I was back in school and in full swing of my mischievous behavior. Once again our lunch program had changed and we were required to pay for lunch, this time rather than bring our lunch to school. We couldn't afford to purchase our lunch or bring lunch, so the principal gave us permission to walk home for lunch. It took about 15 minutes to walk home and 15 minutes back to the school. Lunch was only an hour including recess time. By the time we made it back to school, recess had ended and we were forced to go directly to class. We made it home just in time to remove the potatoes from the refrigerator and allow them to cook for 10 minutes before heading back to school. The potatoes were still raw and I often went back to school as hungry as when I left.

I couldn't take it anymore! After two months of eating raw potatoes I was starving to death. I was only 50 pounds soaking wet and couldn't afford to lose anymore weight. I was bound to come up with a plan. So I ran ahead of my sisters Tiana and Marica, I thought if I could begin the cooking process the potatoes wouldn't be raw and I wouldn't go back to school hungry. So I busted through the front door locking it behind me with the purpose of slowing my sisters down. I filled the pan up to the rim with cooking oil and turned the fire up as high as I could get it. The grease was boiling in no time, smoke billowing from the pan. That was my cue, I grabbed the potatoes soaking water from the refrigerator and threw a stack of potatoes into the grease. The fire shot out of the pan in a roaring blaze scorching the ceiling. I knew this was a bad idea, so I quickly turned the fire off and put a top over the skillet to douse the fire.

The skillet handle was red hot, I was a quick thinker so I opened the back door, grabbed the skillet with a towel and tossed the entire pan, grease, french fries and all into the backyard. As my luck would have it, the first one through the door was Tianna,

" Oh, I'm going to tell mom on you, you tried to burn the house down".

(Marica) "boy what are you trying to do, now we don't have lunch."

I hunched my shoulders, thinking to myself, "It wasn't a total lost" because we never got to eat anyway.

I spent the next four hours of my day anticipating the whipping I knew I had coming. I sat in class staring at the clock, my teacher pontificated nonstop, but I couldn't hear a word she said. All I could think about was the leather razor strap ripping through my skin, leaving marks across my back with every swing.

Finally the bell rang, I was the last one to get my coat from the cloak hall and the last one to form a line along the staircase waiting for the school doors to open. All the kids ran out to freedom. I wasn't running or jumping because I knew I would be running into a beating. My sisters ran home ahead of me, I stayed back and watched them play as I slipped down to the alley of forbidden territory were the bully lived.

I was no longer in fear of his presence, I was only in fear of what I knew was about to happen so I walked the long way home, circling the block where I lived, going up and down the alley and into the apartment where Peanuts live. Eventually I walked down the alley towards my house. From a distance I could see Bryce's white convertible Buick coupe in the back yard where a garage once stood. I stopped by the first tree that I saw and broke a long switch from one of its branches, then stripped it of its leaves. I stepped in the door. My eyes bugged out of my head as I peaked around the corner. He knew I was coming, so he stood there as my eyes looked up and locked onto his unshaved face.

" Get upstairs and take them off!" He said.

I stood in my room butt naked waiting for the beating I knew would come. With every step he made up the staircase my body cringed in fear. I stuck my arm out handing him the switch.

" You won't be needing that" he said.

Folding the belt in half then popping the belt together one time scaring me to death and making me cry before the first lashing. He swung freely, striking me uncontrollably, hitting me in unfamiliar places, putting his 157 pounds behind each blow onto my 50 pound frame. I screamed and yelled bloody hell I thought for sure my mother would have stepped in the room to see what's wrong but she never uttered a word because Bryce was the man of the house and this is the way he disciplined kids. But there was one small problem, I wasn't his kid. In fact they weren't even married.

I never cooked again and we never had to walk home for lunch again. My mother became very creative with her finances and some how she was able to give each of us .20 cents for lunch, allowing us to eat with the rest of the kids in the cafeteria.

Throughout the school years our lunch programs would change. Sometimes we were required to bring a lunch in brown paper bag and the next year we were required to pay .20 cents for hot and cold lunch served in the gym at school #60. In the following year we were required to bring a lunch once again and by this time most kids had a metal lunch box with cartoon characters on the box and a thermos inside for soup or some type of drink. Most of the time my lunch box only contained one sandwich. The other kids in the classroom seemed to have more food than they could eat.

One kid in particular (Edward) sat next to me in the cafeteria, every chance he got he display his wealth of chips, sandwiches, cookies, fruit, and a soft drink of his choice. His lunch box was so full it was spilling over with food. He proudly opened it wide for every-one to see. I open my lunch box just wide enough to remove my sandwich, take a bite then slipped my sandwich back into the box. I took a bite every five minutes trying to make my sandwich last throughout the lunch period. Not only did Edward have an over-ly adequate amount of food, he always wore new clothes on the first day of school. I did not understand it, how someone could be so privileged while others struggle horribly. I was a good kid, at least I thought so. The only troubles I ever caused were troubles for myself.

I believe that I deserve better, but I knew it wasn't up to me. Being poor was one thing, having other students knowing your poor was something totally different. A lot of the children at my school could be mean and spiteful. One day I didn't have clean under-wear to wear to school, so I went commando. Unfortunately for me, one of the kids no-ticed and told everyone in the class. I was totally embarrassed. Not having clean un-derwear wasn't my mother's fault. The nocturnal monster appeared just about every morning right before I awoke. I hid my underwear under the mattress trying not to be discovered until Saturday morning during laundry day. My bedwetting went mostly unde-tected because Denton lived across town with my grandparents.

Bryce was tired after driving his truck all day and never came into my bedroom unless it was brought to his attention by Denton. For some reason my brother didn't like me. I don't know if it was because I was an annoying little brother or because he was forced to live with my grandparents and felt that my mother gave him up rather than giving me up. For whatever reason he continuously tried to get me hurt. One day he was playing football with his friends. I sat on a telephone pole on the sidelines cheering them on as they played the game of football.

" Can I play" I said. "No, you're too little". His friend Bruce replied.

I sat there momentarily depressed and feeling rejected until an older gentleman interrupted their game.

" This little boy and I will take on both teams". The man said.

"We get to run the ball first," he said, handing me the ball.

" Get behind me and hold onto my belt".

He took off running shoving my brother and his friends to the ground, I laughed hysterically as I ran across the goal line smiling from ear to ear.

He said. "come on we're going to go again".

I grabbed onto the back of his belt, and off we went from one end of the field to the other, scoring touchdown after touchdown. I laughed heartily as my brother and his friends lay on the ground defeated. The man tossed them the football, then waved goodbye. Before I could return to set on the telephone pole, Denton and Bruce simultaneously

Said,"Come on, you can play".

They immediately handed me the ball to run, and for some strange reason I got around all of them and scored a touchdown. It was beautiful! Bruce became enraged.

" That was just luck, do it again, I dare you to run it again".

I was having too much fun, smiling from ear to ear. Denton and Bruce walked to the edge of the field, having a secret conversation. I was handed the ball and off I went, blockers in front of me, then all of a sudden my blockers disappeared. Bruce came charging full steam ahead, he hit me so hard, I tumbled in the air three times before landing on the phone pole. Their I lay lifelessly on my back with my neck bent over the phone pole and my arms sprawled out on each side away of my body. He thought for sure he killed me.

" Mikey, Mikey," he said, in a panicking voice.

 He even cried a little, thinking he killed me. When I regained consciousness, Denton said.

" He'll be okay, stand up Mikey, and run the ball again.

I did as instructed and they freely let me make touchdown after touchdown, cheering me alone the away, temporarily rebuilding my confidence. I was an internally tough kid, nothing could stop me from having fun or being mischievous, not even being knocked unconscious. It began to rain and everyone grew tired of playing football, I was still recovering from my state of unconsciousness and wasn't up to running another football; therefore I decided to immediately ran home. Along the way I ran into Sherry standing in the alley holding her bicycle, known as a bus. The bicycle had two huge rubber tires and a thick heavy frame. The bike was called a bus because the tires were so thick they made noise as they turned. Sherry parked the bike by the back steps then ventured into the house.

I quickly jumped on the bike and down the alley I raced off. Sherry chased me around the parking lot of the flower shop, screaming,

' "Bring back my bike!"

I laughed as I rode around the parking lot in circles, laughing harder and harder as Sherry tried to grab the back of the seat. Each time she got close, I would speed up, throwing rain water on her from the oversize tires on the bike. I ride a few feet before slamming on the brakes causing the tire to slide sideways. Sherry became enraged.

" Bring back my bike, you black punk" She said.

I continued to make her chase me. One thing I didn't realize about her bike, it was a kickback, meaning, if you didn't apply the break at the right time, the petal would kick back forward.

I stood up on the bike to increase my speed so I could slide once I slammed on the brakes. I had just reached optimal speed as I stood up I slammed on the brakes. The brake pedal kicked forward and hurled me over the handlebars into the air. Once again I was flipping in circles in mid air. I splashed down in a puddle of rain water, saturating me from head to toe.

" That's what you get" Sherry said.

She picked her bike up, grinning, laughing and snorting her way back home.

I limped my way back home and lay quietly on the couch trying to catch the breath that was just knocked out of me.

Tiana said." Mama and Bryce left a bottle of Kool-Aid on the table, there is some left over, you can have it".

She walked over to the table and poured me a tall glass of grape drink from the bottle sitting in the center of the table.

"This is an odd looking kool-Aid container" I said to myself.

Tiana was my buddy and if I couldn't trust her who could I trust, but she wouldn't explain what the label name meant, (Wild Irish Rose) I decide to drink it anyway.

"Drink it all" Tiana said. "Don't waste it drink the entire glass".

The glass was just about toppling over with Wild Irish Rose running down the side. I had no problem drinking Kool-Aid, no matter how full the glass was so, I choked it down with one swift swallow.

By the time I got to the bottom of the glass I was just about crawling up the steps. The room was spinning out of control, and my eyes rolled freely in my head like a bag of ten cent marbles. Tiana grabbed the empty bottle as she ran past me up the stairs with bottle in hand to present the empty bottle to my mother.

" I'm going to have Bryce beat your ass" my mother said.

For some reason I wasn't scared of the empty threat. I crawled into my bed and passed out for the night. Bryce came to the door, belt in hand. His small frame filled the entry to the doorway and for the first time I wasn't intimidated by him, he stood there calling out my name.

" Mikey, Mikey, you hear me boy."

I turn my head toward him barely able to open my eyes. Then I passed out. For the first time we had a connection, he understood me just for that brief moment in time. He knew what it was like to be stone cold drunk on your face. So he walked away and never spoke of it again. Within a week Bryce was leaving for mechanics school. He would be gone approximately two weeks to a month for training. Miraculously once Bryce left, my biological father appear. Although he hadn't been in my life for years I found it refreshing to have him in the house again.

Within three weeks time, my biological father departed and Bryce returned from his mechanics training. I didn't understand relationships and although my mother told me not to talk about my father in front of Bryce I thought it would be nice to share the fact my father stayed with us while he was away at Mechanics School. Within 10 minutes my mother and Bryce was in a full toe to toe fight. Bryce was very fortunate my mother didn't have a gun or he would've become just another victim of self defense by anger.

I could hear furniture moving and being thrown around the bedroom, they were having a 'Donny brook' (A free for all, knock-down drag out fight). My mother ran downstairs and Bryce came down hurling behind her raving mad. The fight continued into the front room escalating at a fever pitch. Bryce pick my mother up and body slammed her onto the floor. I ran into the kitchen and grabbed a fork. My mother sat lifelessly on the floor trying to recover from the body slam. Bryce reached down and grabbed her by the face then punched her in the eye with his fist. Sherry went hysterically frantic while dialing 911. I stood there tightly clinging onto a fork, tears streaming down my face, feeling defenseless. Bryce stood towering over my mother yelling and screaming.

 I was so traumatized I temporarily went death, then the police rushed in and wrestled Bryce to the ground. Within the short seven year span of my life, the police intervene twice, busting in my house and arresting someone I knew. This time I didn't care if I would ever see Bryce again. Later that evening, an hour after the episode had ended, my grandfather came over to our house. Barely able to walk, he had three Butcher knives wrapped in newspaper.

" Where is he?", he said.

My grandmother ushered him to the nearest chair. Somehow I felt a little reassured even though my grandfather was too old to fight a young 30 year old man.

My grandmother knew we didn't have food to eat and had the wisdom to bring us a bag of potatoes and a stick of butter to assuage my mother's grief. The assuage lasted about as long as it took my grandparents to get back into their car. My grandparents were poor financially but rich in spirit. They couldn't afford to help out much but the small amount of food they gave us left us better off then we were before they arrived.

 Holding the bag of raw potatoes in one hand my mother waved good bye just before preparing dinner. She stood at the stove peeling and frying potatoes, silently crying to herself. I stood squeamishly quiet in the corner of the living room and watched her cry as she cooked what would be our dinner. In a flash she made her way upstairs jumping in the tub to begin the ablution process. The sound of the bath water seemed to splash around for an hour. I guess it provided her anodyne in her time of need.

 I know she was lost in thought, hurt and embarrassed all rolled into one. I couldn't help but feel sorry for her, and I vowed to destroy my step father if he ever hurt her again. Within a weeks time Bryce was back in the house, every time I looked at him I want to stick a fork straight in his back, but I knew he was too strong and would just disarm me. So I stayed as far away from him as I could get. The end of another school year was approaching fast. Denton returned home for the summer, and I knew he couldn't wait to tell Bryce when the nocturnal monster appeared thrusting me back into a life of torment.

Denton took pleasure in monitoring my every move. Every morning as I awoke, Denton stood by the bed waiting for me to get up. Sometimes I could turn the mattress over in the twilight hours of the morning. After two or three times of safely getting away with wetting the bed, he knew it was too good to be true, so he caught on to what I was doing. He jumped out of the bed first thing in the morning, pushed me out of the way and flipped the mattress over displaying the huge spot left by the nocturnal monster. He ran down to my mothers room and summoned Bryce.

" Now you're going to get it" he said, laughing to himself.

I could hear the popping of the razor strap as Bryce's bare feet slapped against the naked wooden floors.

" Take them off". He said.

Bryce stared at me as though he was trying to intimidate me. I didn't bat an eye while stripping from head to toe. Denton ran downstairs snickering and laughing to himself as though this was his greatest achievement. Bryce grabbed me by the arm once again. The swings of the belt were a little more uncontrollable and violent. The whipping lasted a little longer but I didn't move a muscle or flex a bit.

It wasn't long before a new family moved on the block, and occupied a large four bed-room house next to the apartment complex. I was surprised at how big the family was. There were so many kids, that the mother put a chain around the refrigerator and se-cure it with a heavy duty lock.

In a weeks time I became friends with three of the younger children all near my age. Jason was the oldest of the three that I hung around with. His younger brother Meyers went everywhere Jason went, kind of like my brother and I but Jason welcome Meyers presence. His sister Annie was just as crazy as Jason and Meyer. They played games far more dangerous than I would ever consider. They climbed to the top of the attic and jumped off the roof using umbrellas as parachutes.

I climbed up to the attic, looked out the window, I got so dizzy I fell back inside on the floor. I didn't participate in their parachute jumps but I spent many hours playing with them in their backyard. They enjoyed my company so much they invited me to go to the laundromat with them at 8 o'clock the next morning. Trash bags after trash bag, after trash bag were loaded into the back of their dilapidated station wagon. The hinges on the door let out a loud irritating squeak. Once the door slammed closed, particles of rust fell on my lap. I quickly became disenchanted with the idea of helping to wash all those clothes. So I declined the offer to go to laundromat.

Jason's mother made me a special offer, she promised me ice cream if I would go to the laundromat with them.

" How delightful" I thought.

I quickly ran home and begged my mother for the chance to do a good deed by going to the laundromat and helping someone. She didn't even bat an eye, she waved her hand bye and off I went five blocks in a 20-year-old station wagon loaded down with 10 Hefty bags of laundry. The laundromat was jam packed with people. I saw no foresee-able future in ever getting a washer. Every family seemed as though they had several times the laundry we had, as if they were washing for an entire army not a family. We had to wait at least an hour before we got one washer. So the conquest for a washer began. Each of us took a corner of the laundromat, once a washer became available we flag their mother down and she would come running with a garbage bag of clothes.

Three hours into the trip I began to get bored and complacent. I was ready to go home, even if I had to walk. I staired at the five bags of unwashed laundry, opening and closing my eyes wishing they were washed and put away. I knew I would be in for a long night. Annie and Meyer tried to keep me occupied playing freeze tag in front of the laundro-mat, running up and down the street.

but every time I passed the laundromat window, I saw five or six washers and dryers operating at the same time, and there were still three bags of unwashed laundry staring back at me through the window. I couldn't believe it, it was approaching 6 o'clock in the evening and they were just beginning to dry the last five bags of clothes. Finally 8 o'clock arrive. We all gladly piled in the car heading home, but first we made a pit stop to pick up some ice cream. "Oh yes' I thought, smiling from ear to ear, with visions of large bowls of ice cream dancing in my head.

Their mother got out of the car and bristly walked into the store returning with a small bag, small enough to fit in the palm of a small child's hand.

I thought to myself. "This can't be ice cream, ice cream comes in large cartons or large plastic tubs. She must have the ice cream in the refrigerator at home".

We arrived at the house and quickly unloaded the car in anticipation of a large bowl of ice cream. Jason's mother placed a paper bag on the table then pulled out a small quart of ice cream. She took a knife and cut small slits of ice cream and delicately placed each piece on a paper towel. My jaw hit the floor, I didn't want to show disappointment on my face but I just couldn't hide it.

"What the hell is this, before Abraham Lincoln shit, I thought to myself".

I was at that damn laundromat for 12 hours and this is all I get. I grabbed my ice cream and made my way back down the dimly lit street. I was only three houses away and within two bites the ice cream was gone before my foot hit the first step to our house. I had never been so disappointed in my life I would never fall for such a con again. Just like my mother they were preparing their household for Thanksgiving. This was the first time my family would all sit at the same dinner table, including Denton and Rayford. I couldn't believe it. I smiled the entire time, and they both spent the night. I slept well that night and there wasn't any signs of the nocturnal monster the next morning.

In the month of December, 1968 Christmas had arrived, the most joyous time of the year, but the atmosphere was filled with vexation. Martin Luther King was assassinated, tension in this city was at an all-time high. People ran up and down the street, screaming and yelling. My mother told us not to go outside but I snuck out the basement door anyway just to get a peek. People were running and screaming up-and-down 30th St. The glass door to the variety store was kicked completely out. I stared at the Now & Later's behind the untouched glass case. The Now & Laters seemed to call to me.

"Mikey, Mikey, don't you want just one pack?"

Before I could answer the thought in my head the store owner showed up. His head neatly wrapped with a scarf protecting his hair style known as a process.

"Get away from my damn store". He yelled.

As he slipped and slid on the glass, flashlight and gun in hand, making his way to the back of store. I ran back down the block and to my basement door before my mother could detect I was gone. I saw someone standing in the corner of my basement.

He was a tall black man much bigger than Bryce in height and stature. I ran upstairs to alert my mother. She quickly grabbed a butcher knife. Making her way to the top of the stairs, she flipped on the light switch.

"What are you doing down here" she asked while the police sirens blasted up and down the block. "Is that for you?" She asked.

Shaking his head yes.

(Mother) "I'm going to give you three minutes to get out of here, and when I come back downstairs you better be gone or I'm going to call the police and let them know your in my basement".

The man agreed and my mother went back upstairs locking the basement door behind her. I stood in the kitchen and listened for him to leave. I guess she thought it was his imbroglio not hers. My mother made her way back down to check the basement and lock the basement door that leads to the outside. I never told her it was my fault the door was unlocked or the small fact that I ran a block and a half away to watch the riot unfold around the corner from our home.

1968 was so crazy, I scarcely recall any of the gifts I received other than a set of Rocking Socking Robots. It was the year my grandfather walked into the veterans Hospital with walking pneumonia and never walked out. Later that month he passed away. I had just turned eight years old on December 4, the day before my grandmother's birthday. It was cold and the ice covered every open crevice on the street. It was my first time seeing my entire family, micro and macro in one place. It was a joyous time but a sad occasion for me to see my family.

I didn't understand the sadness that filtered throughout the room. I sat in the fourth row watching my grandfather looking placid in his nondescript casket, wearing a freshly pressed blue suit. Sounds of lachrymose sadness echoed throughout the mortuary. I stared it all the faces of my family members, my cousins, aunties and uncles, brothers and sisters. It was unbelievable, we were all in one place for the first time. We stayed for two hours then back home we went to prepare for school the next day. I was scared half to death once again to sleep in the big lonely room.

I was all alone in a big creepy empty room. I was now tortured by the vision of my grandfather lying peacefully in his casket. I scarcely remembered the belt whipping and the unfinished statement about swiping icing from the cake. I wasn't fortunate enough to spend quality time with my grandfather, instead he was born to soon and I to late to form any type of rapport. I scarcely knew of his existence and the fact that he volunteered to watch us while my mother was in the hospital spawning my sister Denise into the New World. But I couldn't get the image of him lying in his casket out of my head.

I lay in bed that night wide awoke listening to the settling of the house and the ice cold air scratching vigorously with its invisible icy claws at the slowly rotting wooden frame temporarily stabilizing the window in one place. Slowly I dozed off, three hours later I was awakened by the forces of nature. For the first time my body summoned me to get up and go to the bathroom. I wiped my eyes trying to refocus my vision readjusting to the light. Standing in front of the toilet I felt re-assured the nocturnal monster wouldn't have a chance to return this night.

As I started to urinate slow footsteps began coming up the stairs. I stopped urinating mid stream, jumped in the bed and buried myself deep beneath the covers. The sound of foot steps stopped, a window closed then down the hallway the steps went. I thought for sure it was spectral visit by my grandfather walking up the stairs securing the house. The image of him lying in his casket and the sound of the footsteps threw me into an overwhelming panic. I shook violently beneath the my blanket.

I was too scared to even peak from beneath the covers, so, I lay there until I dozed off and was awaken by the nocturnal monster early the next morning. Bryce walked into the room, looked at my urine fill mattress.

(Bryce) "Boy you need to get your lazy butt up and go to the bathroom" he said.

Then off he went at four in the morning to work. Bryce had one good quality, he was a functioning alcoholic. No matter how much he drank the night before he was able to get up the next morning at 4 AM and go to work. Other than that I thought he was pretty useless.

He never spoke when he walked into the house. He didn't care whether I got hurt or went to the hospital, he barely helped pay any bills and he was no type of role model for me or my brothers. He lived his life the way he wanted too, which was to hang out on Indiana Avenue, 12 hours a day drinking with friends after work. I didn't understand why it took my mother so long to grow weary of his behavior. He was in it for himself and no one else.

He pushed his head of the household boundaries to the limit. Reclining back in his leather recliner. On Sundays he watched war movies all day long. I sat next to his recliner waiting for him to fall asleep so I could have a chance to watch the wizard of oz that came on once a year the same time every year. As soon as I turned the channel he would awaken and say turn it back. He wasn't even watching the TV but he felt compelled to honor the veterans who served our country, but he didn't have the courage to honorably complete his tour in the military.

I sat behind him with my back pressed against the wall for another 30 minutes until he decided to reside upstairs. I hurry to flip through the four channels including UHF. And their she was making her way to the land of OZ. Life went on like this for the next month and as you would know it another baby was born, January 1969, my sister Rhianna. She would be the last of of the family to be born into this clan, bring our enclave to a total of eight. Another mouth stretching my mothers limited dollars a little farther than they were financially able to go.

Park Avenue

It was 1969 and we were on the move again, unfortunately this time our house was located right in the heart and soul of the ghetto, (30th and Park Avenue). Once again Sam rented us one of his prized rental properties. A big gray double that provided more space than a young mischievous boy in his preteen years could fathom. The street was very long as though it was two blocks made into one. I wasted no time running up the steps and sorted my way through all the bedrooms. My mother stopped me mid stride and said.

"This back bedroom is yours and your brothers."

I stared at her as though I was a deer caught in headlights. Not again, why is it that we always get the bedroom facing the alley? I was thoroughly discussed, I would've loved to have had a bedroom facing the street so that I could yell at everyone that pass by or stare out the window at the neighbors sitting on their front porch.

Once again we were fortunate to have our school #76 located four short blocks from our house. The scenic route provided plenty of distractions for a young boy on his way to school, such as Frogs Record Shop, a variety stores that sold my favorite penny candy. We drove the store clerk crazy. It took us 10 minutes to spend .25 cents . Three pieces of candy for one penny.

"Give me two of them, and two of them and three of those and five of them," I said.

 By the time I was done naming off all the candy I wanted, my small 6 inch tall bag was spilling over with candy. I quickly doubled back home jamming the overflow of candy underneath my mattress.

Here I stood in a 2800 square-foot home. I was shoved to the back of the house, where I was sure to manifest nightmares while I lay in the bed staring at the closet door. The door cracked open to the attic, displaying its endless flight of stairs that stretched into the abysmal darkness of an on unoccupied and Un-interrupted space. I had no desire to venture up those stairs, there was little comfort when my brother Rayford walked into the room and gladly ran up the steps into the attic and turned on the light displaying the empty room. He pulled me up the steps by my hand.

 Rayford said, "See there's nothing here and there's nothing to be afraid of".

 I didn't care I snatched my hand back and ran down the steps. I knew when the hours of midnight came Rayford would not be home and I would be left to fend for myself in the night and in the morning as the nocturnal monster displayed its ugly head, soaking my bed. Bryce's leather belt would once again strike a devastating blow to my young self-confidence and self-esteem. I was shy and had little friend making capably. I set quietly on the back steps watching the squirrels and the birds play in the backyard looking as though I didn't have a friend in the world.

Rayford noticed I was sitting in the backyard, so he began grabbing bottles and cans. Stacking them on a concrete block in front of the trash can, he called me over and show me how to use the cans and bottles for target practice. Before long, two other boys joined in the rock throwing. Then Rayford quietly walked away as we introduced ourselves and became friends. We were having so much fun the day passed quickly then the universal rule signaled us it was time to go in the house.

The streetlights begin to flicker as though they want to come on, that meant we had to go inside the house. I'd be grudgingly walked in the house and to my surprise there Denton stood with his bags in his hands. He was home for the summer and I was glad to see him because that meant I didn't have to spend lonely nights in that huge dark empty grey bedroom all by myself, "So I thought". I was so thrilled that Denton was home I grabbed his bags and carried them upstairs and placed his bags on his bed. I sat curiously by his side as I watched him unpack item by item and place them neatly on the closet shelf.

*R*espect, crying not an option

This must've been the slowest form of entertainment in the world, my eyelids became heavy as I slid back onto the bed. I was awakened by two kicks to my foot. As I focused my eyes, Denton was pointing at the attic door. I rolled over to my right and there was my favorite knit hat lying at the top of the attic staircase. That hat was my security blanket. I could give you one guess as to how it got there.

I stared at Denton and he looked at me hunching his shoulders and said.

"If you want your hat back, there it is, go get it"

I didn't hesitate for a second, I sprang to my feet and shot up the upstairs like a bullet train riding aimlessly on rails, before I knew it the door slammed shut behind me the lock spinning in its chamber, locking me in the dark abyss of the attic. I screamed bloody hell, kicked and beat on the door. I could hear my mother yelling as she ran down the hallway.

"Let that boy out of the attic!".

She snatched the door open and slapped Denton upside the head. I set idol on the bed trying not to laugh. Denton smirked at me and said.

"I'm going to get you back, punk ".

I was hardly worried, but he got his revenge the next morning. The nocturnal monster showed its ugly face. I had awakened to an ugly and wet situation. Denton stood towering over me smiling as though he had won the lottery.

I knew I was in trouble, Denton ran downstairs like a dog at the racetrack giving Bryce the full rundown on my bed wetting activities.

Bryce, "Where's my belt? He yelled.

" That damn boy is too lazy to get his ass out of the bed and go to the bathroom".

I knew I wasn't going to convince him that I was a deep sleeper and didn't know I had wet the bed. I woke up and it was there. This was all too confusing, instead of trying to develop me into a successful Business savvy young man he invested his time trying to beat me to a submissive state, something that will never happen because I was born with an internal strength and a resiliency that wouldn't allow me to succumb to psychological or physiological pressure. This innate ability would serve me well later in life.

At that moment I decided I wasn't going to give him the pleasure of seeing me cry or squirm from the flesh cutting strikes of his belt. Bryce walked into the room he didn't break stride as he grabbed my arm and violently begin swinging his belt, once he realized I still had my pants on he released my arm and said.

"Take them off".

I reluctantly took my pants off and tossed them on the bed, Bryce grabbed my left arm and begin striking me with his razor strap. Denton stood silently by our sister's bedroom door staring down the hallway trying to get a glimpse of his handiwork. For the first time he could hardly crack a smell or pretend that he was getting any pleasure, as I was beaten savagely to a pulp. I stood my ground and I didn't shed a tear or make a sound. Bryce talked and yelled at me as he feverishly struck me with his razor strap. I could smell the stench of alcohol on his breath as the power behind the belt swiping increased with every word.

" Get your lazy butt out of the bed and go to the bathroom".

I didn't say a word. He whipped me for what seemed like an hour and all of a sudden he stopped, he looked down at me then folded his belt in his hand and back down the hallway he went. He turned to look back at me. I stood there with a blank expression on my face displaying no tears, no pain and demonstrating no fear. I had lost all respect for him and I wasn't about to give him the joy of seeing me cry from any more of this unnecessary whippings.

I decided not to stay in my room and pout, I went down the steps and settled down on the couch. The stinging from the belt hurt beyond repair but I didn't give Denton the satisfaction of believing he accomplished his mission. I believe Denton felt bad for once about telling on me, he could see I was hurt emotionally and not physically but my spirit was nearly broken. He could see the light and excitement in my eyes was no longer there and the shift in my personality, the happiness and joy was being beaten right out of my soul. As much as he didn't like having me around him, he left me alone. He never told Bryce about the nocturnal monster again. I made my way back upstairs and lay quietly face down on my stomach.

I could still feel the sting from the razor strap. Denton came into the room and stared at me from the door. I turned my head toward the wall. I didn't understand Denton's rationale, why did he harvest so much hate in his heart toward me, and he was supposed to be my big brother, someone who was supposed to protect me not harm me. I never understood why my mother never uttered a word about her disapproval of the uncontrolled and unnecessary beatings she allowed Bryce to give me. Maybe she believed it was necessary because she knew no other way to prevent the nocturnal monster from showing up. Denton must've felt a tremendous amount of guilt, because the next day he let me walk 10 paces behind him and his friends and never tried to ditch me throughout the day. That was the last time Denton reported to Bryce my uncontrollable bedwetting and it was the last time Bryce ever whipped me.

Camels hump

The summer was still young and the sun shone brilliantly through my window telling me another fun summer day was mines for the taking. Sherry and Marica worked all summer, they were like worker bees busy at work, selling flower seeds and doing odd jobs around the neighborhood, such as babysitting and gardening. Two months into their hard labor they both were able to purchase brand-new bicycles, fresh out-of-the-box. These were beautiful pink bicycles with streamers hanging from the handle bars and glittery pink seats. Pink fenders provided the perfect finish with a mirror on each handle bar and a reflector on the back seat.

Sherry was reluctant to let me ride her bike even though I begged and begged her. She reminded me of the time I took off on her bike in the rain then wrecking the bike before she could catch me. Marica was a little more trusting because she never had a bike and I never borrowed anything from her in the past.

"I'll let you ride my bike" she said, holding onto the handle bar.

Pointing her finger at me, she adamantly said.

"Don't go up camels hump!."

Releasing the bike, Sherry, Jenny and I took off down Park Avenue to Fairfield Boulevard, and there camels hump stood 30 feet tall, cover with the greenest grass I've ever seen with the exception of a thin dirt trail leading up the hill. Camels hump was legendary for sending kids home with scraped up knees and bent bike frames. Camels hump's was well known throughout the neighborhood by any young person with basic bike riding ability. The hill challenged you without saying a word. It's towering presence was menacing enough. No kid ever rode past the hill without venturing up to its peak.

Jenny, a skinny little girl with buck teeth and long hair, yelled out.

"Let's go up camels hump".

I look at her nervously as she started pushing her bike up the hill. Sherry looked into my eyes, then grabbing the bike seat, she said.

"You know what Marica said, don't take her bike up camels hump".

'Jenny' " Come on Michael are you afraid?"

That's all it took and I was off pushing Marica's bike up camels hump. Jenny waited patiently until I reached the top of the hill. Being the responsible young adult she was Sherry waited at the bottom of the hill, yelling

"I'm going to tell on you. She said, don't take her bike up there!

Down the hill Jenny went, nearly losing control of her bike, coming to a sliding stop right as she reached the street. I sat at the top of the hill that seemed 50 feet in the air.

"Holy moly" I thought to myself. "Well, I can't stay here forever" and down the hill I went flying out of control.

The handle bars begin vibrating violently as if they were going to fly right out of my hand. Suddenly, I lost control and the handle bars turned completely in the other direction. I flew off the bike tumbling three times in the air. As soon as I landed on the asphalt I laid on the ground in utter disbelief, trying to collect myself. Jenny went back up the hill for a second run and to add insult to injury she came crashing down right on top of me.

Marica's brand-new bike appeared to be totally destroyed. The handle bars were bent totally in the opposite direction, all the air had been knocked out of the back tire. The fenders were bent and mangled up beyond recognition, the streamers were missing and the frame was scuffed up beyond repair. Sherry laughed and snorted as she rode ahead of me and Jenny as we limped all the way back home. Marica grabbed her bike and went into full shock.

"I told you not to go up camels hump!" She said, angrily fighting back her tears. The bike was rideable I thought, it just needed new fenders and maybe a paint job. Needless to say, she never let me ride her bike again and I was reduced to being a spectator, no one trusted me to ride their bike, because I still didn't have camels hump out of my system. Although I had to crash a perfectly good bike and skinned my legs to the bone, I still had another run in me.

Park Avenue was fun and exciting, and unknown to my mother I spent a lot of time walking in Fall creek River catching goldfish and crawdads. Dwayne, Titus and I were close friends as anyone could get, but during the night they were forced in the house at 7 o'clock and would not reappear until the next morning. Denton and I would slip back outside right after my mother left for work. We walked up and down the alleys, cutting through back yards and occasionally stopping by different homes to see if our friends could come out. Although I told them Dwayne couldn't come out they decided to stop by Dwayne's house anyway. The front porch was dark and rather creepy, two eye laid near the front door glowing in the dark. The closer we got to the door growling noises intensified with every step. Because of the fear factor placed upon me by my brother I didn't back away I kept moving forward.

I couldn't hangout with my brother if I showed any signs of being scared, so I went on the porch as I was expected to without showing the slightest signs of being timid.

Dwayne's mutt of a dog growled as we walked on the porch, everyone greeted his dog by saying, " Hi Champ" then jumping over the concrete divider separating the two porches. I was the last one to greet Champ. "hi Champ!" I said forcefully, pointing my finger toward him. As I turned to walk away, Champ leaped in the air and latched onto my rear end scraping my skin with his teeth. "Wow! I yelled, grabbing onto my butt.

"What's wrong?" Denton asked.

As he continued to walk down the street. "nothing" I said, grabbing onto my butt. The bite hurt for an entire week but I couldn't let anyone know that I have been bitten because I didn't want to go to the hospital again. Two months later the dog was shot by police. According to Denton, he claimed the dog had rabies. But I came to realize it was just another one of his ploys to scare me. My older brothers and sisters took great joy in scaring me, and I took great pleasure in making myself a nuisance around them and their friends every chance I got. That's why they called me Mikey for being so mischievous.

*P*irates booty

The summer was spinning by like a driver at the Indianapolis 500 race track. We were having so much fun we didn't even notice how quickly the fall was approaching. Denton, Vernon, Johnny and I were out late one night after my mother left for work. For the first time I was able to participate in their mischievous escapades. I was over joyed to be a part of their group and thrilled they allowed me to trail close behind armed with my rubber band gun loaded with a bottle cap ready for action. We ran down the alley like a disorganized mob, turning over dumpsters and hurling rocks at streetlights, missing the street lights by a baseball mile. We were moving so fast I didn't notice we were 3 to 4 miles from home. The night was getting long and as scared as I was of the return of the nocturnal monster, I was ready to go home and go to bed.

The hour was approaching midnight and we decided to venture back toward familiar territory, all of the sudden Johnny took off running.

I said to myself "where is this fool going?" he was running towards the bakery glass door.

I thought he would come to a screeching halt but before I knew it, he jumped right through the glass door. Glass shattered all around him. Hitting the ground, he slipped and slid on the fallen glass then ran inside the bakery, grabbed two loaves of bread and ran down the dimly lit street. The alarm sounded, my brother ran but I went to the bakery door in anticipation of grabbing more bread; I knew there was no point in getting the bread other than proving my worth to the bread bandits.

We all started running at a full stride, I heard sirens in the background, and my heart was beating like an African drum. For the first time I feared for my freedom. I just knew we were going to jail. Once we reached our backyard I collapsed to the ground. Johnny was laughing as he tossed his loaves of bread in the air, refusing to share his pirate's booty with anyone.

"Are you freaking retarded or what? I said.

Trying to catch my breath.

(Johnny) "What did you say"

(Mikey) "You heard me, you fucking retard.

Johnny ran towards me so fast I didn't have time to think, so I release the clothes pin on my rubber band gun, and shot him in the eye with a bottle cap. I was as surprised as he was, I didn't even know my rubber band gun had so much power. Johnny screamed in agonizing pain and grabbed his eye. I ran into the house and observed him in pain from the back door.

Tears stream down Johnny's face as he covered his left eye swearing he would kill me when he catches me. I was quick to reload my rubber band gun and dared him to step a foot inside the house. I took my left foot and slammed the kitchen door shut, ran upstairs and listened quietly by the window with Rabbit ears; I could hear Denton and Johnny plotting against me.

(Denton) "I'll get Mikey to come out with us tomorrow night and once we are far enough away from the house I'll let you beat him up".

Johnny rubbed his eye, splashing cold water from the outside faucet on his face trying to relieve the sting of the bottle cap. He agreed to their new plot and began his painful walk home. Denton was thoroughly pissed off at me but he couldn't give his plans away so he didn't say a word.

I was up pretty early the next morning, the nocturnal monster was nowhere to be found. I was pleased with myself and I knew it would be a good day, until I sat at the kitchen table and tried to eat my over cooked cream of wheat Marica had prepared an hour earlier. She was notoriously known for her over cooked or uncooked meals, such as the raw potatoes she prepared for lunch.

There was no happy medium for her, it was well done or raw. I spent the morning with Carvale dragging a wagon down the alley and rummaging through trash cans for pop bottles. Once we collected enough bottles to fill several containers, off to the grocery store we went to collect our five cents per bottle. We wasted no time loading up on cookies, potato chips, and soda, then returned to Carvales basement and perched our feet up on top of empty boxes, reclining back against a dirty pile of clothes while we sipped down Nehi-high grape soda and choked down packages of cookies after a hard day at work. I could see someone's shadow outside the window, there were two heads peeking in and out. It was Johnny and Denton peeking through the basement window, they began beating on the glass begging us to share our pirate's booty with them, so I stood close up on the window and slowly twisted the cookie apart, licked the icing off, then shoved the naked cookie through the dryer vent.

They went ballistic making all types of threats, but I was in sugar heaven and couldn't hear a word; Therefore, I reclined back on my pile of dirty laundry and drink my Nehi grape soda and made the chips and cookies disappear one by one. Before I knew it, the night was upon us once again. I sat on the front room floor watching a rerun of the Wizard of Oz, Denton looked at me and said.

"Come on man let's go".

I sat for a brief second pondering what I heard Denton and Johnny talking about the night before, but if I was to go with them I would surely need an advantage so I ran upstairs reached under my bed and dragged out my PF Flyers. I just knew this would give me the advantage I needed. If Johnny tried anything I could escape with the quickness. Off we went into the night to cause more destruction than the night before. As usual, I stayed behind my allowed 10 paces, but for some strange reason they signaled me to come up with the rest of the group.

Unfortunately for them I had the six sense of a wolf, I could detect what was going to happen before it happened. As they turned the corner I could see part of Johnny's shirt blowing around the edge of the building. Johnny stood at the ready waiting to pulverize me as I turned the corner. That's when my PF Flyers kicked into action. I took off like a bat out of hell, running down the alley, jumping fences and turning corners like I was on rails. I ran into the house and collapsed on the floor laughing to myself.

"They must think I'm the stupidest kid in the world" I said to myself.

Congratulating myself for escaping another one of Denton's plots.

The summer had ended with a bang, capped off by the return of Denton to my grand-mothers house. I started school in September entering the fourth grade. I was dressed to impress, wearing a gold silk shirt; brown pin striped pants and brown patent leather shoes that were two sizes too small. I was always known for fashion, I knew the shoes were too small but it was my first time having shoes with a buckle on the side. I had two outfits to wear for the entire year, my shoes were too small for my feet with only myself to blame. While shopping with my mother I tried on two or three pairs of shoes, they all fit my feet, but the ones I liked were too small, but I was willing to suffer the pain to have style, so I pretended the shoes fit like gloves and persuaded my mother to buy them.

To keep the circulation going in my feet I spent the next few months taking my shoes off once I reached the class room. I was growing up fast, now in the fourth grade but still at an impressionable age. It was the late 1960s and life had not yet challenged me and major life influences had yet to show their face. New friends meant new experiences; tough guys emerged from every hallway, unruly and misbehaved. As part of recess my class would go across the street to Fall Creek park for lunch time recreation. Several classes walked to the park at the same time including one teacher from every class. I was the first to make it across the street because I wanted to be the first one to climb onto the swing sets. There was a wading pool, 2 feet deep surrounded by a 10 foot high fence. I swim in the pool many times but as I grew older the pool became too shallow for my aquatic needs. The teachers were still directing the other kids across the street so this gave myself and my other classmates plenty of time to explore behind the swimming pool and make our way down to the river.

*T*he beehive

Every day at 12 o'clock the class was released and escorted across the street to fall Creek Park. The park was very outdated with limited amount of recreational equipment. There was two sets of swings, a basketball court and a 2 foot deep pool for kids eight years old and under.

The lack of recreational equipment made the young boys restless. A group of 13 boys and I went behind the swimming pool building where we found a large Beehive. Our teacher warned us to come from behind the building and to leave the bee hive alone. All the boys slowly moved from behind the pool wall, except Michael Jones, showing that he could rebel against authority, trying to prove how defiant he was. Michael's brothers had reputations for winning fights, but the talent for fighting was not passed down to Michael.

Michael was not tough but this didn't stop him from living off his brother's reputation for fighting. This afternoon Michael wanted to prove how tough and defiant he was. Once the teacher was preoccupied with the other kids, Michael Jones took a long stick and jammed it right up the middle of the bee hive. The bees went crazy, swarming wildly trying to protect their queen. Forcing everyone back. Michael was trapped, unable to go in any direction and all of a sudden the hive fell straight down on top of his head. He yelled and screamed in agonizing pain, rolling around on the ground unable to escape the beehive trapped under his body, as he rolled around, the beehive rolled around with him. I never saw Michael again. I only heard rumors that he was walking on his toes from that day forward.

Our school had its share of good and bad teachers. One teacher in particular I will never forget is Mr. Schmidt, an unselfish and giving person. These were times where the American color line was drawn in the sand and the twisted face of hate was the mask of the day. The only time a black person got invited into a white person's home was to serve food or clean the house. Sometimes I think Mr. Schmidt did not see the color line or he just ignored it.

On Halloween 1969, Mr. Schmidt, orchestrated a way to take the entire class trick or treating, and during Christmas he invited the entered class to his home, took us caroling door to door and gave each student a Christmas gift. Mr. Schmidt found creative ways to get kids to learn subjects that were not interesting. He did more than his job required and that's what teaching is all about, loving what you do. I learned to see America from a different perspective; this is the second time in my young African American life that someone of a race other than my own showed me kindness, and unselfish love without expecting reciprocity or quid pro quo. Mr. Schmidt kindness and unselfishness was short lived but not forgotten. Over the course of five years my mother had been working double shifts late into the early mornings, and with a little patience and focus, she was able to put away enough money for a down payment on a new home. We soon were moving again, this time into our own house.

2 9Th and Talbott

My mother's diligence was now paying off. Working early mornings and late nights' finally paved the way for her to own her own home. Owning a new home was not without its envious neighbors and family members. We had the newest house in a four-mile radius, and my mother looked the world in the eye, took its best punches and came out smelling like roses. The house was filled with new furniture in every room, one TV in each room and a new car. People no longer looked at my mother in sorrow, but in con-fusion, they wanted to know how one young woman with eight children and apparently no husband or child support could buy so many new things all by herself. Everyone had something to say, the closer the people were to us, the more negative comments we had to hear. How they thought she was going to fail or lose her new car or her new house. What most of these people didn't know is that my mother is a survivor. The kind of survivor that draws from inner strength, the same inner strength that my grandfather had when he raised six girls on dead end jobs that broke his back eight hours a day. This strength moves through the blood of our entire family. Some family members are aware of this gift and some ignore it as though it's the plague.

Moving to 29th and Talbot Street was a big project for my family. Denton and I were in charge of moving the trash barrel from the old house to the new house, because in the early 70's we burned our trash every night between the hours of 6pm and 7pm. Trash pickup didn't come along until 1973 where every house would buy two alumina trash cans. Most trash cans did not last more than three months at any given time, due to the throwing, slamming and mishandling of the cans.

Using the cans for basketball practice didn't help either. 29th and Talbot was a street that welcomed characters. The names alone would scare the average person. Googie, Nene, Nibbles, Cookie, Hippy, Bede, Pewee, pookah, bey,bey. Uncommon names for an uncommon neighborhood. The neighborhood was jam packed with kids, every house had at least five or more kids in the family. The entire block came together over the years and merged into one big family. I made friends fast; the girl next door named An-gela thought I was handsome, she openly demonstrated her affection for me by giving me her older sister's fresh out of the box leather baseball glove.

The glove was new and made to fit a left hand person, which in my case the glove was a perfect fit. Only one day had passed before her older sister Myra saw me in my front yard tossing a ball in the air.

"Hey little boy" she said, "where did you get that glove?"

"Angela gave it to me" I said.

While tossing the ball in the air, Myra ran down the stairs in her bathrobe, the rope flung open exposing her monstrous chest. My eyes went temporarily out of focus and before I could regain consciousness from the site of nudity, she repossessed the glove right off my hand before I knew it. Needless to say Angela was embarrassed, but this did not stop her advances. Candy, kisses and unregulated wrestling matches pursued. She made me wrestle her for candy, but not without a small price. As long as I let her hands, rome free I could have all the candy I could eat. I was too shy to agree to such a deal, so I cut my ties with her not long before she moved to another neighborhood on the West side of town.

Within a week's time I was introduced to my aging neighbors Mr. and Mrs. Jenkins. Mother had a genuine compassion for other people, mostly people that struggle and I would soon be the crusader for her passion.

" Take the lawn mower and cut Mr. Jenkins grass and don't charge them any money because they're on a fixed income". My mother said.

Of course I looked at her with a twisted face, I was dead tired. I just finished cutting our front and backyard. I pouted a little bit but I reluctantly cut their grass. Just as I was finishing Mr. Jenkins slowly made his way down the concrete steps, his aging legs barely able to hold him up. Holding three dollars in his hand waving it in the air signaling me to come get it.

" That's okay, don't worry about it, there's no charge". I said.

Mr. Jenkins slowly made his way down the steps, then shoved three dollars in my shirt pocket.

'No" I said.

Sticking my chest out to ensure the money found its way inside my pocket.

" I can't take this" I said.

Smiling as he turned and went back into his house leaving the three dollars hanging visibly from my pocket.

My mother forcefully reminded me every time I was summonsed to cut his grass, not to take any money from him or his wife. Several months later Mr. Jenkins passed away and his wife moved into a nursing home. Within weeks a new family moved into the large three bedroom double. The family had a young girl and her two brothers. The two brothers were much older than I and their sister much younger. Puppy love was in the air, mostly on her part. Every day she would pop up at my door.

" Is Michael home?", she asked. With a huge smile on her face.

" Mikey's in the backyard" my mother would say.

Unfortunately, for her, I was compelled by orectic thoughts of race cars and burying treasure in the back yard. I had no interest in a pugnacious young lady.

That same week Bryce's son and daughter came for the weekend. Bryce's son Gilbert decided to rummage through my mother's closet. Bryce became angry and just as I thought, he was summonsed to the bedroom for some form of discipline which meant he was going to be whipped with a razor strap. Once the whipping commenced Gilbert screamed and yelled uncontrollably. I stood idling next to my mother licking the frosting off of the beaters she used to stir the cake. She paused for a second from pouring the cake batter into the pan.

"I don't like it when Bryce whips Gilbert, he whips him too hard". She said.

I frozen in my tracks with astonishment, as much as I love cake batter I couldn't even taste the batter anymore. I looked at my mother out of the corner of my eye with distention. All of these years Bryce has been beating the skin off of me and she never batted an eye. So I drop the eggbeaters in the sink, still dripping with cake mix, because it was of no use the taste have left my mouth and so did my sensibility. So I ventured down to the one place I could get it out of my system. The 29th St. basketball courts where I would spend most of my youth, from the age of 10 to the age of 18 years old.

$\mathcal{T}$he swimming lesson

I spent my summers secretly writing notes, placing the notes in jars then adding a few cents to the jar, then I buried the jars all over the backyard. I was ahead of my time, I was creating time capsules and writing down history as if I was a historian. My mother could sense my boredom and thought it would be a good idea to sign my sisters and myself up for swimming lessons at Riverside Park. My mother, Sherry, Tiana, and Marcia went to swim lessons in the evening. Denise and I would catch the bus two days a week for three weeks until the end of our lessons. Denise was separated into a different class than I and for some reason I didn't see her until the end of the swimming lessons. I was the only male in my class and found it very uncomfortable when I had to assist a young girl with her lessons. Sometimes we were required to partner up, to help another student with their back float exercise.

The young girl was required to wrap her legs around my waist as she lay back in the water. There was one small problem. No one told the young girl to shave her pelvic area before putting on her swimming suit. The other problem was her swimming top was too big and once she swim from one end of the pool to the other, her top fell off, displaying her well proportion young virgin breasts. I was caught totally off guard and nearly drowned in 12 feet of water when her breast were exposed and her Bikini top floated past my head.

Denise and I spent the next three weeks catching the bus to and from Riverside Park. After our last day of swimming we decided to celebrate and use the bus money to buy ice cream and walk the two miles home. Being the genius I was, the 2 miles turned into 4 miles. Somehow I got off course and we ended up near Crown Hill Cemetery. I was proud of Denise, she was only seven years old but she showed true heart and endurance and sacrifice for 10 minutes worth of ice cream pleasure. As we approached the house my mother and sister's was standing on the pouch.

'Their they are!" Sherry shouted.

Denise walked next to me dragging her towel, saturated in sweat with total exhaustion all over her face.

Quietly I cruised up to my room. I didn't want to be disturbed but the young girl next-door stopped by to see me. I didn't have time for girlfriends. She wanted a boyfriend, I wanted to ride bikes and play with hot wheels. I asked for hot wheels cars for Christmas but I got Johnny lightning cars instead.

It really didn't matter, either way I was having fun playing with my cars. Tina's brother Dennis was a heavy set kid who loved to wrestle, he reminded me of a young man from my childhood named Buggy. He was obese and slow, I could run circles around him anytime I wanted. One day I found myself in a wrestling match with him on a big grass lot across the street from our house. I could whip around his legs and get away from him easily, but once he fell on top of me, I cried wolf, making him lift his 155 pound body off of my back. Over and over and over again I cried wolf once he pinned me to the ground.

Once he got up I jumped on his back and climbed onto his shoulders, he flipped me to the ground like a rag doll, forcing my legs down and holding me to the ground. Suddenly there was a sharp cut, I screamed and yelled.

" Get up! Get up! Get off of me it's my knee, somethings in my knee" I said.

Screaming and trying to kick. But he wouldn't get up because of my prior attempts at crying wolf. Finally I was able to get him off of my back, blood streamed down my leg as

I gripped and squeezed my knee. Barley able to walk I collapsed on the front porch.

I reached down and pulled a huge piece of broken bottle from my knee. My skin was cut back so far I could see the white meat of my kneecap. I sat on the staircase inside the house clutching my knee. Bryce walked in reeking of alcohol. He staggered right past me to the stove, removed his food from the oven and began porking out on his fired pork chops and mustard greens. Leaving his plate on the table he staggered right passed me, up the steps then plopped down on the bed. He was asleep before his head hit the pillow. The next morning my mother looked at my knee, and was thoroughly disgusted that Bryce did not take me to the hospital. My knee healed with very little medical attention but left a U shaped scar for good luck.

My hair had grown, and so did my popularity. My afro had grown past my shoulders. I had grown at least another foot and I very closely resembled Michael Jackson. My new friends Chris, Enron, Victor, Lundy and Johar didn't think I looked like Michael Jackson. The band down the street thought I looked like him, so they put me up front and center on the microphone. I couldn't sing a note, but I looked the part. Enron and Pier were also in the band, although I couldn't carry a note. Enron and I grow into good fiends because of our participation in the band. Chris and I grow into good friends because we both liked to work on projects, walking in the river or playing basketball.

 For some reason Chris was smaller but always better at basketball than I. Victor and I became good friends because of our mischievous ways. We often responded to life on a day-to-day basis, never planning or preparing, we just acted on our misguided behaviors and impulses. Victor and I would walk around the surroundings neighborhoods looking for mischief; we often founded it not far from our front door. I spent most of my evenings that summer rehearsing the new Jackson Five songs so I could be ready for band practice. I thought for sure that I was famous and had to do something to improve my appearance for my fans. So I decided to blow out my hair so I could increase the size of my Afro. For some reason, young girls found large Afros very attractive and I didn't want to disappoint them.

I was busy one evening blowing out my hair, trying to please the one or two fans I had who screamed my name every time they saw me. I grabbed a huge jar of crown royal grease. With the fire from the gas stove on high I placed the straightening comb directly on the burner. I was just repeating what I saw my mother do to my sisters hair a thousand times. I applied little grease to my scalp, wipe the straightening comb with tissue paper, then ran the straightening comb through my hair. I was just about done, more than halfway finished blowing out my hair. All of a sudden there was a spark, the more I fanned the spark, the more the flames spread. I fell out of the bathroom into the kitchen, my hair burning wildly out of control. Denton and Sherry jumped to their feet, slapping vigorously at my hair, but the fire continued to spread. Suddenly Sherry got the bright idea of grabbing the dish sprayer and soaking my grease filled head with water.

The flames instantly shot to the ceiling of the kitchen. I ran into the front room blinded by flames, all I could see was darkness, as if I was lost in the middle of space. The fire was finally subdued with a damped towel. I walked around in a daze with the straightening comb melted onto my forehead. Denton slapped the comb from my frontal lobe, ripping off a layer of skin from my forehead, displaying 6 inches of white meat. I was barely conscious walking into the ambulance. A crowd began gathering outside, coming from the small two block radius of our neighborhood.

Everyone knew it was me, there was no escaping, because I was paraded from the house into the ambulance, with my hair burnt to the root. The ambulance siren screamed, car's pulling to one side of the road. Once at the hospital I was placed onto a gurney and wheeled down the hallways familiar to my childhood. My mother got word that I would be arriving at her hospital any minute covered with third degree burns. The elevators were too slow, so she ran four flights down to triage where I was once again being held captive by people in white coats.

I was all but shook up, it was a comfort to see my grandmother, my uncle George, and auntie Dorothy in the waiting area. To my very surprise my father was there as well. He gave me hard discerning looks.

" You think it's my fault don't you" he said to my mother.

"How the hell is it your fault Raymond, you weren't even there". She said.

I sat quietly in the backseat of my father's car hoping the crowd in front of my house was gone. I lay in the bed that night with a fan blowing on my fingers trying to cool the first degree burns covering both my hands.

Denton acquired burns as well on his hands and arms and for the first time I was actually glad he was home for the summer. This little incident gave me a short-lived vacation, I stayed out of school for two weeks staring out the window at the kids walking to school. While at home my mother removed the mummy like bandage from my head and cleaned the burned hair from my scalp, I was then escorted to the barbershop. I sat in the chair horrified at my reflection in the mirror. My hair was burned completely down to my scalp. I couldn't help but to cry, I looked like buckwheat. But the barber was an expert, he meticulously cut and styled my hair into a crewcut fashion I've never had before, although I was keen to long hair, my short haircut was very fitting. Teachers told me I looked like a young gentleman and they like the short hair much better than the long, out-of-control Afro.

I returned home later that evening to find my brother and his girlfriend actively engaged in puppy love. I tried sneaking in the front door only to find my brother and his new girl-friend sitting in the red chair next to the door totally engrossed in kissing.

Being Mikey, it was my duty to watch them kiss for what seemed like an hour but was only fifteen minutes before I decided to move in for a closer look. Denton was quick to kick me in the leg, then covering their display of affection with a coat. This sexual dis-play went on for more than a month. Whenever I heard noise and smelled strange scents coming from under the coat they used to cover themselves I would pull the coat off both of them, catching my brother's hands deep down inside his girlfriend's pants. Violence erupted soon after my twenty-five cent peep show. Denton would hit me with his hand covered with secretions, leaving residue on my back and arm. Fortunate for him our mother worked nights, and my stepfather was on the avenue drinking himself into a euphoric state of being. We didn't expect him home for at least five more hours. Bryce, my stepfather was a quiet drunk; he never caused problems or made any ruckus, he was a local truck driver, only leaving the city for special deliveries.

Bryce never gave me advice on life, never forced me to do homework, and never took me out to ball games or showed interest in me other than disciplinary action. Bryce spent his after work hours on the avenue, a place where alcoholics hang out to drink and talk loud about achieving nothing. Every other Friday, Bryce fancied himself the big spender at the bars on Indiana Avenue, It was payday and he was the host for the night, buying everyone drinks, bragging about the new house he lived in, the new car he drove, failing to mention the long hours my mother worked to buy the house and car.

Bryce lived the good life, living in my mother's house rent and bill free, nice clothes, cars, and no responsibility other than to himself and his drinking buddies on Indiana Avenue. My mother was doing financially ok, she maintained and provided for eight children. These were frustrating and difficult times, seeing my mother struggle as so many young mothers do to this day because the fathers lack the where with all to support their children.

Not only was he lacking in the financial area, but also in the area of parenting. I can't recall any special moments between Bryce and I, except once he took time to hand me a towel after I had been in a fight with the kid next door. Although he was not my father I felt that he had a responsibility as a black man to form some kind of kinship with me to ensure that I understood the world around me. The advice and direction I should have gotten, he neglected his duty and left me to experience those growing pains on my own. I was starving for attention and exposure to life. Just a few minutes a week could have made all the difference in my life. Another school year was beginning, I had just survived another summer on 29th and Talbot. New neighbors moved in next door, three boys and two girls.

One of the boys was in the same grade as I and I thought it was nice having a neighbor so close in age and in the same classroom. However; this kid turned out to be a total idiot. It wasn't long before his true behavior and personality came full circle. He spent most of his time starting fights on the playground during recess. During the time everyone else wanted to play, Larry was in the middle of fights at least twice a week. He quickly became a menace to everyone in the class, with the exception of a few boys who had older brothers that were recognized as neighborhood bullies.

These types of boys were high school dropouts who enjoyed hanging around the grade schools when school was out for the day. They bullied anyone smaller than themselves or larger than their brother or sister, enabling their brother or sister to remain the alpha male in school. There was one boundary Larry would not cross. Although, Larry had an older brother, his older brother didn't involve himself in gangs, therefore; Larry had no one to lean on for help. One night during one of the rare occasions when my brothers were both home and sleeping in the same room with me, we had a conversation about women, what women liked and what women wanted. Rayford was the narrator, demonstrating his voyager capabilities, telling us about his legendary sexual escapades and how many women he reeled into his cob web of decent.

$\mathcal{T}$he fight plan

Rayford had a revelation and thought it would be a good idea to show Denton and myself what a real man looked like when he was erect. So Rayford removed the sheets and pulled out his phallic and begin slowly stroking it as he described what it felt like to have sex, Denton was in awe, he leaned over the top of the bed, squinted his eyes trying to get a better view. I was thoroughly disgusted. I reached behind the bed, grabbed one of my shoes and threw it across the room striking Rayford on his penis. He grabbed his phallic and turned on his side.

'Rayford,"if Mikey throws another shoe I won't show you anymore".

Denton reached down from the top bunk bed and stuck his hand out to prevent me from throwing another shoe. Rayford went on stroking his phallic while Denton lay there squinting his eyes in envy trying to get a clear vision. I couldn't take it anymore so I grabbed another shoe and hurled it across the room striking Rayford's phallic once again.

"Rayford, I'm not going to show you anymore thanks to Mikey",

Denton was thoroughly pissed off at this point.

"Denton, "I'm going to tell Larry that you said you can beat him".

I knew for sure that I was in serious trouble, our school administrators appeared to have very little control over classroom and playground activities. Every time I looked out the window and saw a fight Larry was in the middle of it. Larry was not a big kid, but he was incorrigible. He had a house full of brothers. Even his sister looked very masculine. He was surely a troublemaker, the rumors of his fighting escapades were growing and no one was off-limits including me. Later that night I couldn't sleep. I tossed and turn the whole night imagining myself fighting Larry in front of a group of kids on the playground. I knew that Larry was a much stronger kid and had more confidence in the arena of fighting; I didn't know what I was going to do. I stood there staring out the window until the sun light peeked over the top of the Eastside of the Morrett hotel.

I gathered my shoes and clothes as quickly as I could then scurried down the steps to the front door, dashing past Larry's house as fast as my legs could carry me. I made it to the top of the hill of 33rd and Pennsylvania street. Surprisingly, Larry stepped from be-hind the bushes as though he had been waiting there all along. He slowly approached me with a menacing look.

(Larry) "Your brother told me what you said; when we get to school I'm going to kick your ass on the way to the Tabernacle Church for Bible study."

For some reason I wasn't too afraid, but I also knew that I cannot win a fight against this kid, therefore; I was very conscious of his whereabouts throughout the morning.

This was one of the few times during that year that we did have a teacher. Little good did that do, seeing how she was overweight, short, old, and slow. I was like a Klingon that morning. I followed close behind her throughout the morning never more than 3 feet from her at any time. When she went to the chalkboard I went to the chalkboard, when she went to the back of the classroom, I went to the back of the classroom. Larry stood in the background staring at me making faces and slapping his fist into the palm of his hand, and making impressions on his eye with his fist, then pointed his finger at me. I still wasn't overly terrified at the thought of fighting him I just didn't want to get beaten up. The teacher lined us up in the hallway as though we were having a fire drill and out the door to 34th and Pennsylvania Street.

Larry was walking one step behind me, I could feel his breath on the back of my neck, once outside I sprinted ahead of the class towards the teacher, but she was too far ahead, therefore; I stayed 15 to 20 feet behind her. I could see Larry out of the left corner of my peripheral vision walking fast, then turning into a slow jog. All the sudden he burst out into a full stride running right past me. I didn't understand, suddenly Kenny fell into the street clutching his left eye with Larry standing over him looking as if he had seen a ghost. Larry, "Oh I'm sorry man!" Larry exclaimed, "I meant to hit Michael not you".

Kenny continued to lie on the ground clutching his left eye, tears rolled between his fingers as he was trying not to let anyone see him cry, yes it was true, Larry had hit the wrong guy and he would have to pay for it.

The mixup was an easy mistake, Kenny and I both had big Afro's and were about the same height. From behind no one could to tell the difference between us and certainly on this day Larry's adrenaline was running so high causing him to definitely made the mistake of his life. Kenny wasn't in any way a tough guy, as a matter of fact he was a real wimp but he had brothers that were tough guys and notoriously known as gangsters. Once again I was protected by my guardian angels and for the second time Denton had failed miserably at his plans for having me beaten up. We continued our journey to the tabernacle church, once inside Kenny demanded that Larry sit next to him. Each time the teacher would turn her back and write on the chalkboard, Kenny would punch Larry in the jaw.

Larry was too afraid of Kenny's brothers and wouldn't think about striking back because of the ramifications. The Bible study class continued on for 45 minutes and Larry got 45 minutes of consistent right jabs to the jaw. Larry pleaded with Kenny as he confessed.

" Larry, I meant to hit Michael not you; I'm going to fight Michael on the way back to school".

'Kenny' "You better not touch Michael".

At this time I was safe and I had full control the rest of my day. I sat back and smiled and occasionally asked the teacher to write Scripture on the board making the teacher turn her back to us, allowing Kenny to continue to pulverize Larry.

I did my part to ensure that Larry would get beaten half to death by his nemesis. I must have raised my hand 30 times that day, more times than I've ever done in two school years combined. I was the kid with all the questions that day and I kept the teacher facing the board writing down scriptures, as Larry got pulverized for the first time and the shoe was placed on the other foot. After Bible class we headed down 34th street towards the school, Larry slowly approached me from behind, this time I was fully aware of his presence, but he was not there to pursue a fight he was there to strike a deal.

Larry, "I know how you can get out of me beating you up,"

"Mikey, How?"

'Larry' "Buy me some Now & Laters."

Mikey, "Kenny said, ' you better not touch me, so I'm not buying you anything".

I laughed and ran down the street to the head of the classroom as I walked next to the teacher smiling from ear to ear, untouched and unscathed. Kenny continued to punch Larry in the face as we walked down 34th St. Once we were back in our assigned seats Larry was sitting on my right and Kenny sat directly behind Larry. I continued my discord, I was more than happy to change seats with Kenny. I Smirked as I got up and moved to the seat directly behind Larry. For the rest of the day, Kenny continued to beat Larry while our teacher fell vastly asleep behind her desk. She didn't assume responsibility as teachers should do, for averting rancor between Kenny and Larry.

There was no need for Larry to fight Kenny after school because the fight would have been one-sided. Although Larry could have stomped Kenny's lights out with one hand tied behind his back he knew he would have to suffer the consequences of Kenny's brothers beating him up down the road, therefore; he elected to take his beating privately in front of a few students rather than in front of the entire school. This small incident must have taken the fight out of Larry, because I never heard of him fighting again and every day at lunch time I was free to gaze out the window and witness normal play activity on the playground.

There was no more fighting because the charlatan had been shamed in front of 30 students, so I thought. Larry was determined to fight me but he knew the consequences of his actions so he kept his distance and diabolically plotted his scheme. I noticed Larry whispering in a young girls ear. She had muscles like a bodybuilder and was well known for her fighting proweness. She had arms as big as my thighs and her thighs looked like something out of a comic book, big and muscular. She looked like a linebacker for the New York Giants.

I didn't understand why Larry would talk to such a girl because she wasn't his type. The assignation meeting with the muscle bound girl was very unsettling. My curiosity increased because Larry liked slim girls that he could control but she was ripped from head to toe, muscles coming out of every inch of her body. It didn't dawn on me until later that Larry canard a red herring story to get the pugilist well-built girl to fight me. Later that day the young girl walked past my music class, she staired at me with Bette Davis eyes, pointing her finger at me and pounding her fist into the palm of her hand.

"I'm going to kick your ass after school" she said, pressing her fist in her eye.

I wasn't intimidated because she was only a girl but a very large girl with muscles as big as Hercules. The bell rang and their she was posted outside my classroom. I stepped into the hallway and stood close to the music teacher, Mr. Over-by . Deb aggressively walked up so close to my face that I could smell what she had for lunch.

" I heard what you said about my mother". She said, with a disgruntle look on her face.

'Mikey' "I don't know what you're talking about"

'Deb' "I heard you called my mother a whore, I'm going to kick your ass after school".

There was no escaping the flight this time, it didn't matter what I said, she wasn't going to believe me. Throughout the day she stopped by my classroom, snatched the door open and pointed her finger at me. The word of the fight spread around the school like wild fire. Everyone was talking about it. I sat at my desk that afternoon staring at the clock. The clock was moving so fast I thought it was on crack. The bell sounded exactly at 3 o'clock, a huge crowd begin forming outside in the usual place. After the twins stabbed Lala Johnson in the head I never watched another after school fight, I just walked away and pretended it didn't happen. But I wasn't walking away from this fight. For the first time I was the center of attention. I felt like I was standing in the middle of a crowded room screaming and no one cared to listen.

The atmosphere was full of so much excitement you would have thought people purchased tickets to a heavyweight championship fight. Things looked very bleak, my nemesis was at her peak performance, she even motivated the crowd by doing several push-ups. I was in deep trouble, headed down shit creek without a paddle, so I slipped down the sidewalk and passed the crowd.

I reached the top of the 31st & Pennsylvania St.

"Thank God I was out of sight of the crowd" I said to myself.

I was one block from home away from the school, I was home free for the moment until Delvon yelled out.

"Hey Michael!" "There he is right there. Hold on man where you going?"

He ran down the street and stood in front of me simultaneously putting his hands out preventing me from going any farther. Soon the crowd caught up with us. More than 50 kids surrounded me.

The crowd parted like the red sea, Deb walked down the middle of the crowd stopping nose to nose, face-to-face with me. Yelling and screaming but never hitting or touching me, in a minute's time Larry shoved her violently into me. I fell on the ground and she fell on top of me. She began yelling and screaming and hitting me all at the same time. I turned over on my stomach and begin laughing at her lightweight punches which anger her more. She screamed and yelled pounding me on my back. The coup de grace came when she hit me on the back of the head causing my head to hit the concrete.

Enron, yelled out. "Here you go Mikey!"

Tossing me his large Afro pick with 6 inch metal teeth. I recklessly swung the comb over my shoulders striking Deb across the face. She screamed and hollered as I threw her off my back. Jumping to my feet I hit her two more times in the face with the metal afro pick. She screamed and grabbed her face then took off running down the street. Everyone laughed and patted me on my back and I couldn't have felt any lower.

Someone yelled out, "She has a butcher knife".

I took off running home, once again hopping the fence and escaping into the house. The atmosphere was very tense in school the next day, there was a rumor that she wanted to fight again. I had prima facie evidence that Larry was spreading rumors about a rematch fight. Once again after school the crowds begin brewing out front. I wanted no part of it, so I slipped out the side door entrance and took the long way home, down Meridian Street. I took this route home for the next several days to avoid any conflict and within a week's time the temperament of her wanting to fight again faded away. The fight was contrived by a vicious lie spawned by Larry. But as fate would have it he was no longer the king of the playground fights. He had succumbed to being internecine with the female population of the school.

Since he couldn't victimize the young boys anymore he started picking on the girls, any girl that he liked and didn't reciprocate his feelings, he picked a fight with her. Larry began dating Anita, a girl that complemented his personality, her bellicose personality seem to fit his persona, always being called down to the principal's office for behavioral problems. She wasn't really a bad girl. I recalled the time I went to the laundromat with her and her family. I spent eight hours washing and drying clothes just to get a sliver of ice cream. She wasn't a bad girl at all, she wanted to fit in because of her low self-esteem and her need to be liked.

Larry talked Anita into picking a fight with Patrina, a tall beautiful seemingly religious girl who didn't have an enemy in the world. Out of the blue Anita walks over and punches

Patrina in the face. Larry quickly got involved, hitting Patrina so hard she fell lifelessly to the floor, only to be stomped and kicked by Larry and Anita. As she lay there lifeless on the floor, the class began together around as though they were seeing some type of carnival act, no one cared about the poor girl laying on the ground getting stomped half to death, and I didn't have the courage or strength to help her. After three minutes of fighting the teacher from the class next-door finally recognized that there was a fight due to all the commotion taking place in our classroom. She came in the class and abruptly ended the fight and escorted Patrina down to the nurses office.

This type of incident could be attributed to the poor supervision of our class as well as the school districts. Once again we were without a teacher, without supervision, our principal at the time would come up to the classroom, start us on an assignment then disappearing back into the quiet cavity of his office. Our class would go unsupervised for weeks at a time, sometimes we would have a teacher for a few days, but we could go for three or four weeks at a time without having a teacher. This was one of those times that allowed for the bad behavior of Larry to come unleashed, almost snuffing out the life of one of our fellow classmates.

 Larry shifted his focus when another new family moved on the block, a single mother with two kids and a boyfriend. They occupied the other side of the double that Victor and Chris lived in. I didn't pay the couple much attention because their children were much younger than I. Her boyfriend appeared to be strange, I thought so anyway. Every time I went to visit Victor and Chris he stared at me glaringly as if I was a woman. He had a strange name, they called him Fuzzy Pants.

A tall, slim man pretending to know martial arts, gave him ample opportunity to fondle little boys. Larry and his brother grew very comfortable with the hospitality Fuzzy Pants offered them. Fuzzy Pants often had them at his house spending nights and doing minor chores around the house. One day as we were all sitting on the front porch, yelling and screaming begin echoing from the window.

" You're a Fag Fuzzy!".

His girlfriend was reading one of his love letters from another man out loud.

'Fuzzy' "Wait a minute baby, it's not as it appears".

"No Fuzzy, you're a fag! You're a fagg Fuzzy!" she said, yelling and screaming with a 32 caliber snub-nose pistol in her hand.

We sat on the porch laughing and It certainly validated what I believed all along. Fuzzy Pants was gay. The lady packed her kids and her belongings and left Fuzzy to himself. Larry and his brother took comfort in having Fuzzy pants all to themselves. Spending nights and curling up on the couch together. Larry in the back, Fuzzy pants in the middle, and Larry's little brother in the front. Fuzzy pants moved out of the neighborhood as quickly as he arrived, before the neighborhood thugs found out he was a child molester as he would have for surly lost his life or been beaten within an inch of his life.

Before the month was out there was a new kid in town occupying the recently vacant space on the other side of Victor and Chris house. Johar and his brother, sister and mother moved into the three bedroom home. He was a little light skinned wimpy kid. He loved acting tough based on his brother's reputation. His brother was a heavyset Bible thumping tough guy until he met the real thugs of 29th & Talbot Street. Johar often got into trouble, getting into fights with much younger kids, and letting his hands get light, meaning 'he loved to steal', such as the time he stole a handful of valve stem caps off several Indianapolis 500 drag racing cars. Most of Johar's time was spent picking fights in school with anyone he thought he could bully. One day he picked a fight with the wrong kid. The kid was a little wimp but he had bodybuilding brothers to back him up in case of a fight.

Johar's brother, Bunny Rabbit was a high school dropout. Oneday I couldn't help but notice Bunny was pacing back and forth, up-and-down the street outside of school #60.

What's wrong bunny, why are you hanging outside this school?" I said.

(Bunny) "See that little kid over there" I'm going to beat him up"

"Who? I asked, "That little boy with the black leather jacket".

Bunny, "He beat up Johar and now I'm going to beat him up".

"You're not for real, that boy couldn't be more than in the fourth Grade" I said,

"Well, that's too bad, he shouldn't have messed with my brother" Bunny said.

I noticed from a distance a well-known thug in the neighborhood crossing the street. He was the little boys oldest brother. The thug spent most of his free time with his other brother lifting weights, acting tough, and chasing girls. He walked right up to Bunny.

"What's going on man?", he said, looking at Bunny out of the side of his eye.

Bunny was so excited about fighting the little boy that he didn't hesitate sharing his plans. As Bunny talked, the body building thug began removing his belt and wrapping it around his hand, only exposing the huge cowboy buckle.

"See that little boy over there" "I'm going to beat him up, do you want help me?" Bunny said.

The thug looked at Bunny Rabbit out of the corner of his eyes, he took one step back, and yelled,

"No motherfucker that's my brother!" simultaneously beating Bunny in the face with his buckle.

The belt buckle swinging thug chased Bunny back down Pennsylvania Street only stopping a block from his home. Bunny Rabbit never hung out in front of the school again and never respond to Johar's cries for help. That fight would come full circle one week later, when the news filtered through our neighborhood that a local thug from one street over beat up one of the guys from our block. The king of thugs, the alpha male, named Bey lived three doors down from me and found it distasteful that a member of our block was beaten up by a member of another block.

It wasn't long before Bunny Rabbit saw the belt swinging thug hanging out on 30th and Central sipping on a bottle of wine in front of 500 liquor store. "Look he said, there the motherfucker goes right there. Bey casually strolled over as though he was going into the liquor store and before anyone knew it Bey punched the belt swinging thug in the mouth. To my surprise the belt swinging thug ran off into the night he didn't even try to fight back. Bunny Rabbit stood idly by smiling from ear to ear as the belt swinging ran off. The thug ran for help two blocks over and returned with four friends several minutes later. They came around the corner walking at an infantry's pace. I just knew there would be blood shed at hand. This was just like in the movies, just like West Side Story.

Bey, Rayford and two of their other friends were strolling down the street, when the belt swinging thug and his friend blocked the sidewalk, preventing Bey and his group of friends from moving any farther. One of the friends of the belt swinging thug stepped forward.

"Which one of you punched my boy in his mouth?" He said, with an intimidating look on his face.

Bey stepped forward, "I did" he said, with a forceful tone.

The other thug recognized Bey immediately and cowardly stepped back and recanted his challenge.

"I just wanted to know" he said.

They walked down the street as fast as their feet could carry them. I knew the belt swinging thug and his friend from my days of living on 30th and Park Avenue. I've never known them to back down from a fight, they were normally the perpetrators of fights, but now I had a new profound disrespect for their thuggish nature.

School went on pretty much the same for the next three weeks. I didn't understand the system; I wasn't learning a thing, most of the time I sat in the back of the classroom with Jedrek Goodnite drawing pictures from the political articles that I cut out of the news paper the night before. Not paying attention to anyone or anything in the classroom, I was systematically learning how to block out education and the confrontations in the classroom by drawing the atmosphere out on paper.

I don't recall Jedrek ever doing any school work during our class session, the only activity he ever took part in was art. From the time we sat down in the morning until the time the school bell rang at 3 PM Jedrek was engaged in drawing. I didn't realize at the time he was masking the pain that he felt from the recent death of his mother who was an artist as well. I just thought he was another kid too dumb to do the work, therefore; he chose to draw instead. I was never more wrong.

$\mathcal{A}$ bike for Christmas

I spent most of my summer that year trying to piece together bicycles, I spent hours on the patio cleaning up and sanding down rusted out chains and searching up and down allies for bits and pieces of bike parts. I was one of the few boys on the block that didn't own a bike. I would jog behind the other kids trying to keep up with them while they rode their bike's leaving me behind at their will.

I became very discouraged with the idea of not having a bicycle of my own. One morning, Victor, Landus, Enron and I rode our bikes toward the 60th block of Meridian Street. Victor and I rode on the handlebars while scouring the neighborhood for unchained bikes. And there it was, a brand-new Orange Crate bicycle standing unlocked in the bike cage.

The owners, two eight-year-old white boys just walked in the variety store leaving their bikes free for the taking. Victor looked at me and before he could complete his sentence daring me to take the bike, I jumped off the handle bars of Landus bike. I ran down and snatched the bike from the bike cage before the seat was cold. Victor followed right behind me snatching the other bike as the two young white boys ran behind us screaming.

"Bring back my bike, Bring back my bike".

We rode off like bats out of hell, taking side streets ensuring that we didn't run into the police. Victor laughed the entire way home, I was a nervous wreck because I knew I couldn't keep the bike. So I gave it to Victor in exchange for the older disfunctioning bicycle he took from the bike cage. I knew it wouldn't be hard to explain to my mother where the older bike came from because I had been building bikes from scrap all summer but I never had enough parts to complete an entire bike. But she asked anyway.

" Where did the bike come from" she asked?

I pretended like I was working on the bike.

"I got different parts from different people and put it together." I said, looking at her out of the side of my eye.

I felt so guilty about stealing the bikes that within the week I gave the other bike away as well. Every time I went out of the house I was a nervous wreck thinking the police could show up any minute and carry me to juvenile hall. The days I didn't spend at the basketball court I was in search of parts for building a bicycle or walking up to Douglas Park to swim or just relax by the pool. Our summer recreational options were limited. A two-week day camp was the best the city could offer.

We had a basketball court, a sand box, and a couple of horseshoe pits for our entertainment. Anyone with eyes could see that our neighborhood was economically deprived of recreational sponsoring. The city took our taxes and sent the money to the more fluent neighborhoods, allowing them to build cabins and to buy recreational equipment for their summer camps. Occasionally the Parks and Recreation Department would arrange for us to take trips to some of these day camps at Eagle Creek Park and other large parks in the surrounding city. Chris, Victor, Enron and I walked several blocks to 25th and park Avenue to the local pick up spot for day camp.

I thought the day camp idea was great but the recreational instructor was a little too aggressive. He did dangerous stunts and expected us to follow him. Such as going down a steep hill that ended in a 6ft deep marsh. The hill was so steep we could easily lose our footing and end up in the bottom of the marsh with water above our head. The recreation leader ran down the hill and I went right down behind him.

All the other boys took the safe paved road designed for humans to reach the bottom of the hill. But everywhere the recreational instructor went I followed, no matter how dangerous. I don't know why I did it, I just did. After a day of going up and down hills and through marshes, we retired to our own little section of the camp where they serve box lunches stuffed with ham and cheese sandwiches, potato chips and the standard grape drink which lacked vitamins but was a refreshing beverage.

We raced up and down the hills to earn the leftover grape drinks and potato chips. By the end of the day, arts and craft class was the last activity. The instructor was so impressed with my courage he secretly gave me a leather belt craft set while everyone else was weaving baskets or doing paper crafts. After summer camp ended we returned to our routine limited recreational options at our park, playing basketball or horse shoes. Victor and I couldn't stand the boredom of everyday life on the basketball court. So we ventured out of the neighborhood for a more adventurous and exciting life. There was a pool party happening right in front of us at the Stouffer's Inn hotel.

The temptation was too great to let this one pass us by. So, we ran down the alley and climbed over a fence into a neighbor's yard, where we picked a bushel of crab apples. Climbing back over the fence we raced towards the pool party clinging to the crab apples stuffed down our shirts. We took the long way around to the side of the hotel and lay flat on the inclined of the hill. We bit off the stems of the apples as if they were grenades then lay silently on the side of the hill out of sight of the rich and undeserving. They couldn't see us but we could see them living the high bourgeoisie lifestyle, so we begin throwing crabapples in the air. People were running screaming and falling into the pool destroying their tuxedos and spilling their hundred dollar bottles of Champagne. We laughed as we threw crabapples in the air like hand grenades hitting everything that moved. Then we disappeared into the night like the bandits we were.

We ran down Meridian Street laughing to ourselves. At in instant Country western music stopped us in our tracks. I couldn't believe it, there was another party two blocks away at the Children's Museum, jammed packed with Europeans dressed up from head to toe in cowboy outfits. I thought all the whites moved out to the suburbs away from the urban communities. This time it was a country-western party.

Everyone was dressed up in country-western outfits, square dancing their little hearts out. We couldn't resist. This time we made fun of their music by dancing like the Beverly hillbillies and Porky the Pig. Victor would place his finger on the top of my head. I put my hands on my hips while sticking my tongue out and turned around in circles. I couldn't believe it, they loved it. They invited us to come inside the fence and dance. A tall middle-aged white woman came to the fence and handed us five dollars apiece. We stuffed the money in our pockets and took off running down the street never completing our unofficial contract for dancing.

We took our new wealth and went our separate ways for the night, not before stopping by the candy store and loading up for a midnight snack as we once again sat on the neighbors porch to watch the traffic lights, trying to stay awake until the lights started blinking. Once again we fell short of our midnight goal and headed home to the comfort of our beds.

Before the end of the summer the city thought it would be a good idea to host an ice cream social, downtown at the Memorial Park. Ice cream trucks parked all around the square of the park on every corner. There must've been at least 15 ice cream trucks parked in different locations. All the ice cream we could eat was free. I couldn't believe it, I ate more chocolate covered ice cream bars in one day than I've eaten in my entire life. We sat on the grass watching the fireworks and listening to music. I ate and ate and ate until my stomach poked beyond my belt line. I was drunk from all the ice cream I'd eaten. At 9 o'clock that evening the social function ended. The long walk home would give me a chance to burn off the ice cream.

We headed down Meridian Street enjoying the scenic view as we walked home. Suddenly my stomach began to rumble and with every step I begin to fart, then there was more pressure and all of a sudden I had the urgency to go take a number two. I ran ahead of the crowd, trying to make it home before I had a messy accident. My stomach wasn't letting me off the hook from eating all that ice cream. I ran and ran and ran until I was ahead of group by three blocks. I made it as far as the Fall Creek Bridge. The pressure from the ice cream wasn't taking any prisoners, so I had to ditch down by the riverbank, pull down my pants and let it rip. The ice cream blow out of me like an uncorked bottle of champagne. All the ice cream I had just eaten ended up on the bottom of the river floor leaving my carbon foot print for the next generation to find.

My summer ended with a bang and a sense of urgency, but I was the better for. The beginning of school was upon us once again, but the style of dress totally changed. Bell bottoms pants, platform shoes and hot pans were the fashion of the day. I saved enough money to purchase a brand-new pair of Converse sneakers, this time a pair that fit my feet. My mother didn't purchase bell bottoms, however she did purchase two pairs of Wrangler jeans. I pressed my jeans all night trying to get ready for the first day of school. I was entering the seventh grade and had to look the part. I didn't care about my education I only cared about how I looked. My hair grew back in superb fashion, longer than It was before the fire. My mother did such a great job putting the cocoa butter, consistently applying it to my fore head, ears and fingers, the discoloration went away and you couldn't even tell I had ever burned myself.

Winter was upon us once again, Jack Frost was serious this year, the nip of the wind was a little colder, and the temperatures fell a little farther. The coldest day of 1973 was December 22, with a low temperature of-3°F. For reference, on that day the average low temperature is 24°F and the low temperature drops below 8°F only one day in ten. The coldest month of 1973 was January with an average daily low temperature of 23°F. I really didn't care how cold it got, a new bike could cure all the coldness Jack Frost could Manifest. However, Christmas did arrive, my brother Rayford couldn't wait for Christmas morning, so he took a gift into the bathroom, unwrapped it, played around with it, resealed it and placed it back under the tree. I was too scared to try such tom foolery. I waited patiently for the next morning.

I sat in the red chair next to the front room door trying to catch a glimpse of the huge bicycle box stuffed behind the Christmas tree. I was so excited I couldn't sleep. I sat at the top of the stairs listening to my mother and brothers assembling the bike. I practically went to bed around 7 PM trying to rush the night by, leaving the bedroom door ajar just enough to see my mother and brothers busy at work taking Christmas gifts from her closet and placing them under the tree. I fell asleep with my face hanging over the edge of the bed, never seeing Santa or finished seeing the completion of my bike. Five in the morning I was already awake. I sat at the top of the staircase waiting for mother to give the okay to go downstairs.

" Who's on the staircase!" She asked, in a loud but exhausted voice.

No one replied, I sunk back to my bedroom and my sisters went back to their room.

At 6 o'clock sharp I found myself once again sitting at the top of the staircase.

"Go on downstairs" my mother yelled from our room.

All you could hear was eight set of feet tumbling down the staircase all at one time. I rushed directly over to the bicycle, smiling from ear to ear, and to my surprise it was a girl's bike. I was flabbergasted, I didn't want to see any of the other gifts, the bike was the only thing I care about and as far as I was concerned Christmas was over at that moment.

Denise ran downstairs, jumped on her bike and rode it from the front room to the kitchen and around the kitchen table. I sat on the staircase stairing at Denise's bike with a defeated look on my face, watching my brothers and sisters tear into their gifts. It appeared they got everything they asked for. Easy Bake oven's, Barbie dolls, radios, watches, a drum set for Rayford, a guitar and amplifier for Denton. My mother did a great job as a single parent, providing us with our Christmas wishes, but somehow I felt lost in the shuffle of eight children. I received only one gift that I asked for, a digital watch.

The sun came up, and for the first time all week the temperature rose up to 25°, just warm enough for Denise to take her bike out onto the snow covered sidewalks. The streets were jam-packed, kids riding their new bikes up and down icy and snow cover ed streets. Icicles hung from the tree limbs, the sun shone brilliantly, melting the small patches of snow on the sidewalks as if it knew to clear a path for one day of excitement.

I presented a hapless figure as I leaned against the fence in envy, wishing I could've gotten a bike that year. My farouche behavior did not win me any friends that morning. Denise was cognizant of my disappointment, she graciously stopped her bike in front of me.
"Here you can ride it. She said.

I quickly jumped on the bike taking it for a spin around the block, but it wasn't the same and it wasn't my bike. I grew bored very fast riding a girls bike up-and-down the street, being laughed at by my friends. I resigned myself to the house and watched my sisters make cakes in their new Easy Bake ovens.

They put on their little aprons, pour the Jiffy cake mix into a bowl. Once the preparation was complete, they poured the mix into a little metal tray and slid it into their Easy Bake oven. They sat in fornt of their stove's for hours looking into the oven door of their Easy Bake oven watching their cake being baked by a lightbulb. Two hours when by and the cake mix was as raw as when they first put it in the Easy Bake oven.

"Could you watch my cake while I go to the bathroom". Tiana said.

"Sure I'll watch it" smiling from ear to hear with a sinister smile.

As soon as I heard the bathroom door shut, I drank the cake mix out of the metal pan, then tossed the pan back into the Easy Bake oven. I love cake, I didn't care whether it was uncooked batter are completely baked, I just love the way it taste.

I grabbed my basketball and ran down the street toward the basketball courts. I could hear Tiana screaming and hollering from a half block away. I wasn't too concerned because a box of jiffy mix, only costed 15. Cents. I stayed at the basketball court that afternoon freezing half to death. The temperature was no more than 29° but we didn't care because the older boys didn't come out to play basketball in the cold weather. We had the court all to ourselves. One thing that always worked in my favor I had a lot of sisters which attracted a lot of girls. Every time I walked into the house it was like a concert just for women. Girls fill the front room, Cupid, Faye, Diane, Nipples, Kim, Cookie and some other girls I didn't know. I hid behind the couch as a little brother would do, and tossed my shoes at them as they walk past.

Someone suggested we should have a snow ball battle, girls against boys. We all ran outside across the street to the big empty grassy field and began making fortress for protection. Chris, Victor, Enron, Lundy and I rushed to make hundreds and hundreds of snowballs, preparing for the battle we were sure to win. Once the battle began I couldn't bring myself to hit anyone with the snowballs except for my sister Tiana. It took 30 minutes to build a fortress and the snowball battle lasted just as long. The sun began to set, the cold air developed more of a nip with the disappearing of the sun. My tennis shoes were soaking wet and my toes were frozen like french fries. My fingers were frozen in place and I could no longer make a snowball or attempt to throw one.

One by one everyone disappeared into their homes leaving our fortress in place. The snowball battle ensued is everyone went about their way throwing snowballs at each other as they went toward their front door. These were cold but good times, times that we would never relive again. The next morning I searched my pockets for loose change but all I could find was lent filling the crevices in my pocket. Snow was falling by the tone and all of a sudden I had a bright idea.

I grab my shovel, walking house to house charging three dollars a yard to shovel their sidewalk. I worked until I had enough money to purchase a half pint of ice cream, a pack of cookies and a soda. The thought of those refreshments motivate me to walk from house to house until someone trusted me to shovel their sidewalk properly. After working diligently for more than an hour I earned my first $4 and off to the Standard food grocery store I went. I decided to take the shortcut through the parking lot of the Stouffer's in hotel. Something was amiss, there were streamers and declarations around the entry to the hotel.

A big sign with a picture of Jerry Lewis also stood at the entryway. It was the Jerry Lewis telethon. Being the mischievous, curious kid I was I ventured into the hotel. Signs lead me down the hallway and into a big room where Gruff the crime dog was on television taking donations. I sat in the audience watching and cheering before deciding to donate three of my hard earned $4. Every kid that walked up got a hug and a chance to be on TV before Gruff took their money.

I was next in line, Gruff the crime dog looked right past me, I wave my money in the air trying to get his attention but he went right to the next little white boy or girl not bothering to acknowledge my presence. So I tossed the money in the donation can and walked out. I've never been so humiliated in my life I did not understand it and I wasn't going to stick around for an explanation. There were new chips coming out on the market. 'Doritos. .75 cents a bag and I wasted no time being the first in my family to sample the Doritos.

A White Castle summer

Summer was beginning to feel long and drawn out. We were running out of things to do or should I say constructive things to do. Either way I was ready to return to school. Most kids were in the house by 9 o'clock including myself but I would slip back outside as soon as my mother went to work. We settled down for the night on my neighbor's front porch watching the stoplights, waiting for them to start flashing at midnight. By the time 11:30 pm rolled around my eyelids were involuntarily shutting on their own. I had no control or say in that matter so I made my way home and crawled into the bed only to be awakened by the smell of corned beef.

I knew it was my older brother Rayford before I opened my eyes.

"Mikey you awoke? He said, while tapping me on the shoulder.

"I am now, what do you want?" I said.

"Here's three dollars, why don't you go downstairs to sleep".

I gladly grabbed his $3 and made my way downstairs to sleep on the sectional couch. I couldn't believe it the next night he was back again, reeking of corned beef and requesting that I provide him a hotel rate of $3 to sleep downstairs. I gladly rolled out of bed snatching the three dollars from his hand while making my way to the couch.

Night after night it was the same thing, first the awful stench of corned beef smell, then three dollars shoved into my mitts. I couldn't take it anymore! The next night I stayed awake in anticipation of his arrival. He was like clock work, I heard them coming up the steps, two sets of feet pounding on the staircase, as the stench of corned beef preceded him. I squinted my eyelids pretending I was asleep, trying to sneak a peek at the well proportioned female standing next to my bed. "I would take my clothes off but someone's in the room" she said.

"He's asleep" Rayford said.

Bending over looking in my face and tapping me on the shoulder.

" Mikey, Mikey, are you sleep?" I lay still as a rock, pretending to snore.

" See, I told you he's asleep," he said.

Setting his large "20 sack bag" of White Castle Hamburgers on the table with two extra large orange sodas to wash it all down. Ahh, I thought to myself, those burgers smell refreshing. A sense of hunger and thirst rushed through my body like water through the Titanic.

The robust girl climbed under the covers and began disrobing. I squinted my eyes trying to catch a view of what a robust naked female looked like. My brother didn't waste any-time, he went right into it. I squinted my eyes and enjoyed the show. I had a young and limber body so I was able to stick my hand in the big bag of white castles, cautiously pulling out one box at a time. The burgers were still warm. The grilled onions and melted cheese made me salivate as I began porking out on a White Castle hamburger, then tossing the empty box behind the bed. The sex lasted for three minutes and for every minute Rayford was preoccupied, I ate two white castle hamburgers and washed it down with one of his extra large orange sodas. I was thoroughly fed and entertained, there was nothing else I could do. After letting out a loud White Castle fart that could wake the dead, I fell into a deep sleep under my wool Flintstone blankets. The next morning Rayford was up at 6 AM sharp, rushing his latest mistake to get dressed quick-ly. Out the door she went before my mother arrived home at 7:30 AM.

'Rayford,' "There's White Castles in the refrigerator if you want them".

"No, I'm okay, I don't want any." I said, laughing to myself.

$\mathcal{A}$ **fight among friends**

The next morning I was slow getting to my feet, I was still full from the night before so I lay in bed and didn't get up for 30 minutes until the sun was slowly resting comfortably on my face. I wipe the sleep from my eyes staggering from the bed into the bathroom. I was so full from eating six White Castles that I bypassed the leftover bacon, eggs and biscuits left on the kitchen table from my mother's and Bryce's breakfast. I headed straight outside down to the basketball court.

Victor and I played several games of 21 until the teenage boys used their authority, pushing us off the basketball court. We ran up and down the street and through the alleys stopping at a stack of tires, two houses from my home. Suddenly rocks began coming from nowhere, Chris and Enron was in the garage hiding, occasionally sticking their head out and chucking rocks at Victor and I. Within seconds a full all out rock battle was in progress.

Chris and Enron had the protection of the garage, Victor and I stood in the open giving is good as we got. I glanced down looking for a rock, but the glare of a piece of broken glass caught my attention. Rocks buzzed past my head as I stood there staring at the broken bottle. The bottle was staring at me and I stared back. It was as if I was in slow motion bending over to pick the broken bottle up. Before I knew it I had it in my hand. I threw the broken bottle with the intention of making it ricochet off the garage never intending to hit anyone.

Chris began poking his head in and out of the garage as I flung the glass toward the side panel of the garage. Right as the glass was reaching the entrance of the door, Chris stuck his head out and the glass hit him In the eye. He disappeared for several seconds inside the garage and all of a sudden he came charging out of the garage with a brick in his hand. I didn't know what I was doing I just took off running. I climbed up a stack of tires and fell and before I knew it, Chris jumped on my back and smashed me in the back of my head with a brick.

I wasn't physically hurt, just my pride. So I made it to my feet and staggered into the house with blood trickling down my neck.

" What the hell happened to your head boy?" my mother said very angrily.

"Chris hit me in the head with a brick" I said.

Before I could tell her what happened she ran into the street and confronted Chris, then returned to the house to give me a wet cold towel to apply to the base of my head. The entire week when by before my mother allowed me to play with Chris again. I just happen to be in the backyard one day when Chris, Victor, and Enron were heading down that alley into mischief. I was bored out of my mind so I jumped the fence and joined the group. My mother yelled from the door.

"Don't come home crying if you get another brick upside he head" I laughed and ran down the alley with my friends.

Summer was a blast but it blew by as fast as it came, but not before another fight would take place between friends. Early one morning Chris and I ventured out to the basketball court at eight in morning. Just before 9 o'clock we got bored with basketball and decided to make our way down to Enron's house so we could ask him to come to the basketball court. We knocked on his door and his brother, boy George answer the door.

"What do you want this early in the morning?" He said.

While wiping the morning residue from his eyes.

"Where is Enron?" Tell him it's Mikey and Chris and to meet us at the basketball court"

"Enron isn't here," said Boy George.

Then slamming the door in our face.

"You little punk, go get Enron" Chris said.

Continuously knocking on the front door, boy George ran to the second floor and began throwing soap out the window at us. Chris and I began furiously collecting the soap throwing it back at the window. Chris yelled out.

" Enron's throwing soap too, I just saw him" were going to get you Enron when you bring your punk butt out of the house"

Chris and I made our way up the street towards the children's museum. We knew Enron loved hanging out at Ray's service station, so we waited idly across the street lying on the well manicured lawn of the Children's Museum. Enron was so predictable, we could had set our watches by him. Just as we predicted he came marching up the street as happy as a lark.

We jump from our hiding places and surrounded him.

"We saw you throwing the soap at us punk," said Chris.

I stood on his right side looking menacing. But Enron was my friend, I've known him since he was five years old and I was reluctant to fight him, therefore; I did the bare minimum I could have done. I shoved him making him stumble back and before I knew it Chris punched him in the stomach then we fled across the street inside the Children's Museum. Enron cried holding his stomach as he ran home. I feel horrible inside as I watch him cry his way home. I was willing to receive any punishment my parents could dish out.

Chris and I went our separate ways. Chris went to the basketball court and I was told to come home because my mother wanted speak to me. I reluctantly went home and just as I suspected my mother was going to punish me with a whipping. But fortunate for me we were on our way to our grandmothers house were visions of orange slice candy danced in front of my face in a candy dish. Chocolate cake set three layers high on the kitchen table smother with rich chocolate icing. The smell of a three course meal and the fragrance of my grandmother's perfume came home like truth. These were the best days of my childhood, a place I always felt safe and loved.

The beauty of autumn was upon us the leaves were poetically beginning to change into beautiful orange and yellow colors as they fell lifelessly to the ground. New chores immersed as I was given the task of raking the yard and piling the leaves in a stack for burning. My little sister and our dog couldn't help but to run through the leaves creating a small mess for me to rake up.

I love the fall weather and the holidays that came with it. Halloween being my favorite, dressing up and venturing out to receive all the free candy we could eat. I was growing up but I didn't think I had out grow halloween, but due to peer pressure in the neighborhood I was thrust out of halloween by 11 years old. The neighborhood high school dropouts hide in bushes and grabbed our bags as we walk pass. This type of behavior continued and grow from bag grabbing to throwing eggs at trick-or-treaters.

I became so pre-flexed by the entire situation I didn't bother to dress up anymore, I just knocked on doors and stuck out my bag, but the neighbors weren't having it.

"Go home and dress up and I'll give you candy" the lady said.

I was glad she didn't recognize me from the time I threw trash in her yard and ask if I could pick it up for a quarter. These were fun times that became notorious. Running down the street with flashlights, going door-to-door, dressed up like every creature imaginable. Then the infamous bag grabbing and egg throwing began. A tradition that didn't stop until I was well out of my teens or the neighborhood thugs grew up and moved a way or went to jail. The spring and the fall were my favorite times of the year. The summers were too hot and the winters were too cold, but nevertheless all four seasons arrived on time.

The holidays were up on us, I just knew this Christmas I would be riding a new bike, it was one of the gifts I had requested for the past two years. It was the beginning of another school year; the smell of fresh Blue Jeans and new clothes that were traditional for this time of year filled the air. Converses were the popular shoe of the day and every kid had to have a pair. I wasn't so fortunate, my mother was reluctant to pay $15 for a pair of tennis shoes when she was used to paying a $1. 99 for a pair of Buddy Els.

During the fall I would worked all day at Mac's candy store. He was an old nasty bald headed man who had the social graces of a Feral cat. He was a type II diabetic with one leg. He was mean and vicious and often boasted about the days when he had both his legs. He lost his leg when a city bus hit him while he was trying to get into his car. He said the bus dragged him three blocks before coming to a stop. Mac was mean but I enjoyed being around him because he was a character.

My mother questioned the amount of time I spent around him because she saw no good coming from it. Mac's candy store was pretty pathetic, the only type of candy he had for sale was boxes of chocolate Turtle candy. Turtle candy was my favorite candy in the world but even I grew tired of eating chocolate Turtle candy all day long. I sat in his store for hours watching the people walk past his window occasionally staring at the rows and rows of Turtle candy that lined the window sill. One morning I went by the store and Mac wasn't there, he was home lying in bed in chronic pain. His leg had turned black and purple.

"What's wrong Mac?" I asked, with a look of concern on my face.

He rolled back and forth in bed, moaning and groaning.

" It's my sugars boy, it's my sugars". "Handed me that medicine over yonder", he said.

I didn't know what he was talking about but I reached over and handed him a bottle of pain meds. The next day Mac was rushed off to the hospital and he returned a month later with his second leg amputated. By this time he had moved out of Lundy's house and into the back of the candy store, I played nurse maid for his first two weeks out of the hospital. I emptied his bed pan, cooked his lunch and dinner, made his bed and emptied his trash. I did all of this at no charge, I did it because I liked his character. I thought he was funny. My true reward came when he asked me to count out pennies, quarters and silver dollars and put them into rolls. Because the rolls had to have the address of the person turning them into the bank the work became even more tedious and time-consuming.

Mac had a small fortune safely tucked away inside of 10 to 12 five gallon water jugs. I never saw so much loose change in my life. I must've spent the next two months rolling quarters, dimes and pennies in bank rolls, then labeling them with his address. It was very tedious, boring and time consuming work. After stuffing coins for nine hours a day he would pay me one dollar an hour. After working an entire week he only paid me $45 for 45 hours of work. I felt as though I was being taken advantage of, therefore; I began to relieve his cash vault of several silver dollars.

 At the end of the day my shoes were stuffed with silver dollars. I walked as slow as I could to prevent the jingling of coins while departing the store. The silver dollars jingled in my socks no matter how slow I walked. But Mac was no fool, he let me go about my way. He never said I was fired, but he no longer requested that I returned to his store.

 Weeks went by and I would occasionally walk by the store and wave at Mac sitting behind the counter. He sat idle in his wheelchair sucking on a piece of candy nodding his head as if to say.

"Hi".

I couldn't help but to think he was lonely, seeing how no one wanted to buy Turtles candy. The next week he waved his hand in my direction ushering me into the store.

" What's going on Mac?" I asked, trying not to give him any indication I was happy to be employed again.

"Could you empty my bowl for me?"

I looked at him and rolled my eyes, but I couldn't help notice that the store smelled like an unfleshed toilet and burned eggs. Once I emptied his bed pan, he gave me instructions on how to cook hamburgers using two eggs and ground beef. I had to admit it was a little refreshing having my friend back. We kicked back in the store and ate egg cheeseburgers with a side of chips and a tall orange soda.

While lying in the hospital Mac had plenty of time to think, time enough to have an epiphany. He summoned a young man from down the street to drive us to the southside of town to the candy warehouse. I'd never seen so much free standing candy in my life. It must've been a dream, pallet after pallet of candy stacked ceiling high, row after row of Now & Laters. It was insane. I was literally salivating at the mouth.

I felt like I was in a Pavlov experiment. Every time the forklift would lower a pallet of Now & Laters, drool ran down my chin. We loaded the car up with more than $300 worth of penny candy. Once we arrived back at the store kids noticed all the candy and began gathering around. I felt like a celebrity holding back the crowd, they were standing in line just to see me. I removed all the Turtle candy from the display cases, with the exception of two boxes of turtle candy that I put in my favorite hiding place for a midnight snack.

Mac was proud of his new since of entrepreneurship, he just sat behind a curtain in the back room and watch the kids feverishly buy up his candy. Some days he would sit behind the curtain eating candy as he watch me count out and sell the penny candy to school kids. Once his back was turned I pop a piece of candy in my mouth and washed it down with the orange soda that he gave me for slap boxing with another boy for his entertainment. Mac was a diabetic but he ate just as much candy as the kids that came into the store.

Although Mac never caused me any harm my mother was leery of him, she was leery of what he might teach me, some of his bad ways, how to curse and act out. I liked being around Mac because he was a character. Sometimes he'd sit quietly in his wheelchair with his head down while nibbling on a piece of candy. Unexpectedly he would yell out,

"Yee"

He slap the wheelchair twice on the handle, spin around in a circle and fire his gun twice into the ceiling. Then, he would slap the opposite arm of the chair, spin in the opposite direction and fire two more shots in to the ceiling then go back into a slump and continue eating candy.

I spent early mornings and long nights in the candy store selling penny candy to the neighborhood kids. My mother didn't mind that I spent hours working in the store because our house was but an eye shot from the front of the store. If my mother were to step out onto her yard to the sidewall she could see the front door of the store. Every time I arrived home after work she questioned me as to what Mac told me that day.

I would never tell her everything Mac said or did in the store, such as firing his gun into the ceiling while spinning around in his wheelchair. Once again I was working 12 hours a day only to receive nine dollars by the closing of the store. I would've appreciated it more if he paid me in candy. I wasn't too disappointed in the amount of pay I received because I made up the difference with two socks full of silver dollars and all the Now & Laters I could stuff in my pockets.

I was in the sixth grade and as luck would have it Larry was once again in my class, although this time he was inconspicuous and didn't cause much trouble, therefore; I did not mind his presence.

I sat quietly in the classroom and observed the girls in their granny dresses and all the boys with their Converse tennis shoes, displaying different color shoestrings while wearing at least three different pairs of tube socks. Being from a proletarian family my mother was reluctant to pay $15.00 for a new pair of Converses, so I took the lead from my brother. I tried to fix up my buddy El's **(tennis shoes that cost $1.99 with hard rubber bottoms)** by lacing the shoes up with two sets of shoestrings, red and white. This way, no one should know the difference. It didn't quite work out the way I had planned, not only was I laughed at in the classroom, I was laughed at on the school play ground as well. I couldn't take it anymore, so I asked my mother if she would buy me a pair of Converse.

(mother) "Boy are you crazy? I'm not going to spend $15 on a pair of tennis shoes".

That Saturday I took my hard-earned money, and caught the bus downtown. I was so excited, I could hardly sat still in my seat. Within 10 minutes I would be sporting a new pair of Converses. The bus turned right off Meridian Street onto the downtown Circle and stopped in front of Murphy's. I pushed through the doors of the bus before they could open. I burst into the doors of Thomas Ands best known for carrying a wide variety of Converses. I walked into the store and it was like a dream come true, shelves and shelves of Converses, blue, red, white, and black. They even had the thick red, blue or white shoe strings that I'd always wanted, not the thin spaghetti strings that I laced my Buddy El's up with.

I meticulously took my time as I browsed the department store shelf by shelf, checking all the shoes but there was one small problem all the shoes were $15 each. There was only one pair under $15 and they cost nine dollars and some change out the door, but the biggest problem was the shoes were one size too small. I was a size 8 and the shoes were a size 7. I snatched the shoes off the shelf and cradled them under my arm as though I was carrying a crate of Now & Laters. I continued to search the store for my size and a price that could meet my budget. I looked for an hour before surrendering to the fact that this was the only pair of shoes that I was going to get and I wasn't about to place them back on the shelf. I knew this was my only option but I also knew this fashion statement would hurt my feet. I took all the money out of my pocket and place it on the counter. It was just enough money to pay for the shoes.

It didn't matter to me that I had to walk 3 miles home because I was ebullient by the new tennis shoes I just purchased. I carried one shoe in my hand as I walked down Meridian Street smelling the new rubber and playing with the shoe laces. I was so enchanted with my new shoes I didn't even realize I was standing in front of my house.

" (Mother)," Where have you been all this time?"

(Mikey) "I caught the bus downtown to buy some tennis shoes, and I didn't have enough money to ride the bus home so I walked".

(Mother) "Boy your crazy"

I may had been crazy but I had my Converses just like everyone else. I could hardly wait till Monday, I was so excited I began preparing my clothes. I pressed out a pair of blue jeans and a shirt. I hung them over the back of the chair, then I laced my tennis shoes with red and white laces, I washed out two pairs of socks so that my shoes could keep a fresh smell.

Normally it would be a setback for me to walk from downtown but I was destined not to be the odd man out anymore. From now on I was going to be like everyone else with a freshly pressed pair of blue jeans, a white T-shirt and a brand-new pair of Converses. I lay in bed that night curled up with my new shoes next to my nose, smelling the new rubber and dreaming about the impression I would make on my friends. I jumped out of bed the next morning and slid into my freshly starched jeans. The jeans were as hard as boards. I had to do several squat thrusts just to loosen them up. I put on my freshly washed socks and squeeze my foot into the tightly fitting shoe. My shoes were so swollen from the thick socks and the small fit, my feet looked like two pumpkins, but I didn't care, because I had to be like everyone else.

I could hear my friends joyously making their way downed the street approaching the front of my house, so I jumped over the fence striking a pose, displaying my new tennis shoes.

"Oh man, those are nice Mikey". Said Lundy. Smiling from ear to ear sucking up all the compliments, I joined the group and we walked to school, all of us wearing Converses with two sets of shoe laces and two pairs of socks. After one block of cruising down the street my feet began to cramp, my big toe started to bend in places I didn't even know it could bend. The closer I got to Mapleton Fall Creek School the more I noticed my feet were increasingly uncomfortable. My toes were going numb and my feet felt like they were in a vice grip. I dashed up the school steps and into the classroom.

I was just about crippled and couldn't take a step further as I slumped down onto the hard wooden and metal chair. I kicked my shoes off as though my feet were on fire. The circulation in my foot was cut completely off. My big toes looked like two large strawberries and my eyes were almost rolling to the back of my head from the pain.

I was too cool to display such pain in front of my peers, I couldn't let the rest of my classmates share in my embarrassing moment. They would never let me live down that I purchased a pair of shoes that were a size to small. I put my socks back on and slid my foot halfway into the shoe. Every time we changed classes, I put my shoes back on long enough to reach the other class, and once I was at my desk I took my shoes halfway off to give my toes breathing room.

I couldn't wait to get home. As soon as I walked in the door I had the bright idea of throwing my tennis shoes into the washer.

" Maybe this will loosen them up".

I thought to myself. Then I tossed them into the dryer, after 30 minutes of drying I was ready for the big test. I slid my foot into the shoe.

" Oh my god', I thought, these darn shoes must have shrink two sizes"

"What am I going to do? I can't wear these to school.

My Buddy El tennis shoes lay in the back corner of the closet staring at me as though they were laughing. I was so mad and disillusioned by the shrinking of my converses I thought my buddy El's stuck its tongue out at me.

The next morning I was at a Mexican standoff with my new, fashionable Converse tennis shoes. I could envision the painful mile and a half journey to school and back home. Because of the numbing of my big toe the journey home seemed like a 5 mile walk. It was either be in pain and torment and be stylish or be comfortable and wear a dorky pair of tennis shoes. Style won the argument, so there I was once again walking up Pennsylvania Street with swollen feet and tennis shoes that were now two sizes too small. I was so enamored with my feet, Mrs. Wright thought I was ignoring her Socratic method of teaching, so she called me to the chalkboard to write over and over again,

" I will pay attention in class".

While all the students were dismissed for the day I stayed in the classroom to wash the chalkboard and pound the erasers together freeing them of chalk residue.

That Saturday I thought it will be a good idea to break my new tennis shoes at the basketball court. Before we could started playing all the teenage boys showed up taking over the court and forcing us to the sidelines. Lundy stood his ground refusing to leave the basketball court as ordered by the older boys. The game ensued but Lundy stood right in the middle of the court shooting his basketball ignoring the older boys request. Out of nowhere came a 355 pound 6'3' tall man. He grabbed Lundy by the throat slamming him into the fence but Lundy refused to leave the court. He kicked, hit and punched Lundy repeatedly, finally grabbing Lundy's basketball throwing it across the street.

" Please just get off the court man is not worth it" I said.

 Lundy ran across the street chasing after his basketball. Lundy was forced to stand on the sideline like the rest of us until the old boys finished playing basketball.

We stayed at the park playing basketball late into the night. We left just before the street lights began to blink, we sat on Fred's porch looking at porn magazines and lifting weights until the Sandman sent everyone in opposite directions to their homes.

Talbot was a quiet street most of the time, the only noise you heard was the cheerful sounds coming from kids playing up and down the streets. Games like, hide and go seek, red rover, freeze tag, red light, green light, hide and go get it.

Hi and go get it was my favorite game because it had a sexual connotation attached to it. Meaning if you found a girls hidding place she was yours to have for the night. I was too young to think about having any woman for my own, I was still playing with hot wheel cars and rocking socking robots.

 The street light were our curfew. When the street light flickered, we were supposed to be in front of our house and when the street lights came all the way on everyone went into the house except for one exceptional family. I stirred out my bedroom window most nights, dreaming of foreign places I've never been. I often dreamed of California and walking along the sandy beaches, sitting in the shade of the palm trees and roller skating along the boardwalk. It was all a fantasy but for some reason I couldn't get it out of my head. I stared in the mirror at my face trying to imagine what I would look like once I turned 30 years old. Some people thought I was weird but it was early signs of my genius.

$\mathcal{T}$he educational leap

This school year was different, the kids in my class were much older and getting involved in more heinous activities. One boy brought a bottle of Wild Iris Rose wine to school. He led four of us into the bathroom. We stood around a huge metal sink sipping on the bottle of wine. I recognized the bottle from when I was eight, the time I got drunk and could barely walk up the steps. I thought the taste was disgusting then, and I had not acquired a taste for it yet. I stuck my tongue over the whole of the bottle, moving my Adam's apple up and down pretending as though I was drinking.

The other boys drank from the bottle, belched as if they were men or of some importance. Back to the classroom we went, the five of us huddled in the back corner of the classroom. The four boys were for surely high, I just pretended to be high so I could be a part of the tough guy group, but I didn't feel anything because I didn't drink anything.

For the next two months, right before class began I was summoned to the bathroom and presented with another bottle of Wild Irish Rose.

I was the only one in the group that had some form of income. Between my brother's sexual escapades and working in the variety store I had a weekly income of around $45. But I was reluctant to financially participate in the buying of alcohol. I mostly sat in the class and watched the other boys slumping in their chairs. I was no stranger to the effects of alcohol and I refused to be a poster child or accused of being a drunken student. Soon the perpetrator that had the ability to buy the wine was discovered.

He was a young man that everyone knew, he was an alcoholic by the time he was in the eighth grade. He dropped out of school and began a life of drinking and hanging out at the 500 liquor store on 30th and central where most of the would be tough guys found themselves after there was no one else to bully. By the time the young man was 25 he was barely able to walk and soon after he died as a result of his alcoholism.

Later that morning I was escorted to the principal's office by the dean of boys. I thought for sure he found out about our unauthorized drinking in the bathroom.

"Sit here" he said.

I looked through the glass separating his office from the waiting room as he sat at his desk and fumbled with a wooden paddle. I took a deep breath and thought to myself.

"I wish I had taken a sip of the wine, at least I wouldn't feel the paddle".

A heavyset short woman, wearing glasses with pop bottle Lenses tapped me on the shoulder.

"Come this way please" she said.

She handed me four pages of extremely difficult words, words I've never seen before. She asked that I put a check mark by all the words I knew. Then she gave me a puzzle to put together while she timed me. Next she came to my home and discussed with my mother about advancing me to the ninth grade the following year.

"I have to inform you, we're considering advancing Michael to the ninth grade next year" she said.

Staring intensely at my mother while holding a clipboard.

" I don't know about that" my mother said. (mother) "What do you want to do?" "Do you want to go to the eighth grade with your friends? Or do you want to go to high school?" It's your choice" Smiling, I reclined back in my chair.

" I want to go onto high school" I said.

The truth was, I just wanted a break from the people I've known since the third grade. I wanted to see a different crowd and be in a different place. I was excited for change, and couldn't wait for the opportunity to be around more mature individuals. I returned to class feeling uplifted, in truth I felt a little superior to all the seventh graders in my class. I felt more intelligent, one level above my peers. I kept it a secret to myself until the summer break I let it be known to my closest friends that I would not be returning to Mapleton Fall Creek school.

Of course they didn't believe me but the following year when school started in the month of September, I cruised right past their playground. I was proud as a peacock as I strutted past the kids encaged behind the fence. Several of the kids yelled out my name as I waved to them smiling. They couldn't believe I was going to high school. Some of the girls were so full of admiration, I was even invited to walk one home. Every time I walked past the fence, a young girl would approach and ask that I walk her home. She was in the eighth grade and now I was in the ninth and I didn't think it appropriate that I date someone much younger than I.

But she was relenting. After school she would grab my hand and ask that I escort her home. I didn't see any harm and since chivalry wasn't dead I obliged her. Her name was Susan and someone taught her well about how a young man should treat her and the old traditions of walking a lady home. She stopped me in my tracks and moved me to the other side of the sidewalk.

"A man is supposed to walk closer to the street" she said, smiling, she wrapped her arm around mine then shoved her books in my hand.

She was a beautiful girl and well mannered. Everyday was the same thing, I walked her home, then settled down to a nice quiet evening of holding hands on her front porch. Sex wasn't on her mind, but I was being coached by my kids. They advised me to break up with her if she wasn't putting out. Later that year her family moved out on 86 street and that pretty much ended our relationship for the lack of transportation on my part, and I wasn't willing to ride my bike 10 miles just to hold hands on the front porch.

*T*he Baby Fight

Summertime was quickly approaching, I could feel the surge of energy throughout the classroom, everyone seemingly mentally prepared to do nothing for three months but have fun, hanging out at the swimming pools and going to block parties. The last week of school was always fun, only a skeleton classroom was left during the final few days of school. I enjoyed this week because all we did was play throughout the entire week. I never got the privilege of missing the last week like other kids, my mother ensured that we stayed until the last day.

Summer had come and I was surely excited about the opening of Douglas Park and Riverside swimming pools, and the all night escapades of playing basketball with my four closest friends. I would awaken to find one of my friends Victor or Chris sitting outside my gate before I could brush my teeth and wash my face. Chris was a very creative and outgoing person. We spent our time building club houses and jumping ramps with our bicycles. When I was with Victor we spent our time relieving the grocery stores of their striped bubblegum or shooting someone in the neck with a BB gun.

Either way I was having fun. We would make our way down 29th St. on our way to Douglas Park swimming pool, we'd stop by the mailboxes and collect rubber bands to use for slingshots. Victor was a menacing kid but dangerously fun to be around. We made small changes in our plans for the summer each passing year, our old ways had not yet caught up with us. As time passed we matured from walking around with slingshots hanging out of our back pockets, to carrying BB guns. Someone who obviously didn't know Victor very well gave him a BB gun.

Since Victor and I were good friends he had no problem giving me a plastic bag of BBs and letting me keep the gun overnight. I was just as menacing with the BB gun as Victor, but the difference was I would shoot at cans and bottles. Victor shot at people. One day we were hiding on the side of Lundy's house behind some bushes that separated my yard and Lundy's yard. A group of kids were playing kickball across the street on the large paved asphalt parking lot.

Victor cocked the gun 10 times pumping pressure into the chamber. He aimed at the back of the kid's neck and squeezed the trigger, the kid jumped and turned and looked around as we slumped behind the bushes, laughing, covering our mouths trying not to give away our position. Victor passed the BB gun to me, I cocked the gun 10 times, aimed at the back of the boy's neck, pulled the trigger, then missed. I cocked the gun once more, aimed the BB gun at the back of the boy's neck pulled the trigger and once again I missed. I gave the BB gun back to Victor. He then cocked the gun once again, aimed at the back of boys neck and bull's-eye direct hit and off we ran down the alley to our freshly built clubhouse.

Our club house was an empty garage that was too dirty and too full of clutter to park cars in. So Chris, Enron, Johar, Victor and I cleaned up the garage with the permission of the home owner and used it for our own club. Once inside we would tie the door to not allow anyone in.

Later that evening Denton was standing in front of the house with his girlfriend as he normally would do, hugged up kissing, while leaning against the fence. Marica and her boyfriend Carver were arguing on the front porch, at which time Marica was four months pregnant with Carver's baby. Carver decided he wanted to be abusive that day so he shoved her off the porch to the ground. Denton ran over to break to up the fight and then a fight ensued between Denton and Carver.

Denton pulled a box cutter from his back pocket and began cutting Carver across his arms, legs and face, anywhere he could hit him with the box cutter, slicing and cutting and twisting his hand to make sure the box cutter turned deep into the skin. Carver fled down the street and five minutes later he came back with thugess looking friends I've never seen before. Carver walked up and shoved Denton's head. Denton jumped over the fence and began his carving exhibition all over again.

Bryce drove up as Denton chased Carver acrossed the street to the grassy field we played football on. Bryce jumped out of the car and removed the box cutter from Denton's hand. Denton was surrounded by at least 12 boys twice my size, but I wasn't going to let my brother get jumped by 12 guys so I ran in the house and grabbed the longest butcher knife I could find and shoved it into Denton's left hand. Once again in my opinion the fight was unfair, but once again Bryce removed the knife from Deton's hand so I ran back into the house and took out a wooden cane that I've been working on for the past couple of weeks. I went back outside and handed the cane to Denton. He only got two swings striking Carver on the head, shattering the cane into pieces. Bryce halted me steadfast from going in the house to get any more weapons. I watched as my brother and Carver fought heads up. Once the fight was over I went upstairs to console my brother. I couldn't help but to feel sorry for him as he nursed the open scrapes on the right side of his face.

I thought about the times he plotted to have me beaten up and yet he was the one the who ended up fighting. I never started a fight in my life, I've never had a reason to start a fight nor did I want to fight. I did what I had to when I was made to fight. I never fought because I want to prove I could beat someone, I only fought to protect myself.

The next day I noticed Carver walking down the street covered head to toe with bandages. He looked as though he had been in a car wreck. I've never seen one person with so many white bandages. One more bandage and he would've been considered the mummy. I didn't think much more about the fight that day, so I made my journey down the alley to my clubhouse where Enron, Chris, Johar, and Victor were already playing.

Routinely we tied a rope around the door knob onto a homemade latch anchor on the door frame, not allowing anyone in the front or back. We had the rope tied thoroughly around the door. Johar said that he had to leave and be right back. Three minutes later we heard a scuffle in the alley. There must have been more than 10 teenage boys running down the alley headed towards our clubhouse. That's when it hit me, Johar had told them where I was. They began beating and banging all over the garage saying,

"We are going to kill you Mikey when we get inside".

They beat and banged on the door so frantically that the boards began shaking loose. The cans and candles that we had placed on the ledge for decoration had fallen to the floor, the boys behaved like a pack of wolves.

I was so afraid I climbed up into the rafters of the garage. Suddenly my sixth sense kicked in, I felt trapped. The bullies were so preoccupied with trying to knock down the back door of the garage. I frantically jumped from the rafters, 'quickly' I was able to get the rope off the door, then fled for my life. I jumped over 3 fences until I reached my backyard. Once again my guardian angels had protected me, for some reason, it wasn't meant for me to be pulverized. It wasn't meant for me to be kicked and punched, it just wasn't in the cards. The lively street of 29th and Talbot returned to its normal state, kids ran freely up and down the street playing freeze tag and hide and go seek. Weeks had passed deep into the summer and the fight between Denton and Carver was all forgotten. Marica reunited with Carver, aiding him to heal from his wounds, and Denton never defended her honor again.

I return to hanging out at the candy store with Mac. I hung around drinking sodas and waited on some of his customers. One afternoon a well poised, tall africana-american man walked into the store. He was a delivery driver for Jessie potato chips. He walked in carrying four boxes of chips, hoisting them high in the air. His tall stature stretched up towards the sun, with his bald head glistening in the sunlight. One of his hands was three times the size of both my hands put together. He sucked down a soda as though he had a hole in the bottom of his stomach. He set the empty can on the counter and with one juggernaut swing the can was smashed thin as a quarter. I was so amazed I even considered joining his boxing club, but Riverside Park was at least 2 miles or more across town and a mile from my grandmother's home. My mother would never let me walk that distance alone.

$\mathcal{A}$ neighborly ride to the grocery store

By the time I was 17 I'd acquired my operator's license. I had been driving around six months, mostly running errands for my mother to the grocery store on capitol Avenue or to the 7-Eleven on Fairfield. Either way, I didn't care, I just wanted to drive and be seen cruising around by all my friends who weren't driving yet. Friends of the family begin to take advantage of my mother, asking her for rides to and from the store on a daily basis. My mother didn't have the heart to tell them no, so she shifted the responsibility to me. She knew that I had just gotten my license and I loved to drive. All of a sudden it was my responsibility to take all of her friends and friends of the family shopping and other places they wanted to go. I loved driving, I just didn't want to be trapped into sitting on the grocery store parking lot once again waiting for two hours.

One day I was told to take Rayford's girlfriend and her mother to the grocery store. I had to find a way out. After two hours of waiting on the parking lot, the two women emerged from the grocery store. Smiling from ear to ear after a successful Thanksgiving shopping trip, food almost spilling over the top of their cart.

I could not believe it, they just left the bags in the cart and sat comfortably in the back-seat while I begrudgingly unloaded the groceries from the cart into the trunk. I started the car, threw it in gear and slammed on the gas. The back of the car almost did a 180° spin before I could straighten out the wheel. I must've been going 80 miles an hour before I reached the first corner. I didn't even step on the breaks, I turned the corner making the back of the car fishtail around the curve. I looked in my rearview mirror, both women were pinned to the back seat with their eyes bulging out of their heads. They thought for sure they were going to die in that moment.

I thought I heard a prayer coming from someone's mouth, but I didn't let up, as soon as I reached their street I slammed on the gas as I turned the corner. Before I knew it a police car was behind me flashing his lights. Now I was scared. I slowly pulled over to the curb. I took out my drivers license and rolled down the window. Very timidly I asked.

"Is there a problem officer?"

The officer shone his flashlight in my face then asked for my registration. I opened up the glove box, felt around the loose papers for my registration, to my dismay my mother's 22 caliber pistol fell out of the glove box onto the floor.

I froze in position waiting for further instructions from the officer hoping he didn't see the gun lying at the tip of my fingers on the floor. I positioned my body trying to block the flashlight from shining on the gun, then I removed the registration from the glove box and handed it to the officer. He walked around to the back of the car and asked that I step on my break pedal.

Officer: " I didn't see your brake lights when you turned the corner, I wanted to make sure they were operating properly".

He handed me back my license and registration then went about his way. I sat in the car with my head pressed against the steering wheel while the two women expediently unloaded their bags then ran into the house without uttering a word. I was mentally exhausted from the exchange with the police man, all I want to do was take the car back home and hand my mother her keys

The immaculate conception

I was now a sophomore in high school and had the envy of all of my freshman peers. I cruised the hallways of Shortridge High Hchool acting as a guide for the newly arriving freshman, the class of 1979. It was refreshing to see my junior high school classmates finally arrive after standing behind a fence for an entire year waving as I passed by. We were all back together, ready and willing to live as young adults. Sophomores, juniors and seniors stood along the entry to the high school egging the freshmen on. "Fresh men, freshmen! They yelled, laughing and clapping as the freshman filed into the school with apprehensive looks on their faces.

I couldn't help but enjoy the moment, I was an upper classman and very familiar with my surroundings. Sophomores, juniors and seniors didn't wear new clothes on the first day of school, but all the freshmen filed through the door wearing new blue jeans, patent leather shoes, and new Converse tennis shoes. The upper classmen wore clothes from the prior year, we had grown past wearing fancy outfits on the first day of school. Varsity football and basketball players strutted proudly up and down the hallways wearing their letter jackets. I played football in my sophomore year but not long enough to earn a letter. However, I did join the boxing club at Riverside and wore a Golden Gloves boxing jacket for my participation in my 1976 Golden Glove tournament at Tyndale Armory. The school announced the results of my boxing match on the loud speaker for everyone to hear.

I felt like I was in the prime time of my life. It was refreshing not to have fights in school or after school. I was a Captain and platoon commander in the JROTC program. I met several young girls but none held my interest. Later in the school year I begin dating Sarah Gatewood. She was tall, slim, quiet and unassuming. Her huge buck eyes pierced the side of my face as I turned the combination to open my wall locker. Before I knew it I was walking her home from school on a daily basis. In the beginning our initial relationship didn't consist of much. I walked her home from school everyday, played around in the snow and had snow battles from the school to her front door. I was still very immature and had only been sexually active once in my life. I was 17 years old and very shy, not yet a man but ready to try.

I tried having sex once before, but it wasn't a pleasurable experience and I wasn't in a hurry to repeat it, but as fate would have it, Sarah was ready to take our relationship to the next level.

One day after school we walked our usual route home, playing in the snow, wrestling all the way to her front door.

"Come in quickly," she said.

Running to the bedroom taking her clothes off as She ran. I followed behind her as quickly as I could, by the time I reached her bedroom she was totally nude and lying in the bed.

"Get undressed, hurry up before my sister comes home," she said.

I ripped my ROTC uniform off as quickly as possible and climbed into her bed. Two minutes later her sister walked in.

" Oh, oh, oh, I'm going to tell mama," she said.

We both jumped to our feet scrambling to get dressed. I ran into the front room carrying my ROTC shirt and jacket, simultaneously pulling my pants up.

Sarah tried frantically to calm her sister down, telling her we weren't doing anything. I sat in the front room trying to zip my pants up and put my shoes on. I kissed Sarah goodbye and ran down the street like a bullet train. Three days later I got a phone call, Sarah wanted to meet me by the bus stop after school. I didn't think much of it, I grabbed my books and gladly sat at the bus stop watching the pretty girls walk out the back door of Shortridge high school. Sarah arrived with a disgruntle look on her face. She looked down at the ground, and said.

" I'm pregnant".

Then, she hit me in the arm and walked off. I was totally flabbergasted, I was only 17 years old and didn't know what I was going to do with a baby. Within the next week Sarah began demanding that I take on the roll of a father. She forced me to take her to the uptown theater, saying, the baby wanted to see a movie. Once at the movies she said the baby needs nourishment, the baby wants popcorn, a large orange soda and a chocolate candy bar. I was broke as hell! I didn't have two nickels to rub together and this baby was already eating me out of house and home. I went into my emergency stash, a secret hiding place in my bedroom closet and retrieved my jar full of silver dollars and quarters. The uptown theatre only cost $1 per person. A large bucket of popcorn was $1.75 cent, orange soda was $1.50 cent and a candy bar was .45 cent.

It seemed as though she was using the baby to empty my secret stash. The following weekend she said she needed an engagement ring, so we jumped on the city bus and rode downtown to Woolworth's where I purchased her a $13.00 ruby ring. She was very pleased. As we walked down the street, she clinged onto my arm as if we had been married 100 years. I didn't know what to make of the whole situation, and I wouldn't dare breathe a word to my mother until Sarah's stomach begin protruding from beneath her clothes and took all the guesswork out of whether she was pregnant or not.

I couldn't sleep a wink, I stayed awake thinking about the possibility of having another little person like myself running around the house. I couldn't believe I let myself get into such a die or need situation. I didn't take the time to put on a condom but how could I think about a condom, she was naked before I could get in the bedroom, and one thing for sure I wasn't going to turn it down with all her nudity in my face. Fortunately, I was able to get a momentarily mental break at the party Miss Appleton gave for all the kids in the neighborhood. Her daughters were my age and all of us attended the same school. Miss Appleton was a very nice lady and very proactive in giving the kids positive after school activities. Ms. Appleton's party was the biggest social event of our year, all the local girls would be there and fortunately for me the party was right across the alley from my mother's house. All I had to do was hop the fence, walk 30 paces and I was at the party. Of course a party wouldn't be a party without some form of alcohol, so a couple of boys purchased a bottle of Boons Farm wine to bring to the party.

We stood outside passing the bottle around is if we were adults, and to my surprise Sarah arrived with a group of friends. She walked pass me as if I wasn't even their, she headed right down into the basement and jumped right into slow dancing with a boy we called Rook. Rook wasn't very smart. In fact he probably was the dumbest person I knew in my life time. Rook was notoriously known for dating girls much younger than himself, if the girl had a pacifier in her mouth, he wanted her. He was known for having sex with just about anyone, but unfortunate for me he was dancing with my girlfriend and to top it off he had a hard on the size of Mount Rushmore.

I was half drunk but I knew a hard on when I saw one. I stepped immediately between them.

"What the fuck is going on" I said.

Pulling her by the arm, she reached back with one hand and slapped me so hard I thought I was shot.

" Is that the way to treat the father of your baby?" I said.

 Refusing to let her arm go.

 "I'm not pregnant, I got my period this morning," she said.

I didn't know what to think, but I knew I needed another drink, so I staggered back up the steps stumbling out of the basement and into the back yard. The boys were once again collecting .25 cent a piece to purchase another bottle of Boone's Farm wine. I was more than happy to chip in. I wanted to celebrate my new found freedom from father-hood. Sarah and I went our separate ways but she kept my $13.00 ring, refusing to give it back or pay me $13.00. I didn't care because I was just happy to be single, free and childless. She transferred that year to another school and I was the happier for it. I no longer had to worry about bumping into her in the hallway or making unnecessary idle conversation just because I bumped into her. I was totally abdicated of all responsibility, and at last I was able to breathe again and be a 17-year-old boy.

The year moved on, by now Fred and I were full-fledged members of the Riverside box-ing team. We rode our bikes alone the scenic route of 30th St. My Afro fluttered in freely the wind as we rode toward the gym. A young thin girl sitting in her front yard called out to me.

"Hey cutie, come here."

 I hastily stop my bike and made a U-turn in her direction. Fred continued on to Riverside Park. After I stopped in front of her house she jumped up and ran into the house leaving her cousins to answer for her.

"Why did she run in the house?" I said.

(Cousin) She's just shy, hey Lorraine, come back outside he wants to talk to you".

She walked her tall slim frame out of the house. She was tall and skinny, as thin as a rail. Her chest were flat as a board and there was no indentation of a butt to speak of.

Her most glaring attraction was her beautiful smooth skin and her long silky hair. A twisted braid seemingly endlessly hanging down her back hanging past her butt. I've never seen an African-American girl with such long beautiful hair, but she was mixed with another race. Lorraine was soft-spoken, she held her shoulders tightly squared as of her body was full tension. She ground her teeth and wore her clothes as though she was practicing to be a lesbian. I found her pleasant to be around and a far cry from any of the girls on my block whom where loud, out going and vivacious. Everyday on my way to the boxing center I'd stop by her house and chat for 15 minutes, then off I went to Riverside boxing center to receive my daily beating.

My boxing coach was a professional fighter rated 10th in the Junior middleweight class by ring magazine. My boxing coach loved the fact that I was a South Paw fighter. Meaning I was left-handed. In the boxing game most fighters had trouble adjusting to left-handed fighters. This was all the reason he needed to call me into the boxing ring every day to beat me into a new reality. Over the course of one year I developed a knockout punch using the boxing techniques I learned from him through osmosis. He really didn't had the time to train me, all I could do was assist him with preparing for his fights. One day his girlfriend came into the boxing center, she sat idly by the boxing ring observing him shadow box from one end of the ring to the other. I knew it wouldn't be long before I was summons into the ring. He wasn't about to let this opportunity pass. A chance to beat me senseless in front of his girlfriend, but I had other plans. For several weeks I was the first one at the gym. I practiced slipping punches, side stepping moving my head to the right allowing the punches to slip over my shoulder, then I would throw a power shot right down the center of the pike. I watched my boxing coach shadow box and spoil with other fighters. By watching him I was able to learn his timing and pick up on his rhythm. I stood outside the ring and observed how he threw his punches.

Every time he threw his punch I stepped to the right, then came back with a right cross follow by a left to the chin. I practice this move outside the ring unobserved by himself. After three rounds of shuttle boxing he did just as I anticipated he would.

 "Hey Mike, glove up and get in the ring". He said, strutting around the ring waiting patiently for me to glove up.

I stepped into the ring knowing it wasn't going to be another day of just being a human punching bag. The bell rang and we went immediately to it. His 12 ounce glove snapping in my face, slightly catching me on the chin. I wasn't worried, I knew I had his rhythm and his pace down to increments of a second. I knew what he was going to do before he did it.

After three minutes the bell rang giving us a one minute break. Fred cheer me on from the outside of the ring, causing Sammy to looked back over his shoulder at me with a puzzled look on his face. Sammy couldn't hit me, but how could this be, he was a professional fighter with a record of 18 wins and two losses. I was just an amateur who hadn't had my first fight yet. He angrily spit his mouth piece into the bucket, he was amazed that I could move out of the way of his punches. I turned with my back facing him so that he couldn't see I was smiling at Fred. I knew he would come out a little faster and harder this time because he had something to prove. He had an audience of one, one girl with the promise of sexual fantasy if you could impress her with his boxing power. Sammy was rated 10th in the Junior middle weight class but rated as well as the 2nd hardest hitter in middleweight boxing next to Marvin Hagler. Little did his girlfriend know, I wasn't a professional fighter. I was just a kid who rode his bike 3 miles to the gym everyday just to be a living, moving and breathing punching bag for a professional athlete.

The bell sounded and we were toe to toe once again. And just as I thought, his punches came a little quicker and crisper. I was no longer able to move out-of-the-way of his slapping heavy handed jab. Everything he threw landed squarely on my chin but he couldn't knock me out which frustrated him to no end. He began putting all his weight behind his punches, then hitting me straight in the gut. I fell to the floor bent over spitting out my mouth piece.

" You okay boy, I told you to do bodywork," he said.

I eventually stood to my feet.

"Walk around the ring to catch your breath," he said.

He stood in front of his girlfriend leaning over the rope while she stroked his eagle. I took a deep breath, psychologically trying to prepare to go another round. I eventually got to my feet, just before the bell rang giving me a one minute break to shake off the cobwebs. After the break we were right back into it. His crisp snapping jabs were blinding. All I could see was a red glove coming towards my face then drawing back. He was hitting me so hard I was punch drunk before the second round ended.

 I believed he was frustrated that he could not knock me out. I was new to the game of boxing. I wasn't even a contender,   but somehow my chin with stood everything he threw at it. I knew I couldn't take much more of this punishment, I had to focus on his rhythm and timing. I let him hit me with two clean shots to the head, once he got comfortable and felt she could hit me whenever he wanted too I side stepped, slipping his punch. The punch flew right over my shoulder as planned. I responded with a right cross over the top of his punch, then a straight left jab right down the pike. He stumbled back and fell onto the ropes, seemingly shocked by the power behind my punch. I was just as shocked as he, the bell sounded ending the three round sparring session leaving me the Víctor for a day. I didn't have many days like this in the ring. In fact this was the only day I nearly sat him on his butt. During the rest of my boxing sessions he pot shot me with stinking jabs at his pleasure, leaving me bruised and wanting.

I saw myself in a different light. I knew I could take a lot of punishment but now I knew I could dish it out as good as I got. Boxing was fun but it wasn't something I wanted to make a career out of. I just boxed to get respect, and for some reason the boys in my neighborhood and at my school would take their tough guy routine elsewhere. However, there was always someone who want to push the envelope and test my skills. My sister's boyfriend was ripe for the picking. He was a local neighborhood thug who lived off the repetition of his brothers. He wore his hat tilted back on his head, his blue Jeans were pressed and starched as stiff as boards. He wore wing tip Stacy Adams and walked as though he owned the world.

One day Victor and I was engaged in a boxing lesson on my mother's patio. In walked Herd, his hat tilted back on his head, smoking a cigarette. He flicks his cigarette to the side.

" Come on Victor lets box.

(Victor) no that's okay, Victor said, while handing the gloves to Herd.

Herd put the gloves on, throwing a lazy punch in my direction.

"Come on Mike let's go, okay I said.

At that moment a small crowd began gathering at the kitchen door. My mother and two of my sisters watched as the drama unfold. Herd through several lazy jabs barely nicking my chin. I knew I could knock him out when ever I wanted, my eagle was so inflated from the sparring session with my coach I knew Herd didn't have a chance.

He was so arrogant, throwing his punches and talking trash, I couldn't help but to teach him a lesson. He threw a lazy jab without much bite to it. I saw it coming from a mile away, I simply side stepped allowing his punch to fall lazy over my shoulder. I came right back with a 1-2 jab knocking him for loop. He covered his face and began staggering around the patio falling to the ground as though he was drunk. I quickly grabbed him keeping him from crashing embarrassingly to the ground. He wanted to continue but I suggested that he stop while he was ahead. Victor walked off laughing hysterically as Herd try to collect himself. He never challenged me to another boxing match and the story of the boxing match filtered throughout the neighborhood.

I continue my daily pilgrimage to the gym, five days a week for four hours a day of train-ing. Everyday I stopped by Lorraine's house, her next door neighbor was supposed to be some type of martial arts expert, he wore traditional kung fu outfits as well as shoes. He had an incredible kick but nothing else. However Fred did take karate lessons and earned a brown belt in tae kwon do. I could tell this kid never took a karate lesson in his life. However, I do believe he watched too many Bruce Lee movies and convince itself that he was professionally trained.

It wasn't long before Lorraine had us into a sparring session in her front yard. I must say his feet were very fast but I wasn't about to lose. I didn't use any of my boxing training but I did resort to some of the wrestling moves I learned in my gym class.

Once he kicked his foot in the air I simply went under his kick and body slammed him to the ground. He went home limping and I went into Lorraine's house and set on her couch draped with plastic. Her mother yelled from the other room.

"I'm going around the corner to the store, make sure that boy's gone when I get back".

"Ok" Lorraine said.

We set on the couch talking for 2 to 3 minutes and before I knew it we were fully en-gaged in a lip lock.

"Let's go to my mothers bedroom" she said.

I was reluctant to do it but some how the forces of nature put my feet in motion. We struggled for five minutes trying to get into position but it was virtually impossible because she wouldn't take her pants all the way off. I finally surrendered to a sexless night and disappointedly went home. Lorraine called me after words saying that her entire family walked in the door just as I had left. Lorraine and I never became lovers, we stayed friends for the course of my short journeys to and from the gym. We grew in different directions and within a years time I would lose all contact with her.

My life wasn't all stale after training for year I finally had my first boxing match. The Indianapolis Golden gloves held at the Tyndale armory. I walked whether than rode my bike to the center because I wanted to displace all negative or nervous energy festering in my mind. I slowly walked past Lorraine's house, the house was normally teaming with life but for the first time the house seemed dark and abandoned. I took it as an omen and thought whether or not I should even go to the fight but reluctantly I kept moving forward. I knew nothing about boxing, or how to prepare for a fight or what to bring to a fight. My boxing trainer didn't tell me anything. We arrived at Tyndale Armory with a handful of boxing tickets I didn't even know was available that I could have given to my family or my ROTC director Sgt. Woods who loves the boxing game.

I arrived at tyndale Armory early, sitting in the back of the crowd I got to watch all the fights before mines. I was schedule to fight 15th out of more than 20 fights. 12 fights into the sequence I was summonsed to go into the locker room to have my hands wrapped and get dressed for the fight. I sat in the locker room getting my hands professionally wrapped, for the first time I felt like a real fighter. I was presented with a white and green boxing rope, a white pair of boxing shorts and a red, white and blue pair of size 12 boxing shoes. My feet were a size 9, the shoes flopped around on my feet like Bozo the clown. They slid the 12 ounce boxings gloves over my hands, ensuring my fingers were all the way to the top. They pull the laces tight, tying it in a double knot then securing the laces with a piece of tape wrapped around both gloves. Butterflies flattered freely of my stomach, I was a total nervous wreck. It would be my first time fighting in front of a crowd of 200 or more. People were chanting my name as I walked towards the ring, my clown like shoes flapping on the floor in front of me, my non-color coordinated boxing robe and boxing trunks on display for all to see.

 The boxing ring appeared to be lifted high in the air, three huge lights rested comfortably above the ring with smoke circling around the bulbs of the lights giving a nostalgic feeling of the 1940s boxing era. I was in it now I thought to myself as I stepped in the sand box next to the left of steps, then making my way up the steps into the ring. The crowd was so loud I couldn't hear the instructions given by my boxing trainer. People were yelling my name by the hundreds but I was a nervous mess and all I can see were mouths moving muted by the butterflies in my stomach.

 The bell rang and out we came. The first punch was straight to the stomach, a hard slap to the stomach that I was not ready for. I cringed and fault the rest of the round with my right arm covering my stomach. Larry took very advantage of the situation and consistently shot left jabs to my lip. Before the first round was over, my lip was split wide open.

 "You have to do something, you just came take a beating, you got the power let your hands go" my trainer said.

The bell rang for the second round, I knew I was in trouble, I had to find away to work against his rhythm. So I settled in. I let him shoot jabs to my lip. After the third jab I was able to get his rhythm. I side step allowing his punch to go over my shoulder. The next jab I caught with my right hand, I flung it out of the way hitting him squarely in the eye with a left cross. He hopped and staggered across the ring, grabbing his eyes. The referee jumped in front of him holding him by his head to examine his eye. The doctor was called into the ring to determine whether Larry could continue the fight. Blood gust profusely from his eyes while they rush to stop bleeding.

The fight would have been stopped but Larry was too far ahead on the score cards, so they allow the fight to go into the third round. By the third round I was so tired I could barely walk to my corner. I regret the times doing training I would take a shortcut across the park instead of running the entire 4 miles. It was a lesson learned and I vowed to never take shortcuts while training again. Larry won the fight that night, and several years later he went on to be rated number 10 in ring magazine in the Walter weight division. I fought several more times before quitting the gym, boxing wasn't my first love or passion, it was just something I did to fill the empty void in my life.

*O*live Oyl

Boxing was fun but I needed money. It seemed like all the other boys in my school had money except for myself. I was tired of being broke. I was badly in need of new shoes and clothes. The empty spaces in my pockets screamed for relief and to make things worse Rayford suggested that I didn't ask my mother for money, he said she was having a tough time and needed a break. But my shoes were in disrepair and I definitely needed a new pair because my shoes didn't have much milage left in them. One day I arrived home from school and found two brand-new pairs of shoes tucked right under my bed. Rayford took it upon himself to buy me two pairs of shoes. I couldn't believe it, and the next week he informed me about a job at Saul subway.

I ran over to Saul subway as if I had won the lottery. I stood outside Saul's Subway for a brief second, trying to compose myself and catch my breath. The restaurant was choked with customers, waitresses busy serving drinks by the hundreds. Dishes piling up in the tubs located in the waitress bus station. Within seconds I was put to work bussing dish tubs to the kitchen, and cleaning off tables. I was sent upstairs to prepare the kitchen for night dinning. So I shot upstairs into the dining part of the restaurant called the attic. I fired up the dishwasher. While waiting for the dish washer to fill I grabbed a slice of chocolate mousse pie from the freezer, slouched back comfortably against the dish washer and began porking the pie down my throat. Once I had my shot of sugar I began to prepare Julienne salads until the salad prep girl arrived.

 The salad prep girl's name was Eileen, she was a 6 foot tall, slim white girl. She wasn't very attractive, in fact she was kind of homely. I thought she resembled the character from the Popeye cartoons; Olive Oyl. Her body was flat as a surfboard, she had an unassuming nature, with a nondescript personality. She only spoke when she was spoken too. I believed she was borderline developmentally delayed or she was a dull normal. But there was something about her looks that was unescapable, she was soft spoken and had a delicate touch. She moved very slow but was very meticulous in the way she wheeled her knife, slicing every bit of the cucumber as if there was an intentionally diabolical purpose to the way she made each cut.

She applied excessive pressure on the knife and with every cut she ground her teeth. Some how she was able to reveal the softer side of her enigmatic personality. She piled salad on the plate, undulating in her movement, placing freshly cut cucumbers and boiled pickled eggs and generous strips of ham on top of the lettuce. Yellow onions were used to intensify the flavor. Croutons covered the rest of the plate, to enhance the size of the plate making a common salad into a thing of artistic work. It wasn't long before I was summoned to go downstairs and prepare four trays of rosin potatoes. I wrapped each potato in aluminum foil, placing 25 to 30 potatoes on four metal cooking sheets then setting the oven at 350°. I slid the sheets into the oven. It took me about 30 minutes, 30 of the longest most uncomfortable minutes of my life. I was totally creeped out by the stories of other employees being bitten by rats as large as my foot. I've even witnessed large ghetto rodents running freely under the tables, eating the droppings of food left by the rich patriot pigs.

To put it another way, the customers were mostly upper-middle-class professionals and it appeared that they didn't care about the condition which they left the tables and floors or the cleanup that would follow. All they wanted to do was gorge themselves with succulent steaks prepared by uneducated would-be chefs from the ghetto one block over from the restaurant. They porked out on the rosin baked potatoes topped with sour cream and chives, unknown to themselves prepared by a dish washer. The restaurant was famous for its food, often patronized by doctors, lawyers and anyone else of prominence in the city.

I made it my business to cruise around the restaurant in between picking up dish tubs from various stations, I watched the customers and secretly listened to their conversations. I mostly enjoyed talking with Olive Oyl. After six hours working together she began to open up and allow me to enter her cucumber cutting developmentally delayed world. I couldn't help but to listen closely as she laid her life story at my feet. She said she had been raped two years ago by an African American male and since that time she had been trying to find him to force him to be a father to their 2 year old daughter. She talked nonstop for an hour, I passively listened as she pontificated on and on. The longer she talked the more twisted and perverted her story got. She loathed the ideal of searching for her rapists but she felt it was necessary to let him know that he fathered a child.

During her time off she would cruise up and down Indiana Avenue, the last place she saw her assailant. After three hours of walking there he was mindlessly leaning against a concrete building without a care in the world. She confronted him without accusation only with a handful of baby pictures. She beseeched him to come see his daughter but he chuckled to himself with a condescending smile then escorted her to what she thought was his apartment. Instead it was just another vacant building, not as much as a mattress on the floor. He proceeded to rape her once again. I couldn't help but feel pity for Olive Oyl because even after telling me this sad story she punctuated it with.

"I'm going to keep looking for him until he accept his role as the father of our child".

I begin to develop a bad taste and disliking in my mouth for Olive Oyl. When she finally stopped talking I could see the light bulb turn on in her head. At that moment she invited me over to her house but I demurred because of the possibility of our spending the night together. I didn't want her to divulge anymore depressing stories of her life.

I tried to stay out of the kitchen and made it a point to hang out around the bus tub stations, I only went into the kitchen when it was absolutely necessary because I didn't want this woman to soliloquize herself around me anymore. By this time I was tired and pretty much done for the day. My shoes were soaking wet and my fingers looked as though they had been in water for 12 hours. My clothes smelled of corned beef and my pockets occupied empty spaces where tips would normally fill those gaps. I didn't vociferate about the tips that were promised to me by the waitress hours earlier. I was a dish washer and a buss boy, therefore; I only bussed tables at the waitress request, but the request was supposed to come with tips at the end of a shift. One waitress stepped forward and gave me three dollars for bussing 10 tables that were shoved together for a birthday party.

I was young, but I wasn't that young, I wasn't going to put up with the BS. Therefore, I was forced to create my own rules about tipping, and the percentage I deserved. If the customer left $10 I took $2. I didn't enjoyed taking tips but they forced my hand. After cleaning several tables and not being tipped by the waitress I no longer felt guilty about forcing my own tip.

Sunday morning, I was at work for the evening shift which began at 3 PM. The deli and the dining room section of the restaurant were closed for the day because prohibition laws still apply in Indiana on Sundays. No one was allowed to sell liquor anywhere in the city but somehow the alcoholics and the obsessive drinkers would find adventure in seeking out club owners that would risk their license and their business to sell a six pack of beer at twice the price out of the back door of the bar. I couldn't believe people would go through this much trouble just to have a beer because the law said you can't have one on Sunday.

No one ever thought it will be just as easy to buy the liquor on Saturday and put it away to drink on Sunday. Maybe people didn't do that because it would take all of the fun and suspense out of the game. In the meantime I was stuck at work on Sunday, baking potatoes in a rat infested restaurant, looking at my feet and around the machines to ensure that no rats were biting on my shoes. I wrapped those potatoes quick fast and in a hurry, as if I was in a potato wrapping contest. I was totally creeped out, the kitchen was dark and spooky. I took every shortcut possible to get out of the kitchen as quick as I could. Once the ovens were set and the potatoes were baking I'd sneak around to the bar in search of an open liquor bottle or beer tap. Instead I found a bag of lay's potato chips and an open soda dispenser.

I placed my mouth under the Coke tap and drank soda like a horse drinking from a water trough. I was in hog heaven until I felt something squirm over the top of my foot. I threw the chips in the air and jumped over the bar and scurried outside to the sidewalk. Just as my feet hit the pavement two young girls were strolling by, I wasn't really interested in them I just didn't have anything to do at the moment so I persuaded them to come back and talk to me. They kept walking when I called to them, I didn't give up I yelled at them two more times before they turned and began walking in my direction.

One was tall and fair skinned with an awesome figure, the other one was small quiet and reserved, her face was covered partially with a bonnet hat and I could barely get a glimpse of what she looked like. The tall light skinned girl was more of my type. I through out my best lines but after two minutes of talking she mentioned she was dating one of my friends. I didn't want to come up empty handed, therefore; I shifted my conversation to the quiet and reserved one. I didn't care for her at first but she slowly grew on me. I was partially attracted to her because she was soft spoken and appeared to be a very gentle person.

I was loath to give her my phone number because of the crazy cucumber cutting bitch upstairs who was also quiet and unassuming but was prated underneath it all. Cindy and I talked over the phone for the next couple of weeks although I was still technically involved with May. May and I began to drift apart spending less and less time together. Every time I saw her she spoke of moving to Arizona to go to college. Therefore; we ended our relationship on that note the day after our high school graduation. Cindy and May were two extremely different personalities. Cindy was good at math and was very focused on doing well in school, she wanted things in life and was willing to work hard to achieve her goals.

I would sit with her and write out math problems just for the fun of it but there was something mysterious about her that I just couldn't put my finger on. In the meantime her ignorant jackass of a brother would interrupt my thoughts by trying to show how tough he was by punking his friend Jeff, yelling absurdly close in his face and making threatening comments about hurting him physically. I just ignored his dumb antics as well as his dumb comments. He even tried to cajole Jeff to start a fight with me to entertain his sick little twisted mind.

He was a true pain in my butt and I was sure we would lock horns in the foreseeable future. Cindy had four brothers and two younger sisters. They lived in a large rat infested wooden double with three bedrooms on each side. The couch was fitted with the traditional plastic covering that no one would dare sit on in fear of falling asleep and dehydrating to death. Cindy's mother was a very light skinned women closely resembling someone of the white persuasion. She was a country girl from Mississippi with telltale signs of Mississippi culture in her behaviorism.

She wore a gold tooth in the middle of her mouth that was hard to miss because of her infectious smile. She had a way of luring men into her sinister web, destroying marriages along the way. She even had a theme song (clear up women) sung by Betty Wright. She would repetitiously play the same song 24 hours a day until the needle on the record player was worn down and no longer usable. I sat quietly in the living room and watched her dance around in a circle with a glass of liquor in one hand and a half smoked cigarette in the other. I tried not too attract attention to myself but Cindy's sister sat atop the staircase and shot paper spit balls through a straw onto my Afro.

I alerted Cindy to the situation. Before I knew it, Cindy ran to the top of the steps and dragged her sister down the steps by her hair.

"Say you're sorry"

With her foot on her sister's neck, pulling her hair with her right hand, making her apologize before striking her in the back with her fist, then shoving her toward the staircase whining. This was a side of Cindy that I had not yet seen since it was early in our relationship, but I did notice she could go from 0 to 80 in less than 10 seconds flat then back to zero as if nothing ever happened. It seems as though the house was always packed with people or people constantly running in or out taking bites of food here and there eating on the run then back in Streets. This was a very unpredictable place, I never knew when we would get a moments peace to ourselves.

In the month of April my Cindy and I were sitting idly on the couch. Cindy's legs were stretched across my lap, her back resting comfortably against the arm of the couch. We sat around talking while I massaged her feet, purposely hitting the points that would sexually arouse her.

Her brother came back in the room and said,

"What the hell is going on here".

He reached down and grabbed Cindy by the arm snatching her off my lap. But to his surprise my pants were zipped up and securely fastened. There wasn't any sign of for-nication. He looked at both of us with an evil eye, made a moaning sound then walked back out the front door eating his baloney sandwich. Cindy sat next to me smiling, she laid her head on my shoulder stuck her hand out and asked for her five dollars. I whis-pered in her ear.

"I'm still erract".

She laughed, jumped up and sashayed toward the front porch as her brother Robbi walked back and forth peeking in the window.

I cleaned myself up the best I could and reluctantly walked outside on the porch and sat ten feet away. Cindy and I were smiling and laughing to ourselves, as if we had gotten away with the perfect crime. Robbi leaned heavily against the frame of the front door cutting his eyes back and forth at both of us while he devoured his dried up baloney sandwich. I was done dealing with this asshole, I had pressing business elsewhere. So I leaped from the pouch, waved farewell to Cindy then made my way back across the bridge toward my mothers house. I couldn't help but to pass by Sabrina's house. She was the prettiest girl in school but there was one small problem, she didn't brush her teeth. I'd never seen that much food caked up on someone's teeth. I didn't understand how a girl so pretty could miss the most vital part of her conversation piece, her mouth. I thought it was a fluke the first time I saw her, but she was this way every time we talked. Teeth caked over as if she had not brushed for months. I had no time for yuck mouth so I made my way down two blocks to the park on 29th and Talbot.

I was in luck there were two boys playing a game of 21. After playing for 10 minutes we changed the game to a game called booths. Who ever had the lowest score at the end of the game gets kicked in the butt by all the other players. The rules where we could only kick the person with the side of our foot. The game got under way, I played harder than I ever had played before, Victor was the best player and a natural shooter so I tried to keep up with him making basket for basket. The other guy fell far behind on points, I smiled and stepped out of the way as Victor easily ran by me and landed the ball in the hoop making the final point of the game. Victor told the other kid.

" Well, you lost, lean on the fence".

The kid did what Victor asked, placing both hands on the fence. I went first, and did just as the rule said, I kicked him with the side of my foot. Victor got a running start from 20 feet away. He ran as fast as he could and kicked the boy with the point of his foot as though he was trying to kick him to the Moon.

The boy must've jumped 50 feet in the air clutching his butt on the way up and falling to the ground in agonizing pain. Victor laughed and ran through the sand box climbing over the concrete castle and the other obstacles on the play ground trying to escape the screaming young boy chasing him around the park clutching his butt with one hand, seemingly in utter pain. I couldn't help but to laugh at the spectacle before me, although I did feel sorry for the young boy, but he knew the situation before getting involved in the game.

He knew Victor was not going to honor the terms of the game and use the side of his foot. This wasn't his first time he had beeen tricked by Victor. One day we were playing football in the big field across the street from my house. Victor kicked the ball to the young boy then pretended like he was going to let him run by and score a touchdown. Once the boy got side-by-side with Victor, Victor stuck his arm out and clothes lined the young boy making him flip in a complete 360°circle, then took off running down the street laughing. Everyone on the block knew Victor and the type of stunts he pulled. Victor was the most naturally athletic person I had ever known. He could catch and throw a football with little effort. Lundy and Ray had an arm for throwing a football as well, but never pursued or developed their gift. Lundy could throw a football the lenght of the football field and Ray could throw the football like a bullet. My only talent was in my hands 'Boxing'. But I didn't have much time anymore for tomfoolery. I had an appointment too meet with a Marine recruiter that evening.

Once A Marine

I woke up to another exhausting morning, one day closer to being an adult then the day before. I felt my life was at a stalemate and whether I accepted it or not graduation from high school was just around the corner. I knew there would come a time I would have to leave the nest, expand my wings and fly away. I was nervous but excited, I could smell my emancipation floating in the air.

I was mentally exhausted thinking about paying my own rent, utility bills, car payment and other life changing anomalies adults were supposed to do to survive. I was scared out of my mind at the possibility of failing the ASVB exam for the second time. I knew I had to change my methods of study if joining the marines was going to become something more than what I fantasized about in the mirror.

 The recruiter appeared to have more confidence in me than I had in myself, he handed me a stack of loose papers.

"Study this you'll be okay" he said.

Seeing all of those stacks of papers threw me for an educational loop, it was intoxicating, the words over whelmingly covered the front and back of the pages. I was mentally exhausted just thinking of studying all those words, truth be told I didn't know whether I would successfully pass the exam. I wasn't very focus as a student in school. I completed just enough work to get by and to ensure that I was socially promoted out of high school.

I sat in my bedroom for three days not participating in any extra curriculum activities at the basketball court or hanging out with girls or spending time with my friends. All I did was study and pray until I knew the list back and forth. In between study times I would stand in the mirror and imagine myself wearing a set of dress blues. The White hat with a black brim, flank by gold buttons on both sides, placed squarely on my head. The high collar with two gold Marine Corps emblems. The mirror turn foggy then cleared, all the sudden my chin was squared and I was a Marine, a recruiting poster child waiting to be born.

My only focal point at that time was becoming a United States Marine, nothing else mattered, not even getting my high school diploma or the fact that I was leaving my hometown and people that I loved behind. However; I was missing a very important part of the puzzle. I didn't know what I was getting into. I didn't know about the $20,000 recruiting bonus or the difference between an open or closed contract. I just wanted to be challenged. I wanted to see if I could stand on my own 2 feet and take whatever punishment they could dish out. My rude awaking would soon be played out in 16 weeks of boot camp hell.

Growing up without a father created a huge gap of uncertainty in my mind. I question everything I did, right down to the smallest detail. I was never sure if I was making the right decision about anything. I wasn't taught to think on my feet. Everything I learned, I learn from the streets and the people I associated with. However; my mother did teach me how to respect others and things that belong to other people. My mother never overly indulge me, she provided me with the basic needs, shoes, clothing, food, and a roof over my head. Learning how to become a man had a different flavor for me than it did for young boys that had two live in parents. I had to learn from the empty uniforms in the small radius within my enclave. Most of the young fathers worked in plants or some type of factories or as general labors. I don't recall any African American white collar workers living in my neighborhood.

All the young men in my life spent their time chasing women, if they weren't chasing women they were getting drunk at a local bar on Indiana Avenue, or planning some scheme to get some sort of ill-gotten gains. I never saw an example of a black man going to college, medical or law school. I never knew what was possible, other than being a janitor, sport figure, or general labor.

The closest I came to seeing an example of a man working a steady job was my stepfather. He would get up at four in the morning, go to work, then come home sloppy drunk at 10 PM. He found his place at the kitchen table after removing his dinner from the stove's oven. He drunkenly slumped down in his chair, ate his gravy covered pork chops with mash potatoes, then stagger upstairs. He slowly staggered by, brushing against me, not saying a word. He made his way up to the top of the stair landing, turned into his bed room then flopped down on the bed and passed out. He was the most direct example in my life that I had of what a man did on a daily basis. I don't know any better because I didn't have any better examples.

I did have an uncle named George who worked at Regen's bakery, and I'm pretty sure he went to work everyday on time for 30 years, he and his wife Dorothy, my mothers sister always had the newest cars in the family. They had a small dainty two bedroom house with plastic covering the couch and chairs. I found it odd that my auntie was a school teacher yet her husband couldn't read a word, but he was good with his hands and could build almost anything as well as being an excellent mechanic. I do believe he would've been a good role model but I only saw him once every five or six months when he came by the house with a box of stale donuts trying to put a smile on our faces, but I was no longer a little kid I was 18 years old and a box of stale glazed donuts wasn't going to change the dynamics of my life in the next two months.

My life was changing for sure, I was growing as a person and the path that I had chosen I must walk along. Later that day I made my way to the A-fee station were more than 50 other individuals of different ethical backgrounds and genders were all taking the same test but for different branches of the service. I was very proud to be one of the few in the room that was taking the Marine Corps exam but in hindsight I was one of the few idiots that was taking the Marine Corps exam. I finish the exam and was escorted into the other room, anyone that failed the exam was shown the door. I knew the routine from by my pass failures.

I was so excited I couldn't hold it inside, I told everyone, even the people on the bus. I ran down 29th and Talbot as though I won the lottery. When I arrived home I hesitantly approached my front door, I stopped took a deep breath, then walked in as cool as a glass of water in the summer time. I set at the kitchen table, crossed my legs and grabbed a section of the newspaper. My mother stared at me as she stirred her Folgers coffee.

"Where have you been all day?" She asked.

"I was at the recruiting station, I took the Marine Corps exam and passed it, my departure date is July 18."

My mothers eyes got big and suddenly she stop sipping her coffee and begin haranguing me about the corp.

"Why in the hell did you join the Marines? Are you crazy?".

"I want to be tested, I want to know who I am and if I can stand on my own two feet, this is something that I must do alone, "

"I hope you know what the hell you're doing". She said.

"Well, if I don't we're going to find out July 18".

So back up stairs I went. I couldn't sleep a wink. I swear I must have been awoke for five days straight. I stayed isolated for several days, keeping to myself, other than occasional visits to Cindy's house and our well planned 7 PM trips to Riverside Park where I parked, turn out the lights, turn on the radio then climb in the backseat where the seduction began. I grew very familiar with Riverside Park area because I was on the Riverside boxing team. The boxing team, required that I run around the four mile golf course to began my daily work out. I think Cindy liked all the personal attention I was giving her, we stopped at White Castle, pick up a 10 sack and two chocolate shakes. We climbed into the back seat of the car, through our feet up on the arm rest of the front seat and choked down our White castle hamburgers until one of us let out a raunchy fart are belch.

We had gotten very comfortable after stuffing ourselves with hamburgers so we took off our shoes and unbuttoned our pants at the waist to let our stomachs stretch freely. I realize we have forgotten about the time, three hours have passed and my mother had to be at work within an hour so we began scrambling around on the back floor trying to find our shoes.

All of a sudden it hit me she doesn't know I'm moving 2500 miles away. I may as well move to the moon, because the corp doesn't allow phone calls until the 10th week of boot camp. I dropped Cindy at her door then off to the gas station to replenish the tank, arriving home just in time to hand the car off to my mother. I stood on the side walk watching her turn the corner on 30th St. I went one house down the street and plopped down on the steps with my friends, where we sat outside until 12 midnight when the street lights began flashing, then off we all went to our separate homes.

I stay up late that night, wide awake staring out the bedroom window, my mind was going 100 miles an hour searching for an answer about my future in the military and where I would be five years from today. I couldn't help but wonder how my mother sustain herself and eight children all these years. I could barley stomach the fact that I would be expected to support myself from this day forth, it scare me to death because I had always been under my mother's roof, eating my mother's food, and wearing the clothing she brought. All of this will come to an end less than 30 days. I'll be reluctantly cut free of the apron strings.

It has been a month since I enlisted in the Marines and still I cannot muster the courage to tell Cindy. So I just let it ride until that one fateful day. Tiana, Denise, Herb and I was playing cards in the front room, the rules were if you lost a hand you had to drink a glass of water, everyone was willing to comply with the rules except Tiana. Tiana lost a hand and refused to drink the water. I obliged her by pouring a tall glass of water and placed it in front of her.

Tiana said, "I'm not drinking that damn water".

I told her "but you lost, it's the rule, everyone drink water when they loss and you know you better drink the water like everyone else".

She still refused, so I grabbed the pitcher of water sitting at the opposite end of the table and toss it in her face, then jetted up the steps to my room and locked the door.

Denise and Herb laugh uncontrollably. The laughter enraged Tiana even more so she ran up the steps behind me screaming my name and cursing like a drunken sailor. I was quick to slam the door in her face while laughing on the other side of the door which infuriated her more. She began kicking and hitting my door profusely with her fist, she stood there soaked as though she accidentally fell in a swimming pool. She pounded, screamed and kicked on the door until she realized it was of no resolve so she grabbed my brand-new pair of white Converse and flung them outside in the mud, giving my German Shepherd something to chew on. I was so pissed off I ran into her bedroom, grabbed her favorite night gown, tied it in a knot, dipped it in the toilet then flunk it on the roof next door.

Tiana rant and whine until my mother forced me to get a stick and get the nightgown down from the roof and Tiana was forced to retrieve my shoes from the back yard and clean them off. I ran off down the street to the park while Tiana stood outside fuming over the incident and cursing my name as I ran to the basketball court for a brief game of 21. I soon was crossing the bridge on 28th and central to Cindy's house.

As I approached, there was a crowd standing on the front porch, her brothers, sisters, mother and stepfather. I could see something was amiss, and it made me very uncomfortable as I approached the porch. Cindy turned her back towards me as I stepped on the porch then ran into the kitchen and pretended as though she was cooking, at that moment I knew Tiana had called and informed Cindy about my enlistment in the Marines.

Cindy wanted nothing more to do with our relationship and wanted to move her life in a different direction then the path I had chosen, so I walked away with an eerie feeling in my stomach as if someone had kicked me. A month and a half later I was being picked up by my Marine recruiter at 9 AM in the morning to be transported to the recruiting station for final processing and a flight to San Diego California. My mother and I stood outside that morning waiting for the recruiter to arrive, as usual he pulled up in a little ford escort with the Marine Corps emblem on side.

I began dragging my seabag toward the car, the recruiter said.

"Where are you going with that"?

"I said, 'to boot camp"

'recruiter' "You don't need that, I just need you".

So I gave the bag back to my mother and hopped in the front seat of the recruiters car. As the car drove away my mother stood in the front yard watching me drive off teary-eyed with a slight lump in her throat, however; she did summons enough strength to wave a final goodbye. I stared at her out the window until the car turn the corner on 30th Street, I barely caught a glimpse of her struggling to drag the sea bag back up the steps into the house.

I scanned the neighborhood with my eyes hoping to catch a glimpse of someone I knew so I could wave goodbye to them but no one was around, it was as if the streets were purposely empty, no one saw me leave, there was no one there to say good luck or I'll see you when you get back, it made me feel empty, unloved and alone. For the first time in my life 29th and Talbot was empty, there wasn't a soul to be found, everyone had disappeared into their own lives and I was on my way to a new life. There were a lot of first for me that day, first time I've flown on a plane, the first time I would visit California, the first time I would feel what it was like to miss my mother and the first time I would miss someone that I cared deeply about.

The most significant thing of all, I was leaving as Mikey but I will return a Marine. The plane cruised for 6 hrs. at 400 mile's an hour, the plane titled its wing right over MCRD Marine Corp Recruit Depot, several minutes later touching down in San Diego at 7 PM that evening. A green military bus lingered at the corner side walk of the airport.

"This way," the driver said.

I stare at the bus from the airport doors, my life changing with each step I took towards the bus, there was no turning back at this point, I was in it for the duration of four years. The base was ten minutes a way from the airport, I wasn't nervous about boot camp at all because I went through ROTC Boot Camp with real army drill instructors. I thought I was a seasoned vet, and ready for anything the marines could dish out. I sat comfortably in my seat enjoying the scenic view of San Diego streets and towering palm trees I read about in right on magazines.

It was exactly as they described it, women on roller skates wearing bikinis, kids carrying surfboards, and young adults dressed up in the latest Disco attire ready for boogie nights. I was so relaxed I decided to pop a piece of gum in my mouth, reclining back in my chair and taking in the sites. The wheel's slid to a screeching halt. A tall slender Marine wearing a MP patch on his sleeve climb aboard the bus, took a head count then waved us threw the gate.

I quickly canvass my surroundings, looking for signs of drill instructors. The sun slowly set down behind the barracks, it was dark and for the first time I was in a strange place 2500 miles across the country. Thinking about the distance from home left an uneasy feeling in the pit of my stomach. Just as my eyes lock on the yellow foot prints, the bus tilted sideways rocking like a boat on water. A drill instructor stepped on the bus benting his head down, tilting his campaign hat as he stood at the threshold of our new reality.

"You got 30 seconds to get off of this bus, and 29 are up. "Move!"

Feet scuffing threw the bus sounded like a pack of wild buffalo. Simultaneously 12 drill instructor's appeared out of the dark, yelling and screaming, steam coming off their breath while they pressed their campaign hats into the side of our faces.

"In place double time" they yelled.

Making everyone stand in one place for 10 minutes and run.

"Boot top high" they yelled.

Spitting in our faces while giving orders in a harsh and violent tone. The night was crazy, everything was moving at a crazy fast pace. We got our heads shaved, stripped naked, issued and inventoried all our clothing and took showers. I was in the bed by 1 AM. I was thoroughly shaken up, I didn't know what just happened or if I can keep up with this fanatic pace for long. The receiving barracks were located right next to the San Diego airport, I could see the planes landed and take off behind the 12 foot high wooden fence.

The airplanes seemed so close it was as if I could reach out of my window and touch their wings. Glover the kid I flew from Indianapolis to San Diego with wanted to go 'UA' unauthorized absence. We decided once everyone was sleep we were going to jumped the fence and crawl into the landing gear of the airplane. I closed my eyes for a brief second waiting for everyone around me to fall asleep, before I knew it, it was 4 AM, the lights flickered on and trash cans were being thrown about the squad bay.

Drill instructors running, screaming and yelling, getting in our faces, within seconds of waking up we were walking down the street in a big mob, flashlights in our hands, our knowledge and toothpaste in our cargo pockets, our shirts button all the way to the top. Drill instructors yelling at the top of their lungs, calling cadence in an untraditional fashion as we try to get in step while marching down the dim lit streets toward the chow hall.

I was starving and confused, it was dark and cold. I could barley see 3 feet in front of me, we were rushed through the chow hall like cows, given two minutes to swallow whatever food we could get in us. Then pushed out the back door and forest marched back to the barracks at an insane pace. We scrubbed and cleaned the showers and bathroom floors with tooth brushes. Everything was at an extremely fast pace with the exception of getting out of receiving barracks or being picked up by our drill instructors. It had been two weeks and we were still hanging around the receiving barracks waiting for our 82 training days to begin. We practice cleaning the barracks and freeing our uniforms of any iris pendants.

Then all of a sudden there were there three drill instructors kicking our sea bags down the steps, tossing our uniforms and boots over the railing of the balcony. Everyone got treated the same because we look the same in the eyes of the drill instructors, we were all equal idiots.

The torture continued on for 20 minutes as we walked to our new barracks. 20 minutes that seemingly took an hour before we where able to reached the barracks. The drill instructors couldn't resist playing head games, kicking our cover blocks ahead of us as we walked in a disorganized fashion to our new barracks. Walking one right on top of the other, asshole to belly button! They yelled, screaming and spiting in our faces while we locked eyes straight forward on the back of the head of the man in front of us.

The pace was excruciatingly fast, I was beginning to feel the effects of hunger from the corner piece of bread and one spoon of eggs I was able to shove in my mouth before we were dragged from the chow hall and tossed in a half-baked formation. Rush. rush, rush, rush and before I knew it night had fallen upon us. By 9 o'clock pm we were all in bed laying at attention on the top of our olive drab wool blankets listening to the bugle play taps. I tried to stay awake by listening to the comforting sound of the crickets but there were none, all I could here was the planes taking off and landing at the airport next door.

These were 82 of the most intense days of my life but I was made the better man for it. During those 82 days Cindy and I touch bases once again and I had to say her letters did help get me through boot camp. Cindy couldn't help expressing the way she felt about me, she planet kisses on the envelope of every letter. Each time I got a letter with the imprint of lips, the smell of perfume, or salutations written on the outside of the envelope, I got thrashed by my drill instructors. I was removed from the squaw bay and made to roll around in the dirt and perform mountain climbers, side straddle hops and bend and thrust for every salutation or lip imprint on the outside of the envelope.

Over the course of two weeks I became friends with a young marine name Sampson. I thought it was really cool that he was from Chicago and I was from the neighboring city next-door. One day the drill instructors had the bright idea of placing Sampson in charge of the rifle rack, wear more then 80 M16 rifles were locked away. He was also given the responsibility of being the platoon guide on Baron, until one day he lost the keys to the rifle rack. The drill instructors became infuriated and thrash Sampson up-and-down the squad bay, making him do push-ups, setups and mountain climbers until he sweated out a pool of blood. The drill instructor then grabbed Sampson's foot locker and tossed it against the wall, out came the keys sliding down the squad bay stopping at the front of my feet as I stood at attention watching the incident unfold.

Sampson was pulled into the drill instructors office, they slammed him against the wall lockers and bulkhead then tossed him out into the squad bay where he landed on his face sliding almost through the double exit doors. I was glad he was okay, I smiled and chuckled to myself as he ran back and stood at attention in front of his rack. Every morning was the same for the next 82 days, fast-paced, pushing, shoving and yelling. Each day started with a shit, shower and shave. We played mind games, ripping our beds apart and putting them back together as fast as we could. This was our usual 4:30 AM ritual before we went to breakfast. We were marched to breakfast as though we were running the 50 yard dash. We were new to the corp and not yet discipline.

Everything we did we did together in close proximity of one another. They called it ass-hole to belly button. Even in the chow line we were not allowed to look anywhere other than the man's head in front of us. Once we reach the serving line we locked eyes on the wall in front of us and side stepped our way through the chow line. I locked eyes with an authoritative looking Major. Because I had a good nature and wasn't fully aware of Marine Corps policy. As a kind gesture I smiled at the Major.

The major pounced on me like a lion on a hyena, right up to me ass-hole to belly button style, and pressed his nose against mines.

"Do you want to go to jail"? He asked. In a very convincing Voice.

"Sir, no sir" I said, with a nervous expression.

"Then wiped that fucking smile off your face".

My drill instructor stood at the back of the chow hall observing what had just taken place. I could feel the telepathic waves of anger reflecting off the side of my face as my drill instructor ran towards me seemingly at 100 miles an hour then pressing his campaign cover to the side of my head. The pressure was so great I was slightly knocked off balance as he leaned over and whispered in my ear.

"You fucking owe me bitch."

I was so traumatized I could burly eat my breakfast with the thought of going to jail or being thrashed by my drill instructor, either way it wouldn't have a good outcome. Right after we had our limited portions of food we returned to the barracks and change into our PT gear then headed to the obstacle course for a 3 mile run alongside the wooden fence line separating the Marine Corps base from the airport. I couldn't help but be envious every time I saw the naval sailors standing outside smoking a cigarette and laughing at us while we ran 3 miles in 100° weather.

The Navy boot camp was next door to MCRD, there was one small difference, they were on a six week vacation and we were going through 16 weeks of hell. The naval boot camp program was very different, they ate chow whenever they wanted too and wasn't forced to eat vegetables like I was. My drill instructor would stand behind me in the chow line at breakfast, lunch and dinner time and order the line personnel to put stacks of broccoli, collie flower, and carrots on my plate. I would take the vegetables and give them to the Marine next to me or hide them in my ice cream cup or cover the vegetables with napkins. Sometimes my drill instructor would stand by the exit and inspect my tray, if I still had vegetables on my plate he would stand over me until I ate them but most of the time I was able to get away with throwing them in the trash. The drill instructor said I would need the vegetables to get up Mount motherfucker. I didn't understand what he meant at the time because it was too early in my training, and I was still adjusting to all the yelling and screaming at 4 AM.

The sailors stood outside on their balcony's smoking cigarettes, laughing while pointing at us as we ran along the fence line in the sweltering heat. Sampson and I were running neck to neck and all of a sudden he disappear, someone shoved him into a fire hydrant, breaking his right leg. I finished my run around 21 minutes, then down the strip came Sampson, he completed the 3 mile run in 24 minutes with a broken leg. The drill instructor didn't seem to care that Sampson had just broken his leg, he ordered Sampson to continue running until he reached the ambulance, so Sampson limped his way over to the ambulance, and disappeared for three days.

The drill instructors could have dropped him from the platoon at this point but he demonstrated courage and heart when he finished the 3 mile run in 24 minutes with a broken leg. Having a broken leg aided Sampson with skating from a lot of duties. He didn't have to March to church, he was allowed to stay in the barracks and watch all the gear. Everyone went to church, it didn't matter what religion you were, you were forced to attend. After church we spent Sunday afternoon washing our clothes on a concrete slab then hanging our clothes up on a clothes line. We finish the weekend off with polishing our boots and reading our knowledge while the drill instructor paced up and down the squad bay.

After the second month my sleep had a new definition, the definition of military time. I no longer slept until eight in the morning, my mind was now preset to 4 AM. We packed our gear and lined up in formation on the parade grinder, we were on our way to Camp Pendleton for marksmanship training. I was feeling pretty cocky at this point I even felt like I could complete the entire 16 weeks of training. We were allowed to unbutton our collars, roll up our sleeves and blouse our trousers. I had a smile hidden inside that I dare not reveal in front of my drill instructors, but I must admit I was feeling pretty good, so good that I leaned over and spit on the parade deck. My drill instructor saw me out of the corner of his eye. He yelled.

"Get your ass over here private".

I ran over to the drill instructor and lock my body at attention. He leaned forward pressing his campaign hat against my forehead.

He said," lick it up!"

He stare deep into my eyes as I took a deep breath I squatted down and wiped the spit up with my right hand. I locked my body at attention assuming the worst. I thought for sure I was going to jail, but he gave me a stern look and said.

"Get on the bus, crazy one".

The bus ride from San Diego to Camp Pendleton took about 45 minutes. We sat at attention the whole time, locking our eyes on the back of the head of the man in front of us. My drill instructor set at the front of the bus and begin to doze off. I took the opportunity to enjoy the scenic view. I relax my shoulders and shifted my eyes outside of the window getting a quick view of the red roof tops that we stared at from our barracks for the last two months.

It looked just like the pictures in the right on magazine, beaches stretching along the coast of the highways and palm trees as far as the eye could see. My day dreaming came to an abrupt end once the bus came to a screeching stop, all hell broke loose once again. The harassment continued even while we set on bleachers in the marksmanship class. Our drill instructor would tap 10 of us on the shoulder then take us behind the bleachers and thrash us for 15 minutes, making us roll around until our bodies were totally covered from head to toe with sand.

"Make it rain" he yelled as we threw sand in the air.

Once we were filthy from head to toe he would get 10 fresh recruits until he went through the entire platoon. I couldn't focus or learned a dame thing, every time they try to teach us something the drill instructor would fine a way to harass us in the midst of our military education. I was qualifying at the marksman skill level, but I was losing confidence fast. A young recruit next to me have been recycle back two weeks because he failed marksmanship training.

I wasn't about to repeat any cycle, so I pretended as though I couldn't see the target and needed glasses. I was pulled from the firing line and told to guard all the file cabinets and sea bags on the parade grinder. The shooting finally stopped as the young recruits completed marksmanship qualification, everyone lined up to turn in their empty shell casing and wooden ammo blocks. All the sudden there was a single shot fired and within seconds one of the drill instructors came running towards me asking for a file on the private that just shot himself, then ran back to administer first aid.

The young marine recruit that stood next to me killed himself rather than repeat another two weeks of hell. The next morning we returned to San Diego for our last month of boot camp, part of our training included working in the chow hall or working on the lawn maintenance detail. Two weeks after that we packed up once again to return to camp Pendleton for infantry training school. We were still at an incredible pace, a pace that would intensify once we went through the infiltration course with machine guns firing over our heads as we crawled on our stomachs under bob-wire trying not to trip the wires setting off the night flairs. I thought it was easy and fun but other recruits thought it was a horrible ordeal to go through. We slept outside the infiltration course that night and awoke to a mountain towering 10 miles up into the air.

We wore full combat gear including a back pack, helmet and a long wooden shovel that beat the crap out of our leg as we climbed steadily up the mountain at an insanely fast-paced. My drill instructor was right, I did need the vegetables and I was paying the price for dumping them in the trash. The mountain was steep, so steep that my face nearly scraped the ground as I went up. I watched the first platoon flag as it turned the corner and disappear. I thought for sure we were at the top but as I turned the corner the flag was still going up and up. I had no thoughts of home in my head, I didn't even think about finger banging Cindy through her pretty pink panties.

 I was in excruciating pain from head to toe, the Marine that I gave my vegetables to asked if I wanted to grab onto his backpack, but I was too proud, so I sucked it up and picked a focal point and up the mountain I went. As soon as we got to the top of the mountain our drill instructors begin to bin and thrust us.

"Make it rain!"

They yelled as we rolled around in the dirt. The dirt cling to our body because our camouflage utilities were saturated with sweat. Our face was covered with dirt and sweat slowly turning into mud with small thorns from the brush lying on the ground sticking out of our trousers. We stood at attention with our eyes locked on the back of the head of the man in front of us. We couldn't blink, speak or wipe the sweat and mud for our face. All I could think about was I had three weeks left and I be done with this nightmare. We return to MCRD, Marine Corp Recruit Depot two weeks after arriving at infantry training school. All we had left was guard duty, then we turned our rifles in and prepare for graduation. The Marine Corps boot camp definitely change me, my good nature have been soured and my infectious smile had all but disappeared.

I had been beaten on and beaten up for 82 training days in a life I wouldn't recommend for my children or grandchildren, in fact I would recommend it for anyone. Three weeks later I was back in Indianapolis a different man with different perspectives but one agenda. After two weeks of leave I was on my way to Camp Pendleton where my tour of duty would begin. Our routine wasn't much different from boot camp, the only difference was I didn't have drill instructors yelling in my face and the pace was slightly slower, other than that it was still the suck. Cindy and I wrote each other everyday, I'd go home to visit twice a year accept for the summer 1979. I was still just a 19-year-old kid running around the barracks pulling pranks on the older Marines. I always believed it's not where you live but how you live.

Living in Marine barracks was very boring at times especially if you didn't have money. I spend most of my time at the recreation center on base playing pool or watching one of the two TV stations. Sometimes I became very mischievous. One Sunday I had absolutely nothing to do, so I began organizing my room. I was cleaning out an old wall locker. While shuffling through the wall lockers I found a mask of a scary monster stuffed away at the bottom of an empty locker. I put the mask on and walked around the barracks knocking on doors, unexpectedly scaring everyone that opened the door. The biggest, toughest guys in unit would slam the door in my face, until they realize it was just a mask. I went from door-to-door scaring everyone I could until it was my time to return to the duty desk.

It was my turn to stand duty that night but I wasn't sleepy so I sat outside on the steps of the barracks and listen to the quietness of the night. I often thought about Cindy, how much I missed her. I enviously watch the buses leave the base loaded down with Marines trying to escape for the weekend in Oceanside. Later that evening I was summonsed to put on my cartridge belt and sit at the NCO desk, occasionally I would patrolled the hallways of the barracks ensuring that no rooms were broken into and there were no fights. Anything that happened out of the ordinary I'd record it in my duty log and call the duty NCO or Officer of the day.

Having duty on the weekends was a much dislike responsibility each Marine perform monthly. Most of the Marines would offered to pay someone $30 to stand their Post on the weekend, I obliged them as long as they paid me $30 cash upfront. I wasn't familiar with Oceanside nor the people that inhabit the city, so I spent most of my time hanging out on the base and I thought to myself since I'm going to be here anyway I may as well get paid for it. So I sat at the duty NCO desk reading my magazines and counting my new found wealth.

One night while patrolling the barracks I began to smell smoke, I alerted the duty NCO and showed him the location of the fire. We bang on the door trying to wake the sleeping Marine, but to no avail. I was ordered by the duty NCO to climb throw the window and open the door, I did as I was ordered. I climbed through the window and discovered a Marine sleeping on a burning mattress, I open the door, then went back and grabbed the Marine under the arm pits and dragged him in the hallway to safety, then dousing the mattress with several buckets of water.

The next week I was hurled as a hero and given a meritorious mast certificate, nothing change for me at that point I was still an E-3 and performing every shit detail the other seasoned Marines didn't want to do. If the Canon base plates need to be greased, I was sent up the hill to the gun park to grease all six base plates for the cannons. No liberty was granted until all the rust was removed from all six cannons and the base plates were greased for the weekend. So I ran up the hill in the rain, slipping and sliding in the mud as I dug the toe of my boots into the mud, the Marines stood down the hill sarcastically cheering me on

"Hurry up you boot!" "come on get a move on boot"!

Boot was a derogatory term used for Marines fresh out of boot camp, and I was as green as they came. So I climbed the hill and greased all six cannons base plates then I ran back down the hill demonstrating sure footed accuracy as if I was a goat scaling the Rocky Mountains. Back down through the brush cover trench and up the slight incline to the paved parking lot where formation was being held.

My unit was still chanting "boot boot boot boot! I stood there soaking wet listening to the chants, my highly spit shined boots were cover with a clay like mud, my camouflage utilities were soaked from head to toe. It was pouring down rain at this point. We stood at attention silently looking and listening to the first sergeant pontificated the rules of how we should conduct ourselves while on weekend liberty and finally he yelled.

" Dismissed!"

I ran from the formation back to the barracks and began stripping my uniform off as my foot hit the door. I quickly threw my clothes in the washer and jumped in the shower to wash off the grease deep in the pores of my skin.

I could see a person's head poking back and forth on the other side of the shower wall and occasionally peeking around the corner into the shower. I paid no attention because there were no females on base, so I ignored it and finish taking my shower. Wrapping my towel around my waist I slipped and slid my way back to my room, my shower shoes sticking to the floor eventually breaking apart leaving one shower shoe in the hallway as I hobble back to my room on one leg.

I was starving, the aroma coming from the chow hall was fiercely wetting my appetite. I quickly got dressed in my civilian clothes, pausing for a brief second to stare out the window at the line of Marines that stretched around the chow hall. Marines stood in the pouring rain waiting to enter the building. I was very fortunate, I could sit in the warmth of my room and watch the line shrink.

It was an off payday, everyone was broke, this was very typical for young Marines. If you were an E-1 to E-3 you only got paid $600.00 a month. Half our money was spent on the roach coach, a lunch wagon that came around the barrack's blowing its horn at night soliciting snacks and getting Marines to spend the last bit of their pay. The other half of our money was spent at bars in town, movies, and on women at the possibility of having a one night stand. I wasn't broke, I was one of the few young Marines in the camp that had money. I had a pocket full of money and no where to go.

I spent most of my time at the base gym, hitting the punching bag, jump roping or just reading a book in my room. I wasn't familiar with my new surroundings, therefore; I only want to town when I was with a group of trusted friends. Most of the guys I hung around with were young and inexperience like myself. We didn't hang out in bars as the mature guys did. Sampson and I would go to the beach, the mall, the movies, or to Burger King.

He hobbled along beside me, casket on his leg and all. I wasn't a party type of guy, but if I wanted too, I could go in a bar and drink even though I was underage. The bar keeper didn't care about our age, he only cared about how much money they could get us to spend. Every night was the same once we left town, everyone would crowd around the bus stop and rushed the door before the bus driver could open the door or come to a complete stop. The bus driver would just take off and go to the next bus stop making us chase the bus to the next block. Once we got on the bus there was standing room only. When the bus enter the gate to the base the military police (MP'S) made everyone get off the bus, and conducted an informal search of the bus and all the Marines riding on it.

Within 20 minutes we are back on our way. The Marines thought the bus was moving too slow so we rock the bus back-and-forth demanding that the bus driver go faster. The driver pulled to the side of the road and demanded that we stop rocking the bus. The more he demanded the more we rocked the bus almost turning it on its side. The bus driver became so scared he jumped in his driver's seat and race down los pocus road breaking the speed limit by at least 15 miles per hour. Every night it was the same thing, and every night I just sat back in my seat and laugh. We worked hard and we played hard as well.

Most of my free time I spent in the barracks writing letters to Cindy and thinking about my old friends in my neighborhood. What they were doing and who was at the basket-ball court? I thought about my mom and how I've missed living in her house, I thought about my oldest brother and his sexual escapades. I thought about my brother Denton in the army and my sister Sherry in the Air Force. I thought about how nice it would've been if I had stayed home and got a regular job and had a regular life. I had to accept the fact that, that was no longer my life, the corp is my new reality. Something inside of me was changing but I didn't know what it was. Maybe I was becoming a man, or maybe I was becoming a professional killer, whatever it was changing inside of me would alter the way I think forever. I loved the beach and the palm trees and the entire California atmosphere, it was far different from Indiana.

California seemed very fast paced, women would roller skate along the beach wearing bikinis. You would've never saw anything like that Indiana, she would have been arrested and put in jail for indecent exposure. California even have nude beaches that I spent most of my time trying to find but never succeeded. I was told they were 45 minutes away by bus ride. There were orgy houses, where a person could pay $25 to get in and have sex with anyone they saw including someone's wife. California was wild and out-of-control, therefore; I stayed to my boring Indiana ways, watching TV, playing an occasional game of basketball, or spending time in the gym. I stayed in the barracks so long I was beginning to get cabin fever. I just couldn't eat one more burrito from the roach coach or watch one more episode of Gomer Pyle, I had to get out of the barracks and out into life.

A Day of Normalcy

Saturday morning I decide to venture out in town early. I put 20 bucks in my pocket, just enough for a round trip bus ride to and from base and possibly some lunch. I tuck the rest of my money inside of a book hidden in the top of my wall locker. I had a safe proof lock, so I thought. I watched the commercials of a lock being shot with a rifle and still didn't open, until one Marine demonstrated how quickly he could get through my lock with one slap of his hammer, so I relocated my money to another spot. I lifted my bed up and remove the stopper at the base of the bed post, then I shoved my money up the pole of my bed, and off to Oceanside I went. I walked around the town endlessly looking in the store windows, hanging out on the beach or just watching people as part of my weekend fun, finally I went into the barbershop to get my weekly haircut.

This was something new for me, I had never been to a barbershop where all the barbers were white males. I was unsure about the outcome, but I thought, Marines only wear regulation high and tight haircuts, so it really doesn't matter how the hair cut turns out. When he was done he handed me the mirror to check out the back of my head, I noticed a ball spot beginning to form in the center of my scalp, indicating the first signs of alopecia. I was horrified at the possibility of going bald. I must have sat in the chair for two minutes looking in the mirror while rubbing the small circle spot on the back of my head.

I couldn't stay there all day so I jumped out of the chair, gave the barber five dollars and out to the sunny streets of Oceanside I went. The streets were jam-packed with young Marines and young prostitutes relieving them of their hard earned pay. It was a total culture shock, not like Indianapolis, restricted by color. In California more than just black-and-white populated the city, the population of California was well mixed, women from different cultures with long beautiful black hair stretching down their back, laying openly on the beaches in their skimpy bathing suits. I thought I had found a part of heaven, walking along the beach with my tongue dragging in the sand looking at all the beautiful expos bodies as far as the eye could see.

I couldn't stand it anymore so I jumped on the bus and headed to May Company Mall. I couldn't help but notice there was a young girl on the bus sitting directly across from me, her long athletic legs were covered with stockings the had runs in them. I didn't care I worked around men all day, five days a week, so this was a sight to behold. She wore a black miniskirt with a tight white T-shirt displaying her well proportioned torso. She stared at me for a while then struck up a conversation, before I knew it we were walking around the mall together shopping.

She couldn't have been more than 18 years old or the same age as I. We walked and talked for hours prosing through several stores. I was becoming quite comfortable with her, stepping close behind her while she looked at shirts and pants. I seductively assisted her by holding pants to her waistline while she looked over her shoulder into the mirror. I was in hog heaven, I haven't been this close to a woman in months, and I had to say it did feel good. I stayed with her that day for about five hours, looking at stockings, jewelry, and miscellaneous items of furniture. I walked closely behind her heading towards the register so she could purchase a new pair of black stockings.

She lead me into a part of the mall I have never been, then she walked into a secluded corner of the mall placing one hand on my shoulder to bounce her weight, she reached up her skirt and pull off her stockings.

"Hold on to these" she said, laying the stockings on my shoulder.

She remove her new stockings from the packet and begin putting one leg at a time in each stocking then pulling the pantyhose up. She wasn't wearing a stitch of underwear, her skin was smooth and soft as cotton. I felt light headed and unresponsive, I was just beginning to go into starvation mode when she suggested going to lunch. I stood there in a daze staring at her, I could see her mouth moving but I wasn't hearing anything. She snapped her fingers and patted me on the side of my face saying.

"Come on, let's go eat, I know the perfect place".

She grabbed me by the hand, her female touch almost made me drool from the mouth but I stayed in control and off we went back into the mall. She walked slightly in front of me pulling me down the hallway of the mall as if I was her boyfriend or husband. I purposely linger behind her trying to catch a glimpse of those long beautiful legs covered with $1.98 stockings.

The restaurant was beautiful, white table cloths covering every table with fancy napkins made into the shape of animals, with a candle burning brightly in the center of each table.

"What was I doing in a place like this"? I thought to myself.

I began to feel awkward, or out of place, because I barely had enough money to pay for myself and I always felt it was the man's job to pay for the meal, so I told her to give me a second then I ditched around the corner. I begin counting my money, I had $11 dollars to my name, I was so embarrassed I could only afford to pay for my meal, and definitely knew I couldn't pay for hers.

We sat down to lunch, I scooted her chair under her trying to be a total gentleman, it was my first time using an actual menu, I knew I was in a financial dilemma. I scoured the menu quickly with my eyes, the cheapest thing on the menu was a tuna melt sandwich and it cost seven dollars without fries, even the water was a dollar a glass. I frantically calculated the taxes in my head, my meal cost slightly less then I had in my pocket. I had another 1.50 stuffed in my socks but I wouldn't dare use it because it was my only means of transportation back to the base.

She could see the trepidation on my face, she reached across the table and delicately touched my hand.

"We can go Dutch" . She said.

I squinted my eyes indicating I was confused.

"We can each pay for our own meal" she said.

I internally let go of a side of relief, my vertebrae was no longer locked into position and I was finally able to swallow the lump in my throat. She ordered a huge meal costing somewhere around $15, I felt naked, sitting there with my paltry little tuna melt sandwich with garnishment decorating the plate. I pretended as though I hated fries to save my-self the embarrassment when the check came, so I played it smart and just ordered a tuna melt sandwich, and for ten cent more I added a slice of cheese trying not to show that I was totally broke. She sat in front of me with a huge platter of food forking it down, not even catching her breath between bites. She ate fast like she was in boot camp. I nibbled around the edges of my tuna melt sandwich taking my time trying to make it last. I stared across the table at her slim, perfectly built frame fantasizing about the possibility of a sexual encounter.

We talked for an hour and seemingly grew comfortable enough with one another to talk about our heritage and where we were from. She said she was from East LA, she is

Hispanic, she grow up in a dysfunctional family plague by gangs and violence. She needed to get away from the violence of her everyday life that's why she moved to Oceanside California. I'd begin to feel a sense of friendship developing between us, the thought of pulling slick moves to get close to her dissipated from my mind. I gave her space, not even trying to slip my hand around her beautiful thin waist.

Eventually we caught another bus back to Oceanside Boulevard where she lead me into a pool hall filled with young Marines smoking cigarettes and drinking beer, the last place I wanted to be was around a bunch of jar heads. She seemed very popular and right at home as she made her rounds greeting everyone she saw, everyone in the pool hall knew her, a few men walked up to her, picked her up and kissed her on the jaw.

Several man proposition her for dates later in the evening, before accepting, she looked over her shoulder at me then back to business as usual. I observed her for a few more minutes and all of a sudden it hit me, she was a prostitute. I quietly slipped out of the pool hall and walked down to hoagies corner and purchased a .50 cent piece of beef jerky to snack on for the bus ride back to the base. I climbed onto the first bus and stared out the window thinking about my day as the bus twisted and turned down Los pogus dark winding road. It was a long quiet ride, only two other Marines occupy the bus because it was still early in the day, most Marines didn't return to the base until the last bus left Oceanside at 12:30 in the evening. I sat in the back of the bus trying to get clarity about what just happened. I came to the understanding that this young girl just wanted too feel normal for one day. Maybe she want to experience what it was like for other girls her same age who wasn't dating for money or being offered money for sex. I believe this was the closest she would come to feeling normal. This was the first time in months that I had an intimate relationship with the female, a woman's soft touch and the smell of her perfume came home like truth.

It had been seven months since I've visited Indianapolis as well as several months since I had sex. I was 19 years old and horny as hell. I had trouble sleeping at night. I was fine doing daylight hours because I was preoccupied with my job as a Cannoneer. But when the night fell I was alone and didn't have anything to deterred me from thinking about 29th & Talbot.

Every Friday evening we were released to go to chow, then return to begin cleaning the barracks. We scrubbed and polish the bathroom floors for three hours before the first inspection. A tall squared away brass lieutenant walked in as though he was inspecting the barracks at the eighth and I duty station in Washington DC. He rubbed his hand across the wall and under the bathroom sinks, pulling one finger out with less than a microfiber of dust. He said.

"It's not clean, continue to field day and call me when its ready."

Everyone was thoroughly pissed off, the lieutenant wanted to play mind fuck games and keep us cleaning the bathrooms all night. After two more hours of thoroughly cleaning the barracks, scrubbing walls, scrubbing in and behind the toilet, we felt we were ready for another inspection, so we sent the runner to summons the lieutenant. He strutted down the hallway of the barracks, belching from the pastrami sandwich he just eaten. He walked in the bathroom, looked at the roll of toilet paper.

"It's too thin" he said. " replace the roll and call me when you're done".

He strutted out the door as though he owned the world. We replace all the rolls of toilet paper in the stalls, we sprayed windex on the toilets to give them a nice shine and the appearance of being brand-new.

We used our tooth brushes to scrub around the edge of the toilets in any visible seam, we sent a runner into town to purchase civilian bathroom cleaning products. After three more hours of cleaning and scrubbing we sent for the lieutenant. By this time it was 1 AM in the morning, the lieutenant strutted down the hallway as fresh as he was at 5 PM, not a hair out of place. I stood back and observe as he bent down on one knee and wiped his finger around the edge of the toilet, lifting the seat off the toilet he turned and said.

"This toilet is not clean".

Sgt. said, "Pardon me sir the toilet is clean".

"Well, Sgt. This toilet is not clean, and you just failed another inspection, I'll come back at 4 AM." The lieutenant said.

The sergeant said," sir if I can proof the toilet is clean would you releases us for the night?"

"How are you going to prove that" said the Lieut.

The Sgt. got down on one knee, reaching into the bowl with both hands, he scooped out water from the toilet and drank the water from his hands. The lieutenant looked shockingly at the Sgt. and said.

"Your secured for the night".

It was almost 2 o'clock in the morning, the buses were no longer running on the base. I think everyone was too tired to chase women are go bar hopping, we all return to our rooms for a night of well earned sleep.

Saturday mornings were the best of all, it was one of few days the Marine Corps didn't bother us. So I cruised over to the chow hall before catching the bus to San Diego to see a movie. I thought a movie would help distract my thoughts from any sexual desires but the movie had two sexual scenes that had me reeling from the theater in search of a drug store where I can purchase some type of prophylactic for a possible night of sexual ecstasy. Right after the movie I decided to cruise the San Diego strip. I was one block away from the theater before being quickly approached by a young white girl, she was around 25 years old with dirty blond hair, she was a "BWG" Basic white girl with a non-descript body. She looked and smelled different from the girls I grew up with. The girls at my high school smelled like pickles and Kool-Aid, a popular snack in the 70s. The girls carried pickles and Kool-Aid strews in their purses providing themselves with a snack in a moments notice.

The pickles looked as though they were on steroids, they were large and sealed in a plastic bag with juice. The kook-aid strews were long, at least 18 inches, hosting several different flavors. This girl was different, not only was she from a different ethnic group. her blond hair was straight and lifeless, not possessing any body, curl or style. She wreaked of cigarette smoke and seemed very overt and aggressive as she walked upon me fast as if she was trying to beat someone else to the punch.

She said, "I am the best"

I looked at her with a confused look on my face and said.

"You're the best at what?"

She paused for a second, looked at me squinting her eyes while taking a long drag from her cigarette. If I didn't know better I would think she was rehearsing for a Humphrey Bogart movie.

"I'm the best at giving head" she said.

"You're a cop" I implied, and I don't have any time to sit in jail"

She looked at me with astonishment and said.

"I'm not a cop! Just ask the other women around".

So I made my way up and down the strip checking her credentials, after 10 minutes of asking questions while observing her from a distance I discover she was telling the truth, she wasn't a cop.

I slowly made my way back towards her. I leaned over and whispered in her ear.

"How much?"

She said, " It will cost you $20".

" I don't have $20" I said, while searching through my wallet.

"How much do you have?"

"I have $14."

She looked at me disappointedly rolling her eyes.

"That's okay it's enough to buy me a pack of cigarettes let's go" she said.

We jumped into a yellow taxi heading around the corner just a little more than a mile to her house. I was creeped out by the entire seen but I was being lead blindly by my emotional horny state.

I didn't have a clear thought in my head, I was being controlled by my little head not my big head which made me forget about any possible dangers that may have lurked inside of her house. Her room was a very basic set up just for business. A full-size bed shoved in the corner, a cheap night table and a lamp without a shade using a low wattage bulb. After my 10 minutes of passion I got dressed quickly and started jogging back to the bus station before the last bus departed to Oceanside.

2 500 miles away from home

After weeks and weeks of dreaming about going home, July arrived and before I knew it I was 35,000 feet in the air catching jet lag. Over the course of seven months our relationship thrived only on letters and postcards, continuously building on a relationship of infatuation rather than love. I hung out at Cindy's house day and night, her mother never requested that I leave but she listened throughout the night to ensure that Cindy did not slip back down stairs. Unfortunate for her we were young so we did what people do, we fell into the age-old trap of lust and desire. At two in the morning Cindy found her way downstairs.

We spent the next 15 days hanging out at the park, walking, talking, and holding hands where time and space permitted. Cindy loved material possessions, and felt since I was her boyfriend I was supposed to buy her a $400 stereo system. I have just under $300 dollars to my name but I reluctantly gave it to her in hopes it would make her happy. But she was thoroughly pissed off because I was $100.00 dollars short, so she tossed the money back to me and went home. I felt kind of bad about the whole thing, about her not being able to buy her stereo but I didn't feel bad enough to give her the money again. I purchased a ten sack of white castles and a large chocolate shake and sat on my mothers patio and wished I didn't have to return to the base. Before I knew it I had to return to camp Pendleton.

My 15 days of leave came to a bitter end, I grabbed and hug Cindy before reluctantly boarding the airplane. I walked down the lonely 30 foot ramp and took my seat in the coach section of the plane. I raise and lower the window shade on the plane several times signaling goodbye. Everyone else walked away hurrying to the car to claim the shotgun seat ride back home. My mother stayed until the plane back out onto the tarmac, once the plane was in the air she went to her car. I sat on the plane looking forlorn with my face pressed against the window staring at the open sky. The stewardess notice my uniform and the long look on my face. She walked over and asked if I wanted to sit in first class. I looked up at her holding back my tears, I could barely speak but I was able to say.

"No thank you".

I knew I had made a mistake enlisting in the corp for four years. I missed my family, and my friends, it was a part of my life that I could never get back, watching my siblings grow up and my mother gracefully age to the person she became to today. I could feel the distance widening between us as the plane climbed to 30,000 feet. Four years of family memories that would never be realized, only memories of myself and the men I served with in the corp.

Chocolate Mountain

I reported back to my unit and was told to pack my gear, we are heading out to choco-late Mountain Arizona. We loaded our trucks with axes, pics, shovels, a huge camou-flage net, personal weapons including a M-60 caliber machine gun and a 50 caliber anti aircraft weapon. We hitched our cannons to the back of the 5 ton trucks and stage them at the gun Park. We stood in formation to listen to a one hour lecture on safety. Don't play with the rattlesnakes, don't pick up unexploded ordinance, they told us not to do all of the things they knew Marines would do.

The next morning we were off, rolling down the highway at 60 miles an hour, dragging 15,500 pound cannons behind us, trucks stretching 2 miles long convoying down the highway. The ride was long, sweltering heat and hard wooden benches made it very difficult to enjoy the scenic view. Seabags where stack celling high in the back of the truck. The locker meant for storing tools was jam packed with pokey bait, extra food Marines bring to the field to keep from eating C-rations. We became very creative in our boredom, we ripped apart cardboard boxes and wrote messages asking women to pull their shirts up displaying their breasts. Screams could be heard from the last truck all the way to the leading truck as the civilian women passed by exposing their breast.

Two guys in the back of my truck begin to argue about nothing, the white marine repeatedly called the Cuban marine Fidel. They were almost at blows, so I position myself between them to keep the argument from escalating into a fight. It was all I could do to prevent them from destroying the back of the truck. Later that evening we arrived in Chocolate Mountain Arizona. In a distance I could see heat waves floating across the desert. It was seven at night and still 100° in the shade. No one was allowed to bunk down until all the vehicles and equipment were prepare for the training exercise to ensure our readiness. Setting up our nets on top of the trucks, reorganizing the back of the trucks, making room for loading 100 live artillery shells, and stacking case after case of C-rations, as well as four 5 gallon cans of water in the back of the trucks.

The next morning I was awaken by the sound of Diesel fuel coming from trucks reviving their engines, thick gray smoke poured from their stacks. "Amtrak's" amphibious assault vehicles and tanks were the first to pull out, artillery follow close behind. The infantry hit the ground running the same day we arrived, they never stopped humping until they marched 10 miles beyond the artillery and tank units. After hours of driving, we took position in a desolate place in the middle of nowhere. I was given a 5 gallon can of water, a case of C-Rations and a prick radio. I was told to guard the road and not allow anyone to come within 5 miles of the live fire zone. I was left in that desolate part of the desert by myself for four days without seeing another human being. I spent my nights staring at the sky full of stars thinking about Cindy and what she was doing. I spend my days trying to stay out of the sun and the sweltering heat.

My fourth day guarding the road I became extremely bored, so I began to do all the things the Marine Corps told us not to do. I looked for snakes, poking and prodding in the holes hoping to force them out the backside. While walking I nearly tripped over a 500 pound unexploded bomb dropped by one of our Navy Jets. I backed up very slowly, placing 1 foot behind the other delicately on the ground until I was nearly 100 paces away.

I grabbed my prick radio and reported the unexploded shell. Jeeps filled with ordnance personnel appeared out of nowhere as though they rolled right out of the sand. I was transported to the top of a hill and watch as the ordinance crew placed C4 and primacor wrapped around the unexploded shell and destroying the shell and everything within 50 m of it.

An hour later I was returned to my unit three shades darker than when I left. I couldn't help but smile from ear to ear as I tossed my gear into the back of the truck and squatted down next to the tire to prepare a stove made out of a can to heat my C-rations. Just as my food was warming up I heard a loud explosion. Everyone stood up at once trying to get a fix on what direction the explosion came from. We could see smoke coming from 100 yards away, then all of a sudden a navy jet broke through the clouds, swooping down on top of us dropping another shell, a little closer this time within 75 yards of our opposition.

Scrap metal spray the area, ripping through the truck tarps and piercing the metal on the truck doors. Capt. Moore grabbed the prick radio and try to call for cease-fire as the third navy jet was turning the corner. Everyone was running for their life, but there was nothing to hide behind because the shells were falling to close to the trucks to take cover, so we ran as far and as fast as we could from the drop zone before the third shell hit the ground. Three Marines were hit with strap metal and one Marine jumped on a cactus bush. I lay behind a telephone pole that somehow ended up in the middle of the desert.

I bury my face deep in the sand, I could hear the strap metal hitting the pole and grazing the top of my helmet, just as we thought it was safe, another jet turned the corner with its engine roaring. The jet was ahead of its sound but this time I looked straight at the Jet coming down right on top of us preparing to drop another 500 pound shell. My commanding officer grabbed a smoke grenade and tossed it as far as he could into the drop zone, the jets saw the smoke and pulled away from our position.

The scrap metal from the 500 pound shell disable two of the cannons, flatting their tires and shattering the wind shields of several trucks, therefore; myself and another Marine was put on a truck and sent to the rear to guard the ammo dump. I reluctantly grabbed my gear and dragged it over to the ammo dump. I set at the dump for two days with the sun beating directly down on my head, there was no cover, we weren't allowed to put up a tent because the helicopters would come in and kick up so much sand and wind it would pull the tents out of the ground and rip them into shred. So we sat in the sweltering and blistering sun reluctantly getting a complete body tan that we didn't need.

We had only been in the desert a week and already my skin was looking dry and brittle, my lips were chapped and cracking and the lip balm and vaseline provided little relief. The winds were picking up making little sand twisters less than a foot from the stacks of ammunition. There was news of a possible sand storm heading our way, only the news had arrived two minutes too late. I couldn't see one foot in front of me and within minutes our cannons were practically buried up to the top of the tires. All the low ranking personnel were forced to walk guard duty, standing outside in the middle of the storm protecting equipment that no civilian knew was even there. We rotated shifts three hours on and 3 off, no one really stayed awake during the twilight hours, they just pass the fire watch list, watch and flashlight on to the next fire watch. I had the 2 AM to 4 AM shift, I love being awake doing the twilight hours when everyone else was asleep but this was different.

I was totally exhausted from the days activities and quickly fell into a deep sleep. Someone tap me on the shoulder then handed me the flashlight and watch. I shined the flash light on the watch to check the time, then I rolled over and just stayed in my sleeping bag until my shift ended. Wearing nothing but boots, a T-shirt and camouflage utilities I walked 25 meters to the other Canon and handed the watch and flashlight to the next person on patrol. I turned around and took 10 paces and realized I couldn't see one foot in front of me. I waved my hand back-and-forth less than an inch in front of my face. I couldn't see my hand because it was pitch black dark.

I yelled out to the Marines sleeping around my Canon but there was no response, so I walked in the direction from which I came and still I couldn't see anyone. I squatted down trying to see an outline of a truck or tent but there was nothing there. So I yelled out once again and once again no one responded. I began walking in the direction I thought I came from, I must have walk around for more than an hour believing I was walking around my units location but I was at least five or 6 miles down the road where the amphibious assault vehicle division was located. Freezing cold from the bitter night air. My leather boots felt hard as rocks because of the cold weather and the absence of wearing socks. The further I walked the further I was moving away from my unit. I look down and saw grunts lying in their two man fighting positions. I knew I had gone too far so I did a 180 degree turn and went back in the other direction.

More than an hour and a half past and I was finally back to my unit. I located some communication wire in the middle of our camp clearly marked and leading to each canon. I figured out which wire lead to my canon so I traced the wire all the way back to my canon then lifelessly lay down on my cot, closed my eyes for 10 minutes before reveille was sounded. I was exhausted and my misfortune was we just began a three day no sleep training exercise that morning. We moved nonstop all day and silently into the night, dragging our cannons behind us kicking up nose clogging dust, only stopping temporarily to bell from the trucks when the navy Jets flew overhead spraying us with CS gas.

The Marines moved hard and fast stopping occasionally to perform hip shoots, then back on the trucks. The other days were spent performing Hilo raids, pushing the small 105 cannons into the back of helicopters then landing for approximately five minutes, firing off two artillery shells then back in the helicopter to repeat the same raids over and over again until it was time for night fire. The roads were long and hot, I could see heat waves in the distance covering the vast empty desert. As miserable as I was I couldn't help but to have an occasional thought of Cindy and what she was doing at the moment.

My euphoric thoughts were interrupted by more CS gas and the 120° temperature inside my mop suit. The water drinking device on my gas mask didn't work, so I had to go for hours without water because they didn't allow us to remove our gas mask until all clear was given. It was like a scene out of a war movie. As far as the eye could see trucks were lined up along the desert road and the Navy pilots couldn't help but to spray us with gas one last time as we headed to base camp.

We jumped off the trucks and scatter in all directions pointing our weapons in the air and firing blanks at the jets while trying to Don our gas mask and cover ourselves with ponchos to stop the burning effect of the CS gas. Immediately after all clear was given two Marines ran from the road down into a huge crater left by a bomb and began hitting each other with shovels and tent poles and what ever else that was in their reach. Marines stood around the top of the crater taking bets as the two Marines bludgeoned themselves half to death until one Marine Cpl. Stepped in and ended the fight. It was the two Marines I prevented from fighting in the back of the truck on the way to the desert. They finally had enough of one another and decided to settle the difference "Marine Corps" style.

The fight was soon forgotten and before we knew it we were on our way back to camp Pendleton. The ride home wasn't as much fun because dirt soaked deep into the pores of our skin. We choked and threw up in the back of the trucks from remnants of sand caught in our throats and particles of sand trap in the corner folds of our eyes sealing them shut. We had not bathed for eight weeks and the C-Rations give off an awful smell while Marines tried to cleanse their bowels. Grunting and clutching onto the bathroom stall because they were constipation from the military diet of C-rations.

In the Marines we were supposedly guaranteed one hot meal and one hour of sleep per day doing combat conditions, but we never saw the hot meal and scarcely saw one hour of sleep during training. I often thought of Cindy and what she's doing and whether or not she thought of me as often as I thought of her. We were young and in the mist of puppy love. I often thought about the way we were and wished I were more mature and prepare for what was about to take place in my life. I hadn't yet experienced anything compelling or jolting to my character. I have yet to be tested, but I rest assure the test was coming.

$\mathcal{A}$ fall from grace

I was back in the barracks and could easily find time during the quiet hours of the night to write Cindy letters, but to my surprise I was selected for (NCO) noncommissioned officer school where corporals and sergeants went to be groomed for leadership. I was not yet an NCO I was just in E-3 with less than a year in the Corps, the leadership school was eight weeks and a modified version of Boot Camp, fast-paced with a lot of physical activity. There were more than 50 Marines in the leadership school and I was the only E-3 in the entire class. I feel so out of place and so overwhelmed it wasn't long before the corporals and sergeants try to place me on every shit detail they could create, but they were easily reminded that pulling rank wasn't an option at the school but they plotted and threw obstacles in my way trying to find ways to drop me from the program.

From the very first inspection I received unwarranted demerits that other Marines receive a pass on. We were separated into nine man squads no one want to be in the squad with an E-3, they had no choice but to allow me to participate but they didn't make it easy. I was placed with eight other Marines that could run 3 miles in 17 minutes.

I wasn't the slowest runner at the time, my best 3 mile run was 21 minutes. During the final three weeks of NCO school we had a squad run competition, we were the last squad to started the 6 mile course, by the time we reached 3 miles we passed all the other squads and was ahead of them by at least three minutes.

Four miles into the run one of our corporals fell behind, because the pace was very ex-cruciating, we were running at a six minute mile pace. My knees began to feel pressure from the uphill, downhill interchange, causing me to fall back 5 feet from my squad. The other Marine fell back more than 50 yards causing the squad to slow down so that he could catch up. Finally we made it back to the barracks after a 6 mile grueling fast-paced run. Everyone blamed me for the other Marine inability to keep up with the squad. They said.

"If you hadn't drop back he would've run harder to keep up".

Only one Marine came to my defense, saying that.

"It was bullshit and it wasn't my fault that the other Marine fell behind".

I knew I was being targeted for blame and it wouldn't be long before I was dropped from NCO school.

It has been six weeks and I could see the finish line but later that evening I received a letter from Cindy. She reluctantly informed me she was pregnant and her mother was very upset and threatening to call my commanding officer if I didn't marry her. Personally I could give a flying bat butt about her mother being upset, I was more concerned about becoming a father. That night I rode the city bus to Oceanside Boulevard. I walked into one of the sleazy bars, they could tell by my high and tight hair cut that I was a jar head and even though I was only 19 they allowed me to drink my problems away.

I was so distraught by the information of becoming a father, I lost my focus and could no longer study, therefore; I was put out of the (NCO) noncommissioned officer program doing the final two weeks before graduation. I was embarrassed to return to my unit, because I was a failure but I had bigger fish to fry. I had a child on the way and soon a wife, there wasn't any way I was going to let Cindy have my baby unwedded, and my infatuation for her slowly turned into love.

The month of October I receive orders to go overseas to Okinawa Japan the following year, January 5, 1980, and I was given 30 days leave before shipping out. December 1, I landed in Indianapolis, my first stop was my mothers house, then across the bridge I walk to Cindy's house. Her mother answer the door and said.

" Cindy is in the kitchen". She said.

I walked towards the kitchen and in a flash she ran down into the basement then out the side door. She was reluctant to let me see her stomach protruding pass her unfasten blue jeans. So I sat on the living room couch . The couch was cover with plastic, if it were hot outside I surely would have been on my way to dehydration. I waited patiently for Cindy to collect her self, she was being obnoxiously shy, but I understood, so I sat on the couch until she walked into the room and set down beside me. I reached over, opened her coat and rub her stomach, at that exact time I knew I loved her and I couldn't allow her to be an unwedded mother. I stared deep into her eyes while running my fingers through her hair and once again she became soft and melted into my arms. She cried and I whisper softly in her ear.

"Would you be my wife."

She said, "Yes".

We sat a date for December 29, 1979, at Stouffer's Inn a very prestigious hotel less than a mile from my mothers house. I took my last $900.00 and paid for the ballroom and catering. Cindy and her close friend was in charge of the decorations, the room appeared very Idyllic. Many of the wedding party were not particularly interested in the wedding themselves, but attended the wedding to observe first hand the oulchritudinous view of the ballroom. Around 50 people were in attendance for the wedding including my grandmother. Seeing her at my wedding pleased me to see her out and about rather than sitting in the kitchen gossiping with my aunt. Cindy and I were both so young, barely out of high school, naïve, and very uncertain about raising a child. I stood on the left when I should've been on the right which caused me to place the ring on the wrong finger. I just wanted the event over with and to get on with my life.

The thoughts of living in Japan settle quietly into my murky subconscious, we ate cake and slow danced to songs by Earth wind and fire. Everyone seemed to be having a good time until Cindy's stepfather began complaining about the food and how little he was able to get. As quiet as it was kept I spent my last $900 to have the food catered, but Cindy's mother took credit for paying for the food and the ball room.

By the time the rumor made it back to me about who payed for the food and ball room I didn't care, I just wanted the night to come to an end. Cindy and I was whisked away to my brothers small two bedroom house where we would spend the first 24 hours of our marriage. We were reluctant to stay but unfortunately we were short on funds and didn't have many other options, therefore we agreed to stay the night but within an hour we were bifurcate into disagreeable factions. Here we were one hour into our marriage and already had our first fight. Cindy set in the bedroom trying to codify our life while I stared aimlessly out the front room window trying to grasp the fact that I will be more than 12,000 miles away in the next five days.

I believe that's truly what the fight was about. Before I knew it I was sitting on the plane face pressed against the airplane window trying to get a glimpse of my pregnant wife as the plane back out onto the tarmac. The fight was over crowded and It was just my luck to sit next to an obese women wreaking of cheap perfume. I was being mentally tormented, covering my nose with a wet handkerchief. The smell was worse than CS gas because we were in a closed off area. The 22 hour flight laid over in Anchorage Alaska for one and a half hours, then onto Guam airport, a small building, less than Ft 2000.[2]. A barracuda hanging lifelessly on the wall displaying all of its teeth trying to provide some sense of art and style in the dainty little airport. Pictures of the island hung freely on the walls telling the history of the island in the battle it took to keep the island.

Two hours into my layover we boarded another plane for our final destination, Okinawa Japan. I was fortunate to arrive while the sun was still high in the sky. I sat pensively internally feeling the distance from home with every screeching sound of the airplane wheels touching down on the runway. I wasn't comfortable being in another country, so I stuck close to the base my first two months on the island. Occasionally I walked around the perimeter of the fence getting a feel for what it was like to be in a Japanese neighborhood.

The houses were close together one right on top of the other, only a small side walk to separate the tiny houses. Vendors stood on every corner selling sushi and other types of exotic seafood. I thought the people were very pleasant, more so than the foreigners that assimilated while living in the US. I ran around the island like an idiot with a Japanese translation hand book yelling "mushy mushy," meaning hello hello. Once a person stopped to talk to me I thumb through the book for something else to say but they always walked off before I could find the next phrase.

I stayed very close to the barracks, bored out of my mind I watch Japanese cartoons, 'Transformers' in their language. I didn't understand a thing, all the street signs were in Japanese and the streets ran in the opposite direction of the US. I searched the news-paper for criminal activity, picking up a word here and there. I was totally frustrated and felt out of place. Culture shock began to creep in and before I knew it I was shipped to Korea for cold-weather training (Jack Frost). A training exercise conducted yearly throughout the entire fleet Marine force (FMF Pack). I was tired and want to sleep but I was thrown into a group of Marines and marched to the nearest supply room and began withdrawing my substandard cold weather training gear. I arrived in Korea 5 days later and was immediately escorted to a Government personnel tent (GP) where 80 other Marines were suffering the same faith as I. We were living in the chosen frozen, fortu-nately for us it was the Cold War Era. South Korea was at peace but North Korea main-tain a threatening presence just on the other side of the fence line. Marines were stretched out along the demobilizing zone (DMZ) to prevent the occupying North Korea forces from crossing into the forbidden zone.

Most nights the temperatures plummet into-30°. All I could do to stay warm was put two rocks on the pub stoves to get them hot, then place the rocks in the foot of my sleeping bag to prevent my feet from turning into walking ice planks. The ceiling of the tent was covered with 12 inch icicles that hung desperately close to our face as we lay sleeping in our ill-equipped cold weather sleeping bags. I woke up at 4:00 and made my way outside to the tenant covered bathroom just 15 meters from our tent. I was thoroughly disgusted by the bathroom facility. The toilets were knee high, making it difficult to mount and have a seat. Before we could take a dump, we had to remove three layers of clothes, including a parka and snow boots. Frozen feces covered the top of all the toilets from one end of the bathroom to the other, there was at least 10 toilets, two rolls with five toilets on each side. The toilets were wooden with no supporting back structure. We had to use the buddy system, lean against the person behind us or squat on top of the toilet which was what most Marines did according to the evidence they left sitting on top of the toilet. Every morning a maintenance crew with high pressure steam sprayers tried to clean the bathroom using a water hose and scrub brushes, the feces would just liquefied then freeze on top of the toilet leaving a brown slippery residue.

Most Marines got fully undressed so they could balance themselves while taking a dump, there was no place to hang our clothes so we had to be very creative each time we visit the latrine. Holding our clothes in our hand while slipping and sliding on the ice cover rice patties. The Marines believe in teamwork and this was team work at its best. Two men had to travel to the latrine together to assist one another with completing their morning ritual of pinching a loaf. I became so frustrated with the process I grabbed a shovel and began searching for a secluded place bordering the camp. About 100 meters from my tent was the US Air Force campsite. I wanted to see for myself how nice they lived, up to this point I only heard rumors about them living like civilians. So I creeped over to the nearest Air Force building, then peek inside. I couldn't believe how nice their bathrooms were, mirrors on the wall, clean porcelain toilets with wooden floors, and not to mention the bathroom was fully heated. I couldn't believe it, Paradise in the wilderness.

At last I could drop my pants, lay back against the porcelain toilet seat and pinch a loaf as though I was in the civilian world. Although I was in the Air Force plush bathroom, the 12 weeks of C-rations had worked its Magic. It did exactly what it was designed to do, it made me constipated preventing me from pinching a loaf at will. I hated going to the bathroom it was a very painful and unpleasant experience. Although I only had to go to the bathroom once every three weeks I hated stripping down totally naked just to cleanse my colon.

Once I discovered the dietary purpose of C-rations, I stop eating what the military gave me in exchange for carrying my own pokey bait. Food that we purchased from the PX, such as tuna, ramen noodle, cookies, crackers, and other canned foods. I went hungry for my first three weeks in Korea because Lance Cpl. Bird was assigned to mess duty, he would get up at 2 AM and crack eggs all morning long. He was so agitated by the process and pissed off at the world, he'd mix the egg shells in with the eggs, ruining everyone's breakfast.

The bacon was frozen solid, smothered with frozen grease. The grease had to be wiped away with napkins before we could eat it, the coffee was the safest bet, pure black and steaming hot. Bird was a nuisance, no one in the unit liked him, so they send him as far away from our unit as they could. They assigned him to work on shit details just to keep him away from the rest of the unit. Bird was a compulsive liar, he would tell grandiose lies about owning a home on a rotating mountain, marines grew sick of listening to his lies, every time he came around we just walked away.

All of the training and living conditions were very harsh in the Marine Corps, even the showers were run by generators, there was no way for the operators to control the temperature. Scalding hot water was piped through tubes attached to a rod coming from the generator, it was as if we were lobsters being boiled in a pot. Wooden shipping pallets were used for floors. The floors were so cold the hundred degree hot steaming water couldn't prevent the wooden pallets from being covered with ice.

Even the dressing area in the showers were rice patties covered with ice. Everywhere we stepped there was ice under our feet, it didn't matter how hot the shower water would get the ice just wouldn't melt. Every morning for 12 weeks everyone crowded around the small pot stove sucking up all the heat before it could spread throughout the tent. I couldn't believe how stupid I was getting myself in this type of situation, it should be a crime to be so stupid. I couldn't get the fact out of my head that the Air Force camp was just 100 meters across the grinder. They were living a life of luxury in plush two man tent's with real wooden floors, not shipping pallets.

The Airmen had dressers with the mirrors attached and drawers to put their clothes in and a civilian made quilt covering their beds. I envied and I hated them at the same time. Our lifestyles were totally different but our mission was the same, 'keep the North

Koreans in the North'. I spent 12 weeks sleeping on ice covered rice patties, pulling icicles from the ceiling of our tent, using them for water to make coffee. I never drink pure black coffee before this experience, but it was so cold, milk and creamer was a secondary thought. I just wanted something hot to drink, I didn't care what it taste like. I couldn't imagine fighting a war in these type of conditions as the Marines who came before us did. It didn't matter how cold it was, there was always something to do outside in that horrid weather. We parked our cannons in rice fields of some poor farmer. His home was less than 100 hundred meters away from our firing positions, we didn't care whether it kept him up all hours of the night so we shot our live artillery shells over the City highway onto desolate land designated as the live fire zone.

We stood on the firing line for hours in 30° below weather with a windchill factor of 25 mph waiting for a fire mission. The fire missions came few and far between and by 3 o'clock that evening someone got the bright idea to swap off gun sections every couple of hours. We stood out on the firing line until 10 pm at night, my eye sockets were just about frozen in place and my mouth had frozen stiff. I could barley pronounce words or speak. As it got late in the evening Bush bunnies made their presence known, whispering from the bush "GI GI fucking sucky $10".

I just kept walking my post pretending not to notice them but some Marines couldn't resist the temptation of having sex with the young girls, they gladly jumped into the bushes for a cheap thrill that turned out to be a very painful visit to the dispensary. Bush girls weren't tested by the military for sexually transmitted diseases. But prostitution was legal in the bars of Soul Korea, therefore; the military insured that the women occupying the bars got routine physicals or vaccinated for venereal diseases. If the girls refused to be tested by the military the business owner would have to place a pile of salt on either side of the door alerting young soldiers, sailors, and Marines to the presence of sexually transmitted diseases within that establishment. I was married and didn't want to take any chances on the possibility of spreading any diseases to my wife so I stayed away from the Bush bunnies and the bars for the time being. Most of the time I didn't think about sex because it was so cold in South Korea I couldn't occupy another thought in my head other than how to get warm.

My toes were just about frost bitten, frozen with a painful tingling and needle pricking sensation as though I was a sickle cell patient. The doctors were busy treating high-ranking officers, therefore; I was requisite to be examined by a Navy Corpmans with no formal education and just a quick eight week training course in the medical field.

Several hundred of us suffered the same predicament while overwhelming the two corpsmen in their small CP tent. I still had feeling in my feet and the ability to work so I returned to my unit to help tear down and pack away our tents and load equipment onto the deuce and a half trucks. Most tents were frozen solid, a foot or more into the ground. Marines became frustrated, breaking pics and axe handles while trying to free the tents from the ice. We worked at a grueling pace for hours barely make a dent in the ice, it was taking far longer to remove the tents from the ice than anyone expected. To free the tents we begin chopping off the bottom flaps of the tents, using pics, axes, and diesel fuel to free the edge of the tents from the ice covered rice patties. I was sick of this out door ice box and was ready to return to Okinawa where the weather was normal or at least felt normal.

After 12 weeks of taking only one scolding hot shower and sleeping on ice, I fantasize at the possibility of sleeping on a mattress and eating something else besides C-rations. Several days later we bordered a C-130 with our 105 cannons and half ton trucks shoved right in the middle of the air plane, we rode the entire trip with our knees shoved in our chess while holding our seabags on our lap. As uncomfortable as the ride was I was glad to be out of Korea and on my way back to Okinawa to a warmer climate. I couldn't help but to get lost in thoughts of Cindy and my new daughter. How fun it would be to be a father and the possibility of spoiling my daughter rotten. I removed her picture from my pocket, occasionally stared at it creating subliminal thoughts of spending time at the beach and park and celebrating her birthday. Thinking about my family made time pass quickly and before I knew it I was circling Okinawa looking across the vast wing-span of the C-130 airplane. We touch down several minutes later, shortly after landing we secured our gear then was released for the day.

Once we return back to our base camp for a weekend of R&R I found solace just laying on my bunk. Most of the Marines ran down to the USO and stood in the long lines yelling for a honcho (Cab) to whisk them to BC Street or Gate two, known for legalize prostitution and seductive nightclubs. I didn't have interest in such things so I stayed to myself. I sat on my bed and envisioned being with my wife and my new baby girl. A month had past and I still found myself hanging around the base, playing bingo, and space invaders at the USO. I learned to eat with chopsticks, however; the food was still foreign to me so I stuck with the simple dishes. Large bowls of ramen noodles or shrimp fried rice. That's how I visioned myself for the next nine months, spending all of my time on base playing bingo, eating ramen noodle and watching transformers in Japanese.

A week later I was approached by my body building roommate, he suggested showing me the layout and inter workings of the city. I was reluctant and callow, he was very bumptious and churlish refusing to take no for an answer. I got dressed and off we went to BC Street in the back of a honcho. Jackson yelled.

"Coco cing, " that mean play black music.

The ride lasted less than five minutes and once out of the cab we walked at an infantry pace down the crowded military occupied streets of Okinawa Japan. Bars and clothing stores lined both sides of the street, paragon Asian woman strutted back and forth in front of the bars, touching, groping and caressing each soldier, sailor, Airman, or Marine that happen passed.

We walk from bar to bar until we struck gold. A female stripper was about to perform a banana show. I was naïve to the night culture but I was eager to watch and learn of this new culture but I soon discover this new culture would cost me at least two drinks.

A pleasingly 6 foot tall demimonde Japanese stripper strutted out onto the ankle high stage. She concealed nothing. Her well constructed body was on display for all to see as she frolicked on the floor making love to a giant pillow, spreading her legs so I could visually conduct a pelvic exam.

I was unimpressed, although I had never been in a strip bar I thought it was bromidic and mundane. The Marines began to pound on the tables with their fist, yelling.

"Banana show! Bananas show! Bananas show! Bananas show!"

Until the stripper agreed to perform the bananas show if everyone purchased another drink. We were all to happy to accommodate her. I tried to get away with purchasing a Coke but I was forced to buy hard liquor if I want to stay for the show, so I ripped out a few dollars from my pocket and slapped it on the table ordering a rum and Coke.

Most Marines in the club were only 20 years old are younger but it never bother the club owners, they only wanted our US currency and didn't care about US policies regarding age limits placed on drinking. Most of the merchants didn't want their own Yen, they would rather have U.S dollars, so I didn't bother to the exchange my US currency for Yen. I found the money system in Japan to be very strange, 1000 Yen equal $5 U.S dollars in 1980.

The stripper sashayed back and forth on the stage reminding me that I have been without a woman for three and a half months, so I sat anxiously waiting for the banana show to commence. Slight drool leaked uncontrollably down the side of my mouth in a fountain of concupiscence. Suddenly she seductively pulled her see threw gown over her head tossing it on the floor for everyone to pass around the room and smell. She appeared lascivious at least we thought so because she spread her legs wide-open and rubbed her breasts and thighs with coconut oil. She grabbed a banana and began eroticizing it while slowly peeling away the skin. She licked the tip of the banana circularly at the tip then began submerging the entire banana down her throat. We were all in a moment of prurient, moans and groans filter the room as young Marines creamed in their pants.

I clutched my glass of rum and coke nearly shattering the glass from the sultry sex act I just witness, but there was more to come. She laid her head back and slowly slid the banana inch by inch into her well stretched out bottomless pit of a vagina. You could have heard a pin drop as she slowly made the banana disappear into her deeply gorged out wound. Then all of a sudden bananas fell out of her vagina sliced into perfect half inch pieces onto a newspaper placed on the floor beneath her feet.

The slices were passed throughout the club and served on tooth picks as free appetizers for anyone who wanted to add more flavor to their drink. I like to get my freak on but I found this utterly disgusting so I took the party elsewhere. Jackson and I cruised the strip sticking our head's into different hotels and philandering the prostitutes behind the windows until we happened upon a hotel that had women that resemble models. Jackson quickly pulled out a wad of cash, tossing $15 to mama san and said

"Take your pick, I'm paying"

I said, "No man, I'm married".

Jackson looked at me with Betty Davis eyes.

"It's already paid for, don't waste my money".

Then he walked away leaving me standing there staring at 10 Asian beauties in full nudity. I couldn't resist, I ask mamma san could she has them all stand up. Then I chose the tallest one.

Mama san said, "Go upstairs to the last room on the right side at the end of the hall."

Full of apprehension I slowly made my way down the poorly lit hallway. I slid open the door, there was one twin size bed shoveled against the wall, the shower was 3 feet away with a water hoses connected to the nozzle. I was totally naïve, I sat on the bed fully clothed, using up part of my 15 minutes. A minute later a slender graceful Asian female walked into the room and immediately begin stripping, her perky little nipples sprung out like flowers in the springtime.

I couldn't believe my eyes, her skin was as smooth as a manikin and her hair stretch down her back between the crack in her butt. She appeared very at ease as she laid her slender beautiful body stretched across the bed. I froze like a deer in the headlights but she was unwilling to put up with my puerile behavior, she unzip my pants and pulled them down below my ankles, she reached up, grabbed the collar of my shirt and pulled me crashing down on top of her small frame.

I couldn't believe it I was down and out in less than five minutes. She jumped up stepped into the shower and began washing with ice cold water from the water hose. I lay motionless on the bed smoking my mental cigarette, thinking about how good it was but how bad I felt inside. I stood there silently looking at her beautiful smooth skin and long dark soft hair scratching the bathroom floor hanging freely down her back.

I thought for second I could go again but she departed the room as quickly as she had enter. I didn't know what to think, this was definitely a vargary in my life. I didn't know whether to be happy or sad, knowing it was a common practice on the island to pay for sexual pleasure didn't make me feel any better because I had broken my sacred marital vows.

I resorted back to spending a majority of my time at the USO club, playing space invaders, watching TV and participating in occasional bingo games. Fortunate for me our next training exercise was less than a month away and before I knew it we packed up and shipped out to Mount Fuji Japan. This time on a US naval ship called the USS de-buket. The birthing spaces were small and cramp, the Metal bunkbeds were stacked five high with a rope supporting a piece of canvas used as the bed padding. The one man shower stall was very small, the toilets continually over ran spilling all over the bathroom floor due to the rocking of the ship.

This was my first time on a transporter ship and my first time feeling what it was like to be seasick. I laid on my cot for five days, eating only what the more experienced Marines brought me from the chow hall. I eat applesauce and drank water for the next five days. A couple of days had passed and I've grown less weary to the swaying and rocking of the ship. I was summoned by one Marine to follow him into the Weld deck of the ship, I stuck my head out of the Port hold and I couldn't believe my eyes, waves as tall as the buildings in downtown Indianapolis slammed unsympathetically against the bulkhead of the ship. It was as if we were being swallowed up by the ocean and never to be seen or heard from again. I've never seen anything so powerful and overwhelm-ing, it made me realize how small and insignificant my life was and how powerful and forceful the earth is.

I lay in bed that night praying that we would arrive safely on the shores of Mount Fuji. I laid on my cot with my eyes wide open listening to the ship engine and propellers slow-ly whine and the powerful waves slam continuously against the side of the ship. I couldn't help but to think about Cindy in that moment. Her meek but violent nature, just like the ocean she was calm until the plate Tech tonics in her mind change its course, creating friction, causing her to erupt. I didn't know where I was going in this marriage but my first order of concerned was surviving while on the ocean.

The waves simmered so I made my way to the top deck, all I could see were endless waves of ocean as far as the eye could see. I never felt so small and insignificant and so out of place in the universe. I watch the ocean until I fall asleep with my back resting comfortably against a tire on a 105 howitzer. I was awakened four hours later by the coolness of the ocean mist on my face, and their she was, Mount Fuji, her summit peeking up towards the heavens and crested by the clouds more than 20 miles away. I spent most of my life watching the tip of this mountain on TV and postcards, now it was right within my reach, upfront and personal. I couldn't believe it something I have fantasized about since I was eight years old while watching Dean Martin and Jerry Lewis scary around Japan having fun. The moment of truth has arrived and I will be getting to know myself better then I had ever known myself before. Here we were arrogantly occupying another man's country, with rifles, cannons, helicopters, planes, and an occupying force of 10,000 men.

We made an amphibious beach landing on the beaches, smoke billowing from the top of the tanks and Amtrak's as they plowed past the rugged shore line. Landing crafts were the main source used to land the infantry on the beach, others went to shore by helicopters and trucks. It was a most impressive sight. I've never seen so much armor and ships in my entire life. Ships lined up all the way out towards the break of the ocean and slowly disappeared into the fog.

Later that day we convoyed our way up the mountain to base camp, tanks, Amtrak's and trucks stretching from the shore of the beach to 10 miles inland. The base camp look like something straight out of 1950s Marine Corps movie. Metal Quonset hut's in badly need of repair began at the edge of the nearest town, angling up toward Mount Fuji ending at the motor pool. We spent four months in mountain warfare training with Japanese soldiers who were located across the street. Unfortunately we didn't have any women at our base, neither did the Japanese. I don't think the Japanese soldiers mind not having Women as much as the Americans did. Any spare time the Americans had we ventured out to nightclubs located downtown in Tokyo skyscrapers. The buildings contained nightclubs on each of the 25 floors. There was a one time $25 admission fee that allowed us to go from floor to floor, stopping at each nightclub along the way. The native Asian girls were restless, they stood in line just to dance with us leaving their Japanese counter parts standing alone holding up the walls in envy. The young Japanese man appeared reluctant to express themselves freely because of their totalitarian society.

The Japanese army base was not far from the Marine base, right where it was supposed to be far out in the middle of nowhere across the street from the Marine base. I couldn't imagine having a Japanese base across the street from the Marine Corps base in the United States, no other country would be able to set up shop and patrol neighborhoods throughout the United States without being attacked by its citizens. I thought it was very arrogant of the US and I knew deep down inside Japan hated having the US monitoring all their daily activity by foreign occupying forces. In retrospect the base was very small, situated right next to the well-known Mount Fuji volcano. Every morning for four months I stared up at the snow capped mountain wondering when we were going to make our way to the top.

All the Marines knew the Marine Corps could not resist climbing a volcano, it was a small challenge but one we would have to face before leaving the island. The ground was covered with broken up pieces of lava on a concave slope. The motor pool, and gun park was placed at the highest point on the base directly in front of the volcano. The base look very barren, old and run down, there wasn't a woman within Miles of the base. Takahara was the closest town to the base approximately 2 miles away, the perfect walking distance for a fit marine.

There was nothing on base except for Marines. The recreation department try to entertain us by showing old movies in an empty shack and giving us discounted blue ribbon beer. What they couldn't sell they give away for free. Old cable sproles were used for tables which turn out to be a good choice because Marines fought every night over things that wouldn't makes sense to the average civilian. After having a few beers someone would we get liquor courage, stand up and yell out.

"Artillery!", Another marine would yell out.

"Amtrak's"! And another would yell out.

"Infantry!"

Before I knew it there was a full fledged fight taking place. I punch my way to the door and out the back exit before the MP'S arrived.

The next morning Marines were outline up at the chow hall bandaged from head to toe. The commanding officers didn't seem to mind, they were raking in plenty of money, therefore; they decided to let the club continued to operate for the next several months. Every night for four months there was a fight, I stayed in the club long enough for the first bowl of peanuts to be thrown, then I left before the full fight could escalate involving more then 30 young Marines. There was no other form of entertainment, we had nothing to do but drink liquor, eat Ramen noodle, and beat each other senseless. I spent my weekends with two other friends trying to learn the city and figure out how to catch the train to Tokyo.

We got fed up with hanging around the base and fighting in the nightclubs so we got dressed one night and ventured out to the train station in Takahara. We couldn't read the signs, everything was in Japanese, not a single word in English. Unlike the US, Japan wasn't as politically correct as the United States. They're only concern was with their native people and language. No other language could be found anywhere in the city, but we were desperate, so we paid our money and boarded the train hoping to land somewhere near Tokyo. Four hours passed and we were still in the middle of nowhere, all we could see from the train window was farm land and Rice patties as far as the eye could see. We rode from sun up to sund own and never reached anything that resembled a city. We got off the train at several stops, at different stations wondering around like Tourist from another country lost in the US. By this time we come to realize the only way we were going to find Tokyo was if Godzilla were to appear and started chasing Japanese all over the place leading us to downtown Tokyo.

At least seven hours had passed and I was no longer interested in going to Tokyo, I just want to return to the base because. I was starving at this point, even a box of C-rations sound edible. One Japanese citizens couldn't help but to noticed how confused and lost we looked. He offered to help us find our way back on the right course to Takahara if he could practice using his English on us. We were more than glad to oblige him. He spoke English and we complemented his language skills and praised him on everything he said although we could barely understand anything he said. We wanted to make him feel comfortable enough to ride four hours back to Mount Fuji with us. He was a very nice and pleasant man, it appeared that he had just gotten off work heading home with a newspaper tucked under his arms and decided to help a fellow man in need. I thought it was the most thoughtful jester I had ever witnessed.

The other two Marines were flabbergasted by his annoying nonstop talking and the way he pronounced his words, abusing the English language, so they called it a night and passed out on the benches of the train. I tried to be grateful and listen as he talked, nodding my head occasionally as if I was actively listening. I was so focused on getting back to the base I Harley noticed the beautiful Japanese ladies standing shoulder to shoulder less then a foot away. The train slowly pulled into the Takahara station, we gratefully shook the strangers hand, waved goodbye and began our journey back to the base. It was pitch black dark we could only see 3 feet in front of us, fortunately a Japanese soldier happened by.

"Where are you going" he asked.

"We are on our way back to the Marine Corps base"

" This way "he said".

I was shocked by the continued kindness with everyone I encountered at Mount Fuji, each of them went out-of-their-way to ensure that we were okay. I was confused, I thought they would have hated us for occupying their land and forcing our will and the American way upon them, but they were kind and very humble. The train station was only a 20 minute walk from the base, the Japanese soldier walked beside us and began asking us if we would like to sell our high school rings or if he could buy porn magazine from us.

He reached into his cargo pockets and pulled out a Japanese porn magazine. I flipped through the pages, all the women were stretched out with their legs wide open, but there was one small problem, they were wearing panties, only exposing their breast. I immediately understood why he wanted American pornographic magazines, our women weren't so modest, you can see right into their birth canal if you looked in the right magazine. We didn't sell any high school rings that night or give away any American porn magazines. We waved goodbye as we turned left and he turned right, back into our military commands.

The next day I couldn't help but to make my way back out to Town once more but not before stopping and getting a one dollar succulent juicy burrito loaded with unidentifiable meat.

I heartedly chowed down on the burrito while walking towards the front gate. Halfway into the burrito I bit something hard. I reached in my mouth and pulled out a huge canine tooth. I thought nothing of it and tossed it to the side and continue chowing down. I didn't venture far from the front gate, just far enough to browse through a few stores, meet a few of the towns people, then back into the gate I went. Later that day I was informed I would be standing guard duty for the next 15 to 20 days. I didn't mine because my unit was schedule to go on a 15 to 30 mile hike with the infantry division every Friday before securing for the day.

I stood at the armory and watch my unit leave every Friday morning at 5 AM with full gear including backpacks, helmets, rifles, flack Jackets, 60 Cal M and 50 Cal machine guns. I wanted no part of it. They were gone all day until five in the evening. Returning with blisters on their feet, barley able to walk. Somehow I believe the Marine Corps use this as a device to slow the young Marines down and tire them out before letting them go on Liberty. Although the guard shifts were four hours on and four hours off I didn't mine, even when it rained. I would just walk to the back of the armory and stood beneath the shelter we Jerry rigged just for that purpose. 2 AM in the morning hunger would set in, there was no shortage of food because C-Rations for the entire battalion was stored at the armory. All I had to do was pull a case of C-Rations from the stack and take what I wanted out-of-the-box, this was called rat fucking the C-Rations.

The rain poured down unforgivably as I stood under the tarp cutting holes in the bottom of a C-Rations can to make a stove. I shivered uncontrollably from my soaked camouflage utilities and my saturated leather boots. I couldn't believe how cold it was turning, I was hoping we would return to Okinawa before winter weather hit.

I had just come from Korea and I wasn't mentally or physically ready to freeze to death anytime soon. The top of the volcano already had a snowcapped and it was rumored that we were climbing the volcano within a weeks time. Just as I was feeling sorry for myself I heard a banging sound coming from one of the canisters, I reached down into my ammo pouch and remove three 12 gauge shells. I loaded my pump shotgun, cocking it, placing one shell in the chamber. I crapped toward the banging noise, slowly squatted down and peaked around the corner. A hooded man was pounding away trying to break the lock on the canister that house more than 300 weapons.

"Halt!" I yelled as I stood up.

The would-be thief threw the crowbar at me hitting the cocking mechanism of my shot-gun, defensively I let go of a burst barely catching the would-be thief on the side of his face knocking him to the ground, the pumping action on my shotgun had been damaged just enough to prevent me from housing another shell, so I rushed the thief and smashed him in the face with the butt of my weapon.

"Halt" I say once again while pressing the borrow of my disabled shotgun into the side of his face.

Within seconds the reactionary team surrounded us and took the thief into custody. I loved guard duty, it got me out of shit details throughout the day. I was no longer the guy to call when the head needed to be scrubbed down or when the portable toilets needed to be burnt. I spent my mornings hanging around the barracks cleaning my cameras and writing letters home. Cindy often occupied the blank thoughts in my mind during idle moments. I couldn't help but think of her and the mistake I made joining the military. She was always on my mind even at night as I cried in my sleep thinking about her and my daughter. I didn't know this would be a common theme in my life every time were apart.

The nights were cold and silent with the exception of the enlisted men's club, where fights broke out every two minutes. One night I was lying soundly asleep in my rack, the lights flickered on then the reactionary alarm sounded. My guard unit was sum-monsed to the club to break up a fight. We surrounded the building with nightsticks in hand, one white man ran out of the club yelling and screaming, pointing in my direction and yelling nigger! At the top of his lungs, all the sudden there I was staring into the twisted face of hate. I live my entire young life in Indianapolis and only in America do I have to travel 12,000 miles across the ocean, to Japan to be called a nigger by an American Marine.

I wasn't phased by his uneducated remark, I simply tossed him on the ground and cuffed has hands behind his back, making sure he didn't break free I squeeze the handcuffs extra tight, then I locked them in place with my handcuff key. I stood guard for another 10 days before returning to my unit Just in time to go on a 24.3 mile hike with full gear. We were packed up and ready to move out at 4 AM in the morning, the torrential rain was coming down hard in golf ball size droplets that morning. The base was flooded within two minutes of the first rain fall, letting up for two minutes at the most. We held off the hick as long as we could but there was no signs of the rain letting up so we headed out with 50 pounds of gear, 50 caliber machine guns, 60 caliber machine gun, mortars and mortar plates and tubes.

We ran up, down and around the mountains at an infantry pace, if I didn't know better I thought this hike wasn't going to end. Five hours into the hike I begin to feel blisters forming on my soaking wet feet. Temperatures begin to drop as we approach the end of the fall season moving towards the winter. The ground became a little harder and colder and the rain felt like ice water hitting our bodies. I didn't know what hurt most, my feet or the edges of my ears. My camouflage utilities and flak jacket were so saturated they felt like 50 pounds of wet sand. 15 miles into the hike the signal was given for my battery to move to the head of the formation.

That meant we had to run 2 miles past the other platoons while they stood on the side of the road cheering us on as we ran in formation through the entire battalion. Water slashing beneath our boots while dragging the machine guns to the top of mountain. Finally the end was insight. I could see the antiquated barracks as we toppled the rise of the mountain, but the barracks were still at least 3 miles away. One of the commanders got motivated and decided were going to run the last 3 miles and off we went Machine guns and all. We came to a halt in the front of are Quonset huts, I was so exhausted and dehydrated my eyelids felt as if there were glued to the top of my head. We slipped and slid up-and-down the mountains and slippery roads, one Marine took the time to turn around and snap my picture as we came to the end of our hike.

 After we put away our gear we were dismissed for the evening, although our feet were blistered and we were exhausted the entire battalion headed for the showers all it once, everyone scurried into the shower trying to wash up before going to town. We still used the system of showering we learned in Boot Camp. One man jump in the shower and get wet then jumps out and soaps down, while the other man is getting wet. Then the man jumps in the shower rinses off the soap while the other man soaps down. It was a very systematic universal method of expedience showering.

The showers ran constantly until everyone was done, the water on the floor was at least ankle high if not higher, everyone was required to wear shower shoes but Scum and razor blades floated freely in the water left by Marines for the cleanup crew that was formed out of anyone who dropped out of the hike. I was glad I was in top physical condition but due to the scum floating above the water it would be the first time in my life I would contract athletes feet. My feet were blistered from front to back and there was still rumors that we would be climbing Mount Fuji the next coming week.

Most of the Marines got dressed and headed to Tokyo, I stayed around the base writing letters to my wife and playing basketball with two of my good friends. After climbing Mount Fuji we were boarding ships and on our way back to Okinawa, two day's into the trip a typhoon hit and we were force to pull into the naval port in Yokohama Japan. We stopped in Yokohama Japan for three days allowing the storm to pass by. Most Marines took advantage of the military base and PX, stocking up on food to take back to the ship for the two-week ride home. I spend my time running back and forth to 31 flavors ice cream and a Japanese barbecue restaurant. Unfortunate for myself I was constipated, I hadn't taken a dump in 14 days. Due to the lack of proper dietary meals provided by the Marine Corps I was destined to report to sick bay.

The C-rations did exactly as they were designed to do, I sat on the toilet for hours while the boat rocked back-and-forth splashing the toilet water all over my butt, forcing me to call it quits and visit sick day. The corpsman said I was constipated and he needed to give me an enema. I thought it was something to eat like a chocolate candy bar. Smiling from ear to ear I stuck my hand out and said.

"Give it here"

The corpsman said, "no you have to get undressed"

"Just to eat a piece of chocolate?" I said.

He went to his medicine cabinet and remove a plastic bottle with a long stem.

"I will have to fill this with a solution" then you'll lay on your side while I put this tube in your anus and squeeze the liquid from the bottle into your rectum".

While pulling my pants up I said, "I'm feeling a little better now I think I can use the bathroom without your help, thanks anyway"

All of a sudden two navy sailor's blocked the door.

"We can't let you leave we must perform the procedure" he said.

"But I'm feeling okay I don't need the procedure" I said.

While backing up towards the door. Two gay navy corpsmen stood in the room watching, smiling and giggling to themselves. I thought to myself.

"When I get a chance I'm going to throw both of these assholes overboard".

However, I had no choice, so I laid on the table and turn on my side allowing the corpsmen to perform their procedure. It was a valuable lesson learned, the next time I have this problem I would keep my mouth shut and waited it out.

By the time I return to the Okinawa I only had one month left, I spent most of my time hanging around the base and trying not to get myself into anymore quagmires or promiscuous situations. I couldn't believe it January 5, 1981, I was on my way back to Indianapolis, I could burley sat still on the plane. I tried to fall asleep to hurry time alone. I fell asleep for four hours when I woke up I still had 15 hours to go before I even reached Alaska, I counted every second, every hour and every minute until I touchdown in Indianapolis. I walked in the door of Cindy's mothers house and their she was in the middle of the room trying too peek over-the-top of her play pen. She was so pretty with her hair resting on top of her head and a pretty little face any dad would Love.

I Scooped her up into my arms and it was as if she knew who I was the whole time, we immediately bonded, wherever I went she went with me and for a brief second I forgot all about Okinawa Japan and the shame I brought to my marriage.

Later that evening Cindy and I laid in bed staring at one another while our daughter set between us sucking up all the attention. At one moment our eyes locked and I could see the wheels spinning in Cindy's mind, she looked at me with a question mark on her face and I look back at her as though I knew the answer to what ever questions she wanted to ask. She never asked the fatal question, if I had been faithful to her while overseas, she just rolled over onto her side and rub Michaela's back trying to get her to fall asleep. The sun Flickr one last time then closed it's eyes as it set down behind the sky scraping buildings for the night. Cindy laid on her side wearing an inviting pink night gown. I stared at her back inching closer and closer until we were locked into a human pretzel position.

I quickly forgot about her plausible disloyalty and remember my own disgruntled behavior. I couldn't deny it and I didn't want to admit it so I just laid behind her as if I never heard a word. My mind ran wild thinking about her intimately making love with another man.

The next 29 days would be more of the same, I felt the boundaries of our marriage had been breached at both ends of the spectrum and no one was innocent. Three weeks later I was on my way to Camp Pendleton to report for duty. My family would arrive at the base within the matter of two months so my first order of business was to buy a car because the base was more than 14 miles away from base housing. Although the city bus was walking distance from my front door I wanted the luxury of leaving the house at the last minute and not having to leave two hours early just to catch two city buses and one military bus before reaching my barracks.

One evening I decided to leave the base and cruise Oceanside Boulevard for a car lot. After visiting several car lots I determine they all were selling junk, so I reluctantly purchased a 1972 lavender blue Cadillac El Dorado, it was a piece of junk, the car had no problem leaving me stranded. The first week the engine caught fire, then the transmission went out, the horn didn't work and the gas guzzling piece of junk only got 12 miles a gallon. I couldn't have picked a worse car if I try. People seem to be impressed that I was driving a Cadillac and often question whether the car was mine.

Cindy arrived right on schedule two months later. I wasted no time preparing the house, making it livable and comfortable. We didn't have many friends, therefore; we would occasionally walk to the beach or take trips to the mall. I was excited for Cindy to experience California, it would be her first time traveling this distance from home. I knew I had to make personal adjustments, making sure she was comfortable, but those adjustments wouldn't last long.

Sometimes doing the quiet hours of the night when Michaela was in bed sleep, Cindy would lay on the front room floor and talk about missing her brother, as tears stream down her face I didn't know what to do in this type of situation so I just listen, once in a while I would try to redirect her thoughts toward other things. Later that month came the news, She was pregnant again, I wasn't surprised by the news since we just came off of a 30 day sex Benj. But I would have to start making plans for the near future because I would be getting discharged within 15 months. Cindy didn't care for the military life, she never got use to me being gone for extended periods of time. I did understand her reasoning so I offer to send her back to Indianapolis for 12 weeks are until she was ready to return. In two months she was on a plane back to Indianapolis and I was on a 5 ton truck heading to 29 Palms California for 12 weeks of desert training.

The training was gruesome, and dirty. The sand stung my skin like bits of broken glass. There wasn't many places to take cover from the sun beating down on us mercilessly not giving us much of a break doing the waking hours. During night training the sky was lit up for miles covered with illumination shells floating in the sky long enough to light a target area more than a mile long or at least several grid squares. Before the illumination Flickr out we unleashed over 1000 artillery, tank. Mortars, and aircraft shells across a mile long stretch of desert. Tanks sat 100 meters in front of our cannons, dug deep into ditches, they would roll up on top of the ditch long enough to pump out one shell then back down in the ditch they would go. Helicopters were next, they would fly in and shoot up the area with 1000 rounds then spin off Just in time for the low flying jets to drop a quick 500 pound white phosphorus bomb in the target area, next artillery pumped out five shells from each canon simultaneously firing a 50 Cal machine gun from the top of the trucks.

We repeated this operation over and over again until we had it perfect. We called this the iron curtain. This was a last ditch effort when all at else had failed and the enemy seemed unstoppable. The constant firing drove the canon spades deep into the ground, I knew we were set in for the night not making another long dreaded road trip to the next position or so I thought, until someone yelled out the word "CSMO" that meant to pack your gear and move out quickly. Everyone began slinging artillery shells, shovels, pics, and axis onto the back of the half ton truck, tanks came out of nowhere as though they were hidden in the ground, smoke billowing from their stack, helicopters hovering above escorting us to our next position. Jets buzz the ground leaving trails of CS gas and the young marines scrambling to don their gas mask and cover themselves with their ponchos.

The CS gas burned our eyes causing us to choke and vomit as we hurried to displace our weapons, the sun flickered one last time before it hide its fiery face behind the settle slopes of the mountains. Everyone was lined up on the road ready to move onto the next position, everything was on the truck. The spades of my cannon were stuck deep in the sand. This was quite the conundrum, all the other trucks were lined up on the role and slowly pulling off. We had to dig out a spot beneath the trail of the canon and place a jack under the trail of the canon and dreacinate the spade far enough out of the ground to allow us to move the canon trail slightly toward a closing position. After 20 minutes of furiously digging out the space of my canon we got the cannon hooked up to the truck. I looked up and my unit was gone as well as the sun. I broke out my night vision goggles, map, compass and combat flashlight then navigated my way to our new firing position.

At one point during the drive I thought for sure we were lost, It seemed as if we had been driving all night into the morning. I didn't see my unit for hours, but I knew how to effectively read a map and use a compass. Finally arriving at the new position only minutes behind my unit, everyone was so exhausted from the long drive and the late hours, no one seemed to notice that I was not in the proper truck line order.

We repetitiously emplaced and displaced the canons several times throughout the night. By the time I had a chance to look at my watch it was close to 2 am in the morning, everyone was just concerned with getting their cannons in position for the next artillery barrage. The entire firing line was quiet and pitch black dark and all of a sudden at 3 AM in the morning some young private got the urge to make coffee. The inexperience marine lit a heat tap which illuminated the entire gun line. You could see the men walking around the cannons from a mile away.

A dust storm with feet scurried across the desert yelling and screaming while walking at an infantry pace. Gunnery Sgt. Jef-fords came yelling down the gun line.

"Who the hell lit that fire?

"Put it out god damnit, put it out".

He said, while walking at an infantry pace with his hands shoved deep in his pockets and the light of the Moon refracting brilliantly off of his bald head. It was freezing in the desert and at this time we were on our third day of training with no sleep, everyone was on edge, we were a bunch of walking time bombs waiting to explode. Our physical condition and stamina was being tested in every sense, heat exhaustion in the afternoon and freezing half to death at night. I just about had enough of the desert and military training. The wind was beginning to kick up again, my goggles couldn't prevent the sand from edging its way into my eyes. By the time reveille was sound my eyes were woefully swollen shut. I made my way to sick bay located in the back of a supplies truck, not before emptying two canteens of water on my face loosening the sand that scratched the cornea of my eye.

The Navy corpsmen only care about getting to the chow truck early in the morning so he just poured water on my eyelids and told me to report back to my unit. I prided my eyes lids open with my finger, once I cleaned the sand from the corner of my eyes I was able to see well enough to set the deflection and quadrant on the canon sight for the next fire mission.

Once again the sand kicked up creating a small tornado but this time it was due to the helicopters that came out of the sky like locus and landed 50 feet from my firing position. I was ordered to push the cannon into the back of the helicopter and carry one case of artillery shells. Off we went flying to another desolate place in the desert to conduct what we called a hip shoot. Once the helicopter landed, we push the cannon out of the rear of the helicopter at an exaggerated pace. I shot a quick asthma with my compass, pointed the cannon in the designated direction then we pumped out two artillery shells, then back on the helicopter as quick as we landed.

This was called internal raids, because the canon was placed inside the helicopter rather than being towed from the bottom of the helicopter. We landed back in our staging area, connected the canon back onto the truck and off we went down the road to our next firing position. I was starving, so I dug into my cargo pocket and pulled out a piece of Poggie bait. I ripped a piece of jerky apart with my teeth and chewed on it to get some type of nutrition I could barley eat while the truck raced down the desert road at 50 miles an hour, tossing artillery shells around in the back of the truck while the man got swallowed up by the desert sand.

It was a tremendously fast pace and very early in the morning, it was barley 4:00 AM and I hadn't had breakfast, I hadn't got a shave, nor had I taken a dump. We continued at this pace for the next 12 weeks. I was truly physically and mentally beaten up and drained, at the time I didn't believe anything in my life could have matched what I was going through at this time. The more training I had the further remove I was from Society. I didn't think I could ever be a civilian again, I could only exist in the civilian world in a physical state, but my true heart and experiences and life lessons would come from what I experienced in the Corp.

After 12 weeks of eating nothing but C-rations my digestive system was permanently damaged. I haven't taken a dump in 8 days. Subliminal thoughts flashed before my eyes, there I was in the middle of the desert visiting an oasis of regular food, even the food from the chow hall seen appetizing to me at this point, if we were fortunate they would give us one hot meal from the main base. But that was wishful thinking, C-Rations was the only meal we would see until the end of this 12 week training, because C-rations were designed to clog our system, making us constipated so that we wouldn't interrupt our work by running to the bathroom once a day.

This gave us more time to focus on our job. It took most of us 12 minutes to take a dump so the order of the day was too carry a stack of newspapers or magazines to provide a distraction so we would focus on something other than the pain while cleansing our colon. The portable toilet was crafted out of an ammunition box with layers of duct tape used for padding the seat. It was a hard way to live and I promised I would encourage any young person to go else where, the Marines weren't the place to be, living in dirt and squalor, sleeping one hour a day and working 18 hours a day was the norm during training.

This life was certainly not for the weak at heart and for the moment I didn't think it was me. I had approximately 13 months left in the corp and I lost plenty of sleep thinking about the possibility of becoming a civilian. Working a 9 to 5, no NCO duty, no field ops, and no unit rotations or oversee deployments. I was ready for the real world and for the civilian minded attitude that would come with it. The Marines had maded me into a very punctual and dependable person, it would be a hard adjustment to be around people who just cruise through the day. The Marines function on high-energy and fast-paced, slowing down to a civilian pace would be mental torture. I didn't have any idea of how to be a civilian again but I was willing to give it a try even if it meant I will lose some of my military bearing. I was ready to try something different, something that didn't require me to polish my shoes or press my uniform. I was thoroughly tired of the bullshit and ready to resume my life as a civilian, with a civilian job, and civilian ideas.

The me nobody knows

After 12 rugged weeks of dragging our cannons behind half ton trucks in the desert we packed up and headed back to Camp Pendleton, so we thought. Right before Our convoy was rerouted to the San Diego Pier we received two new privates fresh out of Boot Camp. We boarded a troop transporter ship headed overseas and private Dunbar one of the new privates was assigned to my section. He was kind of a goofy kid and if a strong wind came along it will blow his hundred and 110 pound body right over. I didn't think much of him and my presumptions were right. He immediately began to get into mischief and I found myself standing in front of the captains door explaining why I didn't have control of him. I had to manually resolve this issue, therefore; I placed him on every shit detail that came down the pike. It was time to depart and as the ship slowly back away from the port the entire battalion stood on the deck of the ship while being dragged out to sea by two tug boats. Dunbar stood next to me practically leaning against me as the wind blew violently across the deck of the ship loosening some of our cargo straps.

I didn't know where we were going nor did I bother to ask, once aboard the ship I settled into my birthing area and sack down for the night. I stayed in the bed during most of our two-week trip except during the times we held formation or when I had to stand guard duty. I found the ship to be very peaceful, the quietness in the night gave me a chance to think clearly about what I would do after I left the Marine Corps. Sometimes I would set on the top deck from sunrise to sunset watching the ocean and the Dolphins swimming along side the ship. After about a month of floating around aimlessly on the ocean a small rise of land appeared out of nowhere, I could hear the captain of the ship talking to my Company commander.

" That's our next objective" he said pointing to the barren land.

I started preparing my section by taking an ammo count and ensuring that we had night vision goggles and binoculars. I sent private Dunbar to the armory to secure two pairs of night vision goggles, but he took the liberty to tell the armory sergeant he was promoted to squad leader and was to be issued a .45 caliber pistol with four magazines along with several pouches of ammunition. Dunbar returned to the squad equipped with two pairs of night vision goggles smiling from ear to ear as though he had just won the lottery. With his 45 caliber pistol tucked safely out of view he became mysteriously quiet and off to himself. I was rather pleased and thought I have broken him from his bad habits and childlike behavior so I left him alone until it was time to board the landing craft.

Three hours later we were shoved into a landing craft, and once again the onslaught of ocean water spilling uncontrollably inside the craft. I was hoping it wasn't another training exercise where they made us jump out of the landing craft and swim ashore, but this couldn't be a training exercise because we were carrying full clips of ammo. After wandering aimlessly around the ocean for several hours we began our journey towards the shore, the landing craft went up and down the shore trying to bypass the coral reef but we had no such fortune. They had to let us out about 100 yards from the beach. The door fell and the Ocean water rushed right inside the landing craft soaking us up to our knees. From the back of the landing craft I got a running start and jump 3 feet out into the Ocean. I Kicked my way a shore pulling private Dunbar and one other marine right along with me, whom were struggling to stay afloat because of the heaviness of their camouflage Utilities and flak jacket.

After reaching the staging area we quickly divided our sections into two squads, this time we didn't have our cannons, we became instant infantry men gearing up to head out on a recon mission. We were divided into two small nine man squads. After staging we quickly wiped the salty ocean water off our M-16s, just as my M-16 was wiped down and oil, it was snatched from my hands and replaced with a 12 gauge pump shotgun. "Gray take this compass and map your on point." The staff sergeant said.

I only have 13 months left in the suck and I wasn't trying to get killed with a little more than a year left in the Corp. I couldn't help but to ask.

"Why am I on point, this job is reserved for a private not an NCO!". I said.

"We need someone that knows how to competently use a compass and read a map". The staff sergeant said.

I loaded five shells in my shotgun, orientated my map and shot an asthma towards the designation.

We formed a line on each side of the road, I thought for sure we would ride a portion of the way but instead we humped on foot like the infantry. The American arrogance was upfront and on display for everyone to see, we were in Country less than 12 hours and we walked around like we own the place. The sun fell down behind the landscape before we could walk our first 20 miles, It was instantly dark. I couldn't see 2 feet in front of my face. The marines behind me watched the reflectors on the back of my helmet, every time I stopped, both squads would stop then moved to the side of the road until I started moving again. We must've walked for hours, my mouth was dry like cotton but we were prohibited to drink from our canteens to prevent water from splashing around. We stop for a minute and set up on the side of the road, they said there was troop movement coming our way, a small group of about 15 soldiers, so we position ourselves to set an ambush.

Two hours went by and still there were no soldiers. In the meantime Dunbar laid at the rear of the squad off to the side of the road in his own world, playing with and polishing his new .45 caliber pistol, loading and unloading it unbeknownst to the rest of the squad. Suddenly a group of undisciplined Lebanese soldiers were patrolling directly toward us, I signal for both squads to standby. The moment intensified with each step. I was so nervous, every step they took echo like big drums pounding in my ear. I could hear my-self breathing heavily the closer they got. I slowly began to get into a kneeling position, rotating the butt of the weapon into my shoulder and positioning my finger to squeeze off the first shut.

Just as I was applying pressure to the trigger, an unauthorized shot was fired from nowhere making the soldiers turned and ran the other way. Dunbar had accidentally discharged his unauthorized .45 caliber weapon. My first response was to send him to the rear and placed him on a shit detail until we return to the rear and process him for NJP 'nonjudicial punishment'. But that didn't happen, because we were too far out into the sticks, to far from the closest town and there was no turning back at this point so we were forced to allow him to continue on with us. We walked four more hours before the rock in my boot begin bruising my foot. I was just about growing tired and weary of playing Marine when all of a sudden I bumped into someone coming from the opposite direction. We stood facing one another for what seemed like an hour but it was less than 15 seconds. I didn't know how he felt but I didn't want to die nor did I want to kill another person. I couldn't see him and he couldn't see me. I knew all the friendly's were behind me, and not coming from the other direction. We stood so close I could feel his breath, his clothing smelled of burnt wood. It was so quiet I could hear his heartbeat.

My palms were dripping with sweat, I was gripping my shot gun so tight I accidentally force the cocking lever up, the shotgun made a clicking noise in the echoing atmosphere of the night so loud it could be heard from a Mile away.

"I was in it now" I thought to myself.

I felt his arm make a slight shift and before he could complete his motion I leveled my shot gun pulling the cocking mechanism home letting go of one shell. Everyone scattered to the side of the road, the silence was palpable, my heart was racing 100 miles an hour as I lay silently in the ditch trying to slow down my breathing but nothing helped. I thought for sure there would be more of them and an all out gun battle would ensue. No one spoke a word, everyone lay silently in the dirt until the next morning. The sun rose slowly that morning as we all emerged from our ditches onto the road to witness what was no surprise from the night before. A young soldier laid alone, spread Eagle on the road. Half his face and hand blown off. I thought it ironic, I hated the arrogance of American but I got the first American kill. Everyone thought it was cool that I killed someone, I was bona fide, the first kill of the day they said,.

"You're going to get a medal for this one!" one private yelled. As they all took souvenirs from the young soldier's body.

I stood there staring at the body, I didn't have time to process what happened before I was summons to the rear of the squad.

One Marine broke his leg jumping in the ditch, he was being medevac back to the ship so I reluctantly swap my 12 gauge shotgun in exchange for his M 16 rifle then returned to my position as point man. Within the hour we were walking over the ridge into a small village, the war between Israel and the PLO have not yet started but it appear that all the buildings in the Village were practically burned to the ground. We broke into two squads of nine and enter the Village from two different directions, to prevent crossfire the first squad moved towards the South entrance of the village, my squad headed in from the West.

Since I was still on point I was the first man into the building, I wasn't worried about the possibility of occupants because the buildings were supposed to be empty, from the looks of the town no one could possibly exist in such a barren and burnt out place. The first building had holes blown in the wall big enough to walk through. I stuck my head through the hole in wall, without being too temerity I judiciously made my way up the steps, one of the privates tap me on the back of my leg indicating that he heard a noise coming from outside, being a de facto leader I sent two Marines to check the noise then preceded up the steps. As I turned to look up the staircase a grenade was tossed over the balcony striking me in the face then rolling under the staircase and exploding. I fell from the second flight of the stairs losing my helmet. The hand guards on my M-16 shattered into pieces as I hit the concrete. Unexpectedly another small explosion went off just big enough to knock me crumbling back to the floor. Before I could get my focus someone grabbed me by my flack Jacket and began dragging me out of the building across the street to another building and threw me down a flight of stairs into the basement.

"What the fuck!"

I thought, as I struggle to get to my feet. I was struck in the face with the butt of a rifle, I was struck once more before blood started trickling down my face blurring my vision, I laid very still on the floor pretending I was helpless and unconscious.

I reach under my T-shirt and placed my hands on my palm size combat knife, I listen for how many people were in the room, one soldier walked over and placed his foot on my head, he raise his machete high in the air then suddenly the wall exploded, giving me time to spin around and shove my knife into his thigh. I twisted the knife into his leg and pulled out a chunk of flesh, suddenly his head disintegrated into small chunks of flesh, he was shot several times in the face. It was Dunbar, he unloaded an entire magazine into the soldiers face, within minutes the room was filled with the first squad. Helicopter transporters were called in and I was medevac back to the ship. I wasn't hurt, I just had scratches and cuts here and their but I was glad to be out of that desolate place and back aboard the comforts of the Navy ship. Our Recon mission was successful, we provided solid evidence that the enemy materiel have been occupying the town for sometime.

I sat on the top deck of the ship and read my novels, with Dunbar locked away in the ships Brig. Later in the month he was given an other than honorable discharge. I was so disenchanted by the war I harley notice rockets fired back-and-forth across the vast wasteland. In two weeks time the islands slowly disappear as we set sail out to sea as another group of carriers arrived. We were relieved and rotated back to the states. The ocean was angry once again, slapping its waves harshly against the ships bulkhead.

I didn't mind the slumming of the waves this time, it seem to provide a calming effect from the shotgun blast ringing in my subconscious, the rifle butt to the face, the exploding walls and the falling pieces of facial flash. I sat on the top deck of the ship wishing I was somewhere else. From a distance I could see my luminary platoon sergeant coming in my direction, assigning guard duty to anyone on the top deck. He walked towards me at an infantry pace scribing as he walked. He got within 6 feet, bent over bonhomie touching me on the shoulder staring me in the face, then he walked over to another marine assigning him to guard duty. I guess he could see I've been through enough in the last month so he was magnanimous and avuncular at a time I needed space and clarity of thought.

Although it really didn't matter whether I stood guard duty or not, I would've still stayed on top deck and off to myself but I was appreciative of his kind gesture. For the next week I sat in the weld deck of the bottom of the ship, I climbed into the back of one of the deuce and a half trucks, where I could get a good night of uninterrupted sleep, and no one would hear me crying in my sleep. Everyone seemed to be having a good time, drinking beer, eating lobster and steak, celebrating our last day on the ship. I was suffering a guilty conscious of my American sin. I knew that sins pay wages, even though I was following orders it didn't abdicate me from the responsibility of taking another's life. I secluded myself from others, staying in the back of the truck for the next week. I only went to the top deck three times a day for roll call, then I would climb back into my truck and think about home.

Slowly I began to mentally metamorphosis from the sound of the shotgun blast torturing my murky subconscious, the sound became more dense with each passing day. I made my way up the metal steps clinging to the hand railing preventing myself from slamming into the bulkhead because of the violent rocking of the ship. I made my way to the top of the deck, and for the first time in two weeks birds begin landing on the bowel of the ship. I knew we were within eyesight of land and right before I could complete the thought a city emerged out of nowhere. I could recognize the coast of San Diego from 100 miles away, it was the most beautiful thing I've ever seen and I was grateful to see the coast once again. Every minute seemed like an hour as the ship slowly dock, we unloaded our trucks and other equipment then convoy back to camp Pendleton. The long trip back home was physically draining, we were too tired to hang signs out of the back of the trucks asking women to show their breast. Before we made it back to the base there was rumors that one Marine walked in and caught his wife having sex with three men at the same time. Infidelity was very common around base housing units, it was the closest thing to Peyton Place I've ever seen.

At last we were back in the familiar and secured surroundings of our base, we secured our gear and was awarded a 72, meaning we were off for three days. I spent my 72 hours relaxing, stretching my feet across the front room table and for the moment I forgot about Beirut. I placed my short live combat tragedies deep in my subconscious and wouldn't speak of them again for 40 years.

Even though Cindy was not home I couldn't wait to get in the house and allow euphoria to set in. The house was quiet almost to the point of being ghostly, there was no laughter of children, not so much as a mouse squeak, but my neighbors were loud and up notches, letting their children run wild on the playground unsupervised, seemingly only hearing and not seeing them. I sat quietly on the porch sipping on a beer, free from the thought of Amtrak's and tanks rolling pass my head or an aircraft spraying me with CS gas, or the dead soldier staring up at the sky on the dark desolate winding road in Lebanon. I was in a moment of euphoria and all the sudden out walked an attractive young Puerto Rican girl seemingly focused on herself, cleaning and grooming her fingers and toe nails to perfection, looking as if they were professionally manicured. Her small 5 foot frame was athletic and well proportion. The red tube top she wore could barely contain her 36 double D's breast. I looked at her like a man in the desert without water, seeing an oasis of fresh spring water for the first time. I knew if I stared long enough she would become my next mistake, so I got up and went in the house, shut the door, grab another beer, and plopped down on the couch for another episode of the Andy Griffin show. My friend Richie came by later that evening to borrow my car and ask if I wanted to go to the nightclub with him.

I said, "No" " I just want to stay home and relax and listen to the sound of crickets and allow the cool breeze to blow on my face".

The breeze felt so good blowing through the door I walked outside and sat down on front porch, once again, the breeze on my face was suddenly blocked. I looked up and their she was standing 2 feet from me with a deck of cards in her hands.

She asked," do you want to play cards" " we can play goldfish"

I said, " no I just want to sit here quietly"

She was persistent. She asked three times in an insidious way, this time bending over hanging her huge 36 double D's in my face, my eyes went cross as her breast hung less than an inch from my mouth. It was all I could take so I reluctantly caved into her well proportioned body and submitted to playing cards with her. There was nothing I could do at that point in time, the blood had already left my head, so I was no longer thinking clearly. I couldn't get up and run in the house because the blood left my feet as well and began to centralize once again in my pelvic region. I was in a temporary trans, she beat me five games straight. I found it hard to focus on anything but her perfect body. She was killing me, I couldn't take it any more so I excused myself and limb into the house, closed the door leaving her on the porch to play solitaire by herself.

I must admit that I am week for the flesh and I loved wild passionate uncontrollable sex but I was certainly no lothario. Five minutes later there was a knock at the door, she was definitely indomitable, their she stood with a bowl of blueberry pie.

"Would you like some pie" she asked.

"No, I'm good, I'm just going to watch TV.

" Are you sure? It's really good" she said.

She asked over and over and over again. I begin to have visions of smearing blueberry pie all of her huge naked breasts, so I submitted to her request once again. I open the door and walked out on the porch. We ate blueberry pie with a scoop of vanilla ice cream, my imagination began to run even wilder, we talked for about an hour.

Once again I excused myself and limped my way inside the house, this time I close the door to ensure that no one would bother me. Once again she was knocking on my door, I pull the curtain back and peeked out the window, this time she had nothing to offer so I let her knock on my door two more times, before she could knock the third time I'd open the door, grabbed her by her tube top and pulled her into the house.

The sexual experience mint nothing to me, it was just another proverbial $15 on the table and no emotion required.

I never heard from her again, but Unbeknownst to myself her sister-in-law was listening at the door, she could hear the yelling and moaning as I was breaking her young sister in law off something proper. The next week after pulverizing my opponent in a boxing match I was walking down the side walk toward my house when the young girl older brother was coming down the side walk from the opposite direction with his wife. His wife was clutching his arm, digging her finger nails into his flesh preventing him from attacking me.

I wasn't worried because I knew he saw the first marine division championship boxing trophy in my hand and realize that he could get the brakes beat off his dumb ass, so he just walked by looking angrily at me out of the corner of his eye. Our sexual escapade would never happened again, soon after her brother was discharged from the Marines within three months of our xxx one night stand.

Cindy return home shortly after, by this time she was more than seven months pregnant with our second child and more than ready to drop this load. I did feel guilty about my sexual promiscuous, I didn't have any real excuses for messing around I suppose I just did it because I could. Most of the time I thought I cheated because I got married too early, or it was because I was like my father, or I was just bored, or it was because I wasn't in love when I got married. I was trying to do the honorable thing by marrying her, at the time I thought the honorable thing was the only way.

Our life became routine, going shopping on the weekends, walking on the beach or walking around the part of the base called main side located near the PX. We took pictures standing in front of the armored tanks and later that day we drove from one end of the base to the other just taking in the sights. One morning I was getting dress for work.

Cindy said. " My water broke, I am having the baby"

She said it so calmly I didn't believe her so I kept getting dress.

 She said, "take care of Michaela I'm going to the MP gate for an ambulance"

 I got dressed and hurried Michaela to the baby sitters, by the time I got to the MP gate she was gone. Miya was born November 1, 1980, in the Naval hospital on the Marine Corp base Camp Pendleton. She had dark black eyes with beautiful curly hair, most people thought she was a Hispanic baby. She was the first in my family to be born in another state are on a military base. Cindy and I were very happy and content with our life style, we attend church every Sunday one block from our base housing unit. Miya was the star of our church. Everyone wanted to hold her, before I knew it she was on the other side of the church, being passed around from women to women. I had to go get her from some women I had never seen before. I must say she was an attractive little girl with curly coal black hair, and big black eyes.

I believe those were just old Family genetics popping up to say we're still around. I didn't think I could make something so beautiful all by myself. After all the excitement of church I forgot It was Easter Sunday and I was supposed to be sitting at the barracks behind a desk as the duty NCO. I totally rebelled against the idea of standing duty after 12 weeks of being in the desert and spending a month aboard ship and in another country. I knew I would have to pay the consequences for not showing up too stand my Post but I also knew the Gunnery Sgt. was wrong for continuously placing me on duty every weekend. After returning home from church I was informed by one of my Friends that the first sergeant was banging on my door, I knew at that moment they were going to try and court-martial me when I arrive at work the next morning.

I arrived at work anticipating the worst, before I could get in formation the first sergeant called me into his office.

"Stand at attention!" he yelled.

Reaching into his desk he pulled out a short three foot wooden club and slammed it on his desk. He stared at me as if he want to kill me while rolling up his sleeves.

"I'm going to kick your ass!" he said. "Where the hell were you Sunday?"

I stared at him for brief a second.

"I'm not afraid of you first sergeant". I said.

He yelled. " Stand at ease!"

Then he marched out of the room into the Captains office next door.

"Report to your Capt". He yelled.

I came to attention and marched into the captains office.

"Go back out and report in right!", the first Sgt. said.

I did an about face walked outside then pounded heavily on the hatch.

"Sir, Cpl. Gray reporting as requested sir!

Captain, "Why didn't you report for duty on Sunday Cpl. Gray?

"The gunnery Sgt. repeatedly put me on duty every Sunday for the last two months and all the other NCOs had duty one weekend per month" I said.

Captain "well that's no excuse".

I said, "Sir before we go any farther I would like to request mass to see the commanding general".

Captain, "Step outside Cpl. Gray"

I stood outside for two minutes that same like an hour after which time I was order back into the office. They decided to give me duty one more Sunday before I was discharged. I begin packing my house and returned the furniture to base housing and the rental stores. I sold my car for slightly more than I paid for it, therefore, I spent the next six months riding my bike to and from work 14 miles each way. The road was long and dark, my power generator light provided very little reflection making the ride more difficult while the wheel of generator rub against the back tire creating energy for the light. I tried to cover the hard bicycle seat with a specially designed seat cover made of rabbit skin, but to no avail, my testicles banged against the seat like a pinball machine. By the time I got to work it was time for morning PT, physical fitness training, included 80 sit up's, 20 pull-up's, jumping jacks and a 3 to 6 mile run.

I ran my last (PFT), physical fitness test without motivation as if I didn't care, my platoon leader yelled at me as I just about walked across the finish line completing the 3 mile run in 22 minutes.

"You're not even sweating!" he yelled.

I just looked at him and walked over to the barracks. I was a short timer with less than three months left in the corp and I knew there was nothing he could do to help or hurt me. Three months later I had served my four years and my contract was over. I reported to the main side base at camp Pendleton to receive my final pay and discharge papers. Their must've been over 50 of us getting discharged that day, we were so happy, we stagger the line and talked loudly about our civilian plans. A Sgt. began yelling from the top of the steps.

"Shut the fuck up and get in a straight line!"

The voice was so distinctive I recognize it right off. It was Sgt. Hondo, he had returned to his old job in finance and no longer was a drill instructor. After waiting 45 minutes I stepped in front of his window and said,

" Sgt. Hondo" he looked up at me with a stern look and said,

"Were you one of mine's?".

"Yes, sir platoon 1059".

I couldn't help but feel good seeing the beginning and the end come together. I smiled as I went down the steps after receiving my pay and completing my final act in the Marine Corps. Just seeing my drill instructor again reminded me of what I had achieved.

I was discharged from the United States Marine Corps with an honorable discharge and returned to civilian life ready to be placed in a job I thought I rightfully earned. But I soon found out that was not the case. I spent the first couple of weeks back in civilian life walking around the old neighborhoods on Delaware St. and Park ave, reminiscing about old times. I walked past John's old house on Washington Boulevard, remembering it wasn't long ago that I sat on his steps begging for candy. I even took an occasional trip to riverside park hoping to catch a glimpse old friends. I didn't have a car so I just rode the bus every where I traveled, enjoying the nice quiet ride while touring through familiar places. I even passed Saul Subway, I couldn't help but to stop and peak in the window. It had only been four years that I was away but it seems like so much had changed, the only thing that remained the same was my family. They worked the same jobs, living the same life style, not traveling, or making any big plans, they just continue to live the same day in and day out routine. All of a sudden it appeared to me, I could see why I left Indianapolis.

The routine was stale and the City seemed slow and less progressive than California. Jobs were very scarce and I was in for a big surprise when I went looking for one. I thought being in the Marine Corps would give me the advantage, employers would just love to have a young fresh marine straight out of the military. I couldn't have been more wrong, no one cared that I was an ex-marine. I was just like everyone else, if you didn't have a skill or a college degree you didn't have a job. I worked in field artillery for four years and had trouble matching my skills with any civilian employers qualifications, therefore; Civilian life was a big adjustment. I had to get use to unorganized and slow moving civilian behavior, the other bad news was we didn't prepare for the move back home so we moved in with Cindy's mother until we could find our own place.

I wasn't over joyed with the decision so I hung out at my mother's house most of the time. Miya was too young so she stayed at home with her mother while Michaela went with me to the park and to play in her grandmothers backyard with her cousins. I hung out in the front yard with my brothers drinking beer and talking about old times. Cindy called two hours later requesting that I bring Michaela home to eat dinner. I didn't think much of it so back over the bridge I went to her mother's house. I found it difficult to stay in a strange place not knowing whether I was really welcome but it seemed Cindy was right at home, cooking dinner and seemingly more alive then she was just a week ago in her own home. Her conversations had more of an edge to them, because her mother play with her mind. She tormented Cindy with conversations about my escapades in Japan and how I probably left children in Japan waiting to come to United States.

I didn't think it was funny at all, as a matter of fact I believe Cindy was taking her mother serious and began to show signs of jealous impulse. Any time I left home she wanted to go with me, even a casual stroll a half block down the street to the variety store she want to go with me. I was beginning to feel smothered and overwhelmed by the entire situation, so I escaped into myself, playing with my kids on the couch and riding them on my back around the room. I looked through the newspaper everyday for work but was sadly disappointed by the lack of job opportunities in the capital city. I began to pound the pavement, newspaper tucked under my arm. I wanted to impress employers so I wore a pair of Stacy Adams and a pin strip suit I had made while in Japan.

I headed to the downtown circle where multiple businesses lined the Streets. I when door-to-door but had little luck finding a job, but the day wasn't a total waste. I bump into a couple of old flames from my high school days, they saw my wedding ring on my finger but didn't care if I was married and invited me to come by after hours. They even gave me their phone numbers but I drop them in the trash before I reached home. I didn't need any more drama in my life than I already had. I escaped unscathed from my extra marital affair with the Puerto Rican girl and I just didn't need the hassle, so I kept pressing forward trying to find a job. After several days of walking around I just couldn't get any traction, I wasn't making any ground because most of the jobs have moved to Carmel Indiana or out toward 86 street. I was destitute, without a car securing a job was next to impossible.

I returned home that evening less confident than I was before I left. Fortunately for me my wife was big on saving money but we had to dip into our account sooner are later. We discuss buying the car Cindy's Brother had for sale, a 1976 Burgundy cutlass supreme with a half white top and burgundy crushed velvet interior. Her brother kept the car in immaculate condition, the paint was flawless as well as the inside of the vehicle. He wanted two thousand dollars but I Waved $1600 in his face, he didn't even break stride as he ran across the room grabbing the cash tossing me the keys as he walked into a corner to count his new found wealth. I couldn't wait to take the car for a spin and to my surprise Cindy let me take off by myself. I drove to my mothers house showing off the car to my brothers. My eldest brother Rayford con me into buying two old antiquated speakers, he even made an honest attempt to install the speakers but hardly had a clue how to mount them properly in the back of the car. It took three hours and finally they were installed. My sister Sherry yelled out the door, Cindy wants you on the phone, she said bring the car back to the house.

I thought to myself now it starts, I didn't want to look like I was weak are hen pecked by my wife so I hung out for another hour with my brothers, besides I haven't seen them in 18 months. After downing a couple more beers I headed back to Cindy's mothers house. I was greeted at the door with low key aggression as I stepped onto the back porch. Cindy reaching and clawing trying to snatch the keys out of my hand, I shoved the keys deep inside my pocket follow by her hand probing deep into the pelvic region of my pants trying to retrieve the keys. She won that battle, she ran upstairs and hid the keys in a secure place insuring that I would not journey out of the house again that night.

I could understand how she felt but little did she know the more she tried to control me the more she pushed me away, after spending four years in the Marines I wasn't taking any more orders from anyone else. I didn't like being controlled nor did I understand why her mother felt it necessary to talk about me going back to Japan to be with Asian women, it didn't make sense. I thought she was childish and insensitive and only serve the purpose to make Cindy angry. Cindy became more and more of a Klingon refusing to detect herself from my every move. I felt the walls closing in on me. I laid in the bed staring at the ceiling while everyone else slept peacefully. I began suffering from sleep deprivation, I laid in bed listening to the mouse traps snapping the necks of mice foraging for food. I felt totally out of place so I walked downstairs in the middle of the night, staring out the front window onto the quiet peaceful but unsafe streets of 25th and central Avenue.

I knew somewhere among all those thousands of buildings, there had to be a job for me. I felt responsible for my children, I wanted them to live in their own house, sleep in their on bedrooms and eat what they want without having to ask permission from their grandmother. I want my wife to be the woman of her own home and not feel as though she has to tolerate the behavior of her crazy ass mother. Occasionally Cindy showed little respect for her mother, engaging in toe to toe arguments, something my mother would never let me get away with, and I would never disrespect my mother in that manner in the first place. For the most part I thought Cindy was a sweet loving girl until someone did something not to her liking.

I began to grow increasingly tired of staying around the house day in and day out. I didn't have a life and it was getting old, quick fast and in a hurry, but Cindy loved the ideal of me being around the house day after day, 24 hours a day. She loved having me within eye distance and all to herself. I went along with it for as long as I could but I couldn't stand it anymore, so I grabbed the car keys and off I went cruising around parks, hanging out with buddies that I hadn't seen in years. I played a few games of basketball, drink a couple of beers. Just as I was beginning to feel good about my new found freedom it wasn't long before Cindy grew short of patients of my absence. In a fit of rage she walked over to the park, concealing herself well behind a big oak tree and waited for the moment I turn my back to run to the other end of basketball court, then she made her move. She ran to the park bench grabbing the car keys, she jumped into the car and fled back across the bridge toward her mother's house.

I ignore her for the most part because I knew she wasn't going anywhere out of reach so I continued to play basketball until everyone decided to end the game for the night. I was somewhat embarrassed as everyone jumped in their cars and headed off while I had to reluctantly walk home to a place I didn't want to be. I stepped through the front door, the house was very quiet to the point of being eerie, normally her mother was re- peatedly listening to renditions of the song 'clean up woman'. I didn't even smell her cigarette smoke or food cooking in the kitchen. The house was surprisingly quiet, I asked myself.

"Where are the kids?

I noticed the car keys lying on the fireplace, before I couldn't reach them Cindy beat me to the punch, she ran around the chair and jumped over the back of the couch. Without breaking stride she very athletically snatched the keys off the mantle all in one motion. She stuffed the keys in her pocket, wink at me, give me a half smile then pranced her way into the kitchen, summonings me with her finger to the dinner table.

The meal was exiguous, a pair of pigs feet laced with bar-bare cue sauce, macaroni and cheese and collard greens. I thought this meal should be served on Sunday considering it was the beginning of the week. I set at the table and watched Cindy's youngest sister devour her pig feet, bite after bite, ripping the skin away from the bone like a carnivorous prehistoric animal. Cindy prepared a plate of two pig feet and all the trimmings, then proudly slit the food in front of me as though she had prepared a meal fit for a King. I didn't want to be ungrateful but hell would freeze over before I ate those big feet. A knock at the door temporarily distracted Cindy so she left the room for a split second giving me time to shove the pig feet back into the pan, her younger sister watched as I slid the pig feet off my plate settling deep into the barbecue sauce.

"Here, I said, you can have another pigs feet go-ahead take it.

She grabbed the pig feet with her baby hands, and within seconds she begin ripping meat right off the bone.

I gave her a half smile and pat her on head. I put my finger to my mouth signaling her not to tell. I didn't want to hurt Cindy feelings. She was from Mississippi and pigs feet was their traditional type of meal. I had never eaten pig feet in my life, as a matter of fact I have never seen a real pigs foot on anyone's plate before that night. I only saw pigs feet attached to the pigs bodies. The macaroni and cheese was filling enough for me, so I retired upstairs and Cindy followed close behind being ever so demonstrative, slapping me on my butt as I climb the stairs to our room. We sat on our bed occupied by nothing but time, we talked and try to come to a decision about the use of the car.

I felt it was my car because I used my money to purchase the car. Cindy was very pugnacious by nature she couldn't let go of an argument until she believed she won, and other times she would have an affable personality. I told her.

"I don't care about what she thought, I was going to do what I want"

I slipped my pants off and laid back on the bed in my boxer shorts. Cindy casually got up and disappeared into the hallway. I didn't trust her, I knew to stay awake even if I have to use my night vision technique. Several minutes later she came back into the room wearing a provocative night gown totally distracting me from any signs of danger, but I noticed she had one hand behind the her back. She slowly caress my thighs and before I know it she grabbed my penis as if her hands were a pair of vice grips with locking channels, she pressed a razor sharp meat cleaver against my penis.

I didn't care whether she was seriously or not her wish was my command, at that point she totally had me by the balls "literally". I couldn't move or barely breathe, she looked at me with vengeful eyes as she grind her teeth, she leaned forward and whispered in my ear.

"I ought to cut your Dick off"

I jokingly reply" then you won't get any either"

She press the meat cleaver deeper into my flesh angle down as though to make a final cut. She began to draw blood then I let out a hi Octavio Yell that could wake the dead, she released my penis and toss me a towel while shoving the meat cleaver under the mattress. I thought to myself.

"I have agape love for her but I'm not trying to die for it".

I got to my feet and hurried downstairs applying pressure to the wound, trying to stop the bleeding, Cindy came downstairs, place her head on my chest, laughing to herself .

She said, "I'm sorry you'll be okay baby".

To be honest her crazy ass turned me on but she was crazy to the 13th degree and I knew if I didn't get away from her she would do more physical damage and damage that may not be repairable. I didn't know what to do, I was at a total loss. I didn't want to leave my kids, although I trusted Cindy to raise our girls in the past but now I was beginning to have serious doubts about her mental state of mind. She definitely appeared to be quick to anger but she could always sucker me back in two minutes after our fight once she's back to being the sweet angel that I met outside of Saul's subway. She knew where to touch me, and how to touch me, and what to say when she was touching me, yes she had my number and she knew it. I stayed awake most nights thinking about our marriage and how long can I go on facing knives every time we get into a minor argument.

I just didn't know what to do. I was very attached to Michaela but I haven't yet had a chance to bond with Miya. For some strange reason I knew our marriage wouldn't last because Cindy was still mentally wounded by my sexual escapades in Japan. I didn't know what to say or how to say it. Every time we made love she commented on how much better I was at having sex after I return from Japan, therefore; I must've been having sex with a lot of women to develop that kind of sexual prowess. I was pleased that she thought I was good in bed, but I was tired of sleeping with one eye open. I was no longer in the Marines, there was no reason to conserve my night vision by closing one eye while keeping the other one open. I slept with both hands covering my growing, I even thought about wearing a jock strap with a protective cup. Sleeping nude with this woman was a thing of the past, I went to bed fully clothed and slept on my stomach with one eye wide open scanning the area for meat cleavers or flying knives.

Over the next several months I tried everything to be on my best behavior, I stayed at home, not only at home but in the house, only going on the front porch and occasionally to the variety store visible from the front porch. I wanted our marriage to work so I was willing to sacrifice myself but there was one small problem. I needed a job. I couldn't stand being caged in, depression slowly creeped into my murky subconscious. I felt as though I was losing myself for another human being. I felt trapped and couldn't breathe because the walls of Un-marital bliss we're closing in. It was the month of August and I had been out of the military 30 days, my travel had been limited to my mothers house and back home. I couldn't take it anymore so I took off walking until I walked the bore-dom out of my system. I walked up to school #60 just to sit on the steps and reminisce about my childhood. I didn't know how long I was gone or how far I went I just kept walk-ing. Finally I arrive back home three hours later. Cindy was standing in the kitchen with a scarf tied around her head. She stood at the stove boiling hot water with a box of grits in her hand.

She said" These or for you"

I said to myself "I never had grits before this might be a nice change"

I sat on the couch anticipating eating something other than pig feet. Five minutes later Cindy came around the corner with a pot of boiling grits and before I knew it she was drawing back to throw the grits at me. I flipped over out-of-the-way just as the grits splash on the wall. I try to get to my feet but I slipped in the grits and fell back to the floor on one knee. Before I could stand up she came charging out of the kitchen with a butcher knife. Something clicked in me as though it was an automatic reaction. I grabbed her knife wheeling hand and flipped her over my back disarming her of the butcher knife. I tossed the knife on the floor and made my escape out the back door while her brother held her long enough for me to get in my car and drive off. I truly don't think she would've hurt me with the knife but I wasn't going to stay around and find out.

I believe most of the time she was just acting out, putting on a show for her mother or whatever family members she could use as an audience, but unfortunately for her I grew very tired of being in survival mode all the time. I spent one night at my mothers house which didn't make any difference in regard to my sleep deprivation. I still stared out the door at 4 AM, my mind raced like the cars in the Indy 500. I couldn't hold a single thought in my head, I worry about everything, work, or where I will be 20 years from now, my marriage, and mostly about my children. I knew deep inside I couldn't stay away from Cindy no matter how crazy she was, I've grown to love her and it deeply saddened me that we were apart, it bother me more not knowing if we would ever re-pair our marriage.

I spent the next several months living in my oldest brother apartment, off 38th St. We were living the bachelors life, he had an occasional girlfriend spend the night and I had an occasional old flame from my boxing years drop in for the night of sexual ecstasy. I wasn't mentally attached to any of them, my mind was still on my wife, so I shared with all the women before any sex took place that I was married and wasn't going to leave her. I didn't care how they felt or if I hurt their feelings because it was just sex, a cliché, something for the moment and nothing more.

I wanted to give my marriage another chance. Cindy would have to prove her anger was under control and she let go of my past sexual escapade in Japan as I let go of her pass sexual relationship she had with her old boyfriend when I was in Japan. She had sex with one person and I had sex with many and I believe that's what upset her. After end-less months of scouring the newspapers and pounding the pavement I was hired for the graveyard shift as a security guard at a helicopter engine manufacturing plant. It was definitely the good old boys club and I knew in certain terms, I wasn't welcome. They were just filling a quota by giving me the job, either way I didn't care. I just wanted to work. I never thought it would be this difficult for veterans to find work. I was under the illusion that veterans had preference.

That fantasy flew out the window along with all the other idiocies that I learned about being a patriot, serving in the military and waving the American flag with pride. My mili-tary service didn't mean much to employers and it was beginning to mean even less to me. I spent four years operating million dollars worth of equipment, firing artillery shells over the head of troops, coordinating fire, and being a section chief of a 12 man crew service weapon, but none of this could be applied to a civilian occupation. I received $1 million worth of training in the military, but the training was valued at $3.25 an hour in the civilian world. I walked around the helicopter plant as though I was standing guard duty on a military post, with a meter clock neatly strapped to my shoulder, my clothes were finely pressed, my choler fram shoes were buffed to a high gloss.

Every hour I would cruise through the plant. When one guard return to the guard booth the other guards would walk around the plant, punching his clock at selective stations. I hated this job but I had to support myself and my children. I stopped by every weekend to visit with my kids, Cindy was on her best behavior because she wanted me to return home but I was still skeptical of her unmanaged and displaced anger. So I visit my kids then back to my brothers house for a night of running the streets and club hopping. Those nights were beginning to remind me of my old days in Japan, I was free to do what I want and I didn't have to answer to anybody as long as I came back to the base sober. All the club hopping we did didn't amount to much. I never picked up a woman in any of the clubs and over a period of time I was beginning to lose interest. I start staying around the house more. I worked, I went home and every weekend I would visit my kids and take them to the park. I felt empty inside I want to be with my wife but I didn't want to argue and fight.

One day out of nowhere it started pouring down rain, the rain was so heavy I was forced to pull to the side of the road. After five minutes the rain began to lighten, I still could only see 20 feet in front of me, so I drove slow and cautiously taking my time because I had nothing to do and nowhere to go. I saw someone standing on the bus stop in the pouring rain wearing white pants, totally drenched, soaking wet from head to toe. I pulled over and asked her if she would like a ride.

She said, "No thank you"

I said. "Stop playing and get in this car"

At that moment lightning crack across the sky like a whip, she folded her umbrella then quickly jumped in the car. She removed her scarf. She was young and attractive I wanted to see where she lived, so I offer to give her a ride all the way home. In my mind I thought she lived where every other struggling young adult lived, in the Grass Moore Apartments, but she lived on 38th and Emerson much further than I could afford to go so I looked at her, then at my gas gage. I had a fourth of a tark of gas and I didn't want to waste it on someone I had no intimate connection with, but I was overtaken by the size of her perfectly round butt and I wanted to see more so I sacrificed my last drop of gas so I could sneak a peek.

I slowly creep up to the front of her apartment taking my time to make the day last a little bit longer. We sat and talked until the rain stopped, she hopped out of the car and made her way down the long sidewalk toward her Apartment coor. She waved goodbye but I didn't move an inch, I was too busy watching her wide 40 inch butt switch back-

and-forth. She looked back over her shoulders to see if I was enjoying the view. I was not only enjoying the view, I was in total amazement. Once again the blood left my feet and my brain, centralizing in my pelvic region. I got dizzy but was able to refocus before driving off. I knew when and where to pick her up so I made it a habit to cruise by her job everyday in the same place at the same time. I was very friendly, lets make no mistake about it, I wasn't simply rescuing her from a bus stop, I was trying to take one for the team. We dated four weeks but she wasn't giving me any signals about the direction our relationship was going.

I began to wonder if I was wasting my money and my time on her, she was eating me out of house and home. She loved McDonald's barbecue rib sandwiches, I bought her three barbecue rib sandwiches on three different days and still she didn't even let me smell her panties. I was getting sick of her begging ass, she was getting free meals and free transportation home everyday, at this point our relationship was purely platonic. The onus was on her to make the first move. To my surprise she invited me into her studio apartment she shared with her brother. The apartment was arranged like any young persons apartment, quite empty, nothing on the walls. A couch in the middle of the room was the only piece of furniture occupying the two room apartment.

The peep hole on the door was jammed with a wod of paper to prevent anyone from looking inside. The apartment was dimly lit as if they were trying to save money on their electric bill. We sat close on the couch and talked for what seemed like hours. I was close enough to her I could smell the absence of perfume on her body, her lips were chap and dry and she squinted her eyes as she bit into the cold barbecue rib sandwich she had left over from the day before. She offered me a bite but I shook my head no as I watched her savor every bite, as if she hasn't had a meal in weeks. She let out a belch and wiped the barbecue sauce from her mouth with her sleeve then headed into the bathroom closing the door behind her. I sat anxiously on the couch anticipating her next move. The bathroom door was slightly ajar I could see her reflection in the mirror, first she took off her blouse, then her pants, intensify each moment as I watched her like a peeping Tom. She undress all the way down to her black satin panties clinging to her beautiful brown skin. I move to the edge of couch, I wanted so bad to shove the bathroom door open and claim my prize, but I was going to be a gentleman that night so I waited patiently for her to give herself to me.

Suddenly I was summonsed to the bathroom, I leaped through the bathroom door as though I was shot out of a cannon, pushing the door back she was lying in the tub naked as a Jaybird, body shaped like an hour glass, with skin ike Queen Nefertiti. She reached up grabbed my hand.

"Take off your clothes and get in" she said.

But I was too shy to comply with what she was asking because the apartment was too small.

"No I don't feel comfortable and what if your brother comes home " I said.

She pulled me closer and said.

"Don't worry about him he always comes in late"

I still didn't get in the tub but I did help her dry off, taking my time rubbing the towel all over every inch of her well proportioned body, my sexual appetite was being fed.

I felt her warm breath on my neck, I became so concupiscence my eyes went cross and I loss conscious for a couple of seconds. When I came too their she was standing in front of me disrobed, her beautiful brown skin on display, not a blemish are unsightly mark to be found, her coal black hair hung slightly past her shoulder only serve to accentuate her hour glass frame. All of a sudden I no longer felt the financial loss of three barbecue ribs sandwiches, I was about to get paid in full and with dividends. It was my birthday I believe that was the reason she let me make love to her or a better term Break her off something proper.

I didn't love her, at least not yet, we were getting acquainted with one another, one sexual episode at a time. I didn't know if I would ever love her, I was still married and had no intention of leaving my children for her or any other women, as bad as my marriage was I still thought about Cindy and my two girls all the time. I wasn't a perfect husband but I wanted to be a perfect dad. After several months of dating, Gina and I moved in together. I don't know what the hell I was thinking or if I was thinking at all.

She was so toothsome and voluptuous my hormones ran wild not allowing me to think clearly, not with common sense anyway.

Gina and I were both very fortunate to have full-time jobs, our combining incomes didn't even equal $10 dollars an hour. I work for a security company and she worked at a dental office making false teeth. We were doing okay for a while, we went to the movies regularly, and out to dinner on several occasions. I got to meet a few of her girlfriends. One girlfriend in particular (Pat) Gina thought I was having an affair with her but there was nothing between us. She was attractive, very well groomed as if she live at the beauty shop. She had a long slender body with big 36 double D breast. I could see why Gina was a little jealous, it was competition and Gina knew what parts of women I liked. Pat would often come over strutting around the apartment wearing tight blue jeans and her stylus white silk shirt, showing off her figure, knowingly driving me crazy while she set on the end of the couch allowing the sunlight to penetrate through her shirt giving me a view of what she thought I was missing.

After six months of living together I lost my job and so did Gina, and to make the situation worse my car transmission stop working. My car broke down right in front of the transmission shop. I had no choice but to push the car onto the transmission repair lot. The shop wanted $400 to repair the car, I didn't have two nickels to rub together so I left the car at the transmission repair shop and walked 6 miles home. Gina and I spent the summer searching for jobs. I worked for manpower day labor, she worked various jobs throughout the city never finding steady work. We got bored sitting around the house so our sex life blossom. We had sex everyday, sometimes twice a day. Our refrigerator was empty but somehow we seemed to be able to feed ourselves at least once a day. I found myself walking everyday looking for work, sometimes I walked 7 to 8 miles each day wearing a three piece suit and Stacy Adams shoes.

Once I took a bus to apply for a bus boy job at a popular restaurant on the East side of town, to my surprise the line of people stretched around the corner for one busboy position, the word got out that someone already got hired for position through nepotism. I couldn't believe it I'd come all this way for nothing, no money in my pocket, 85° outside and I have to walk home from 56th and Keystone to 30th and Post Road. I was tired of being broke, not having a penny in my pocket. I needed my car out of the shop so I could expand my job search. So I sat outside on my apartment steps contemplating about my life and where I would get the money from to get my car out of the shop. I went for a walk around the block to clear my head. I couldn't help but notice that one man was working at the gas station by himself and then it hit me that's how I could get some money. Rob this gas station.

The next day I walk to my brother Denton's apartment. We sat and talked for a while before he offered me one of his beers.

I said, "Sure I'll have one"

I opened the refrigerator door and to my surprise all the cans were yellow with one big word on the can. 'Beer' I took a sip and tasted nothing but barley. I held the can of beer up in the air and stared at it, there was no inscriptions on the beer can other than the word beer. I try to drink it, making polite conversation then ask if I could borrow his gun. He didn't ask any questions, he open the gun chamber to ensure it was loaded, closed the chamber and handed me the gun.

All that day I cased the gas station across street from the apartment complex, I watch the movement of the men inside, one man went home and the other stayed to close the stop.

"This is it"

I thought to myself putting my ski mask on my head. I slowly made my way across the street towards the gas station. I opened the Chamber of the gun to ensure that it was loaded, suddenly the chamber fell on the ground and the bullets scattered all over the sidewalk.

 It took me 10 minutes to recover the bullets, by that time I could see clearly this was the wrong thing to do so I put the gun away and walked back to my brothers house. I set on the balcony and drink one of his generic beers and handed him back his gun.

The balancing beams of my life were knock off their axles, things were starting to get uneasy around the apartment, our relationship had run its course. Gina and I was spending too much time coupe up in our small apartment, we were beginning to slowly drift apart. Sex couldn't make up for the discontent in our relationship. I try to make our evenings more interesting. I had my daughter come over and spend the night. Cindy did mine Michaela spending the night with me, but she let her come over anyway, and it wasn't without reciprocity. She wanted a full report once Michaela got home the next morning. 6 AM the phone began to ring, it was Cindy requesting that I bring Michaela home right now. I told her I'll bring her home in two hours when I get up but she kept calling and calling until I agreed to take her home.

I arrived at Cindy's mothers house at around 7 AM I knocked on the door then turn the knob. The door open and I stepped inside the house.

"Go up and get in the bed Michaela". I said,.

She ran towards the staircase, she reached the top of the steps then stop and came down midway. She set down on the steps and stared at me as if she was looking right through me.

I waved bye to her and said.

"It's okay baby, go on up to bed"

She got up and made her way up the steps. At that moment Cindy step from behind the door, jumped on my back and place a butcher knife to my throat.

"I ought to cut your fucking head off" she said.

While applying pressure to the knife placed against my throat.

In a split second I did what was natural for me to do, my mind clicked over and I flash back to my hand-to-hand combat training. I grabbed her knife wheeling hand, took one step back flipping Cindy over my shoulder onto the floor. I tossed the knife on the floor then headed for the door. Before I could reach my car Cindy began throwing knives and bricks at me from the front porch. I stood there blocking the bricks and knifes with my hands. She was out of control and I didn't know what else to do so I walked up to her intending on slapping some sense into her but as I swung my hand didn't open. I ended up striking her just below her left eye with my fist. I felt horrible, I felt so bad I grabbed her, hugging her and said.

"I'm sorry I didn't mean to do that, I'll let you hit me back"

Before the words cleared my mouth she cold cocked me cutting my eye in almost the exact same place as hers, but she didn't stop there, she ran to the kitchen grabbing more knives from the kitchen drawer. This give me time to make my get away, as I drove off she ran behind the car throwing bricks, barley missing my driver's door window as I skid around the corner. It would be a month before I went to visit my children again, the meeting would have to be in a mutual place not at a mothers house. I spent most of the summer looking for work or hanging out at the apartment doing nothing. I was extremely bored, some days I would walk from post road to 29th and Talbot St. to visit my mother, then I would walk home later that day. The Marines prepared me very well physically, but not so much in the area of employment. The Marines didn't provide me with any transferable skills, everything I learned in the Marines or thought I knew, I can't use in the civilian world. I was forced to look for low income jobs or to go to college, something I wasn't prepared to do.

I was struggling in all areas of my life, I couldn't see anyway out or any possibility of improvement. I was stuck. Here I was, I had just served my country for four years and I couldn't even get a job as a bus boy. The time we spent clamored in our apartment began to develop into a unrestful situation. Gina and I was beginning to really get on one another's nerves, the sex had run its course. She was young and inexperienced and couldn't take me sexually where I need to go. After having sex five or six times a day, in 3 to 4 hour sessions for six months straight, we both were bored with it. I began to see another side of her, a very childish side of her that would irritate me to no end. She would do little things to try to pick a fight but I would just ignore her and watch TV.

One day she was picking with me just out of spite.

" I never see you get upset" she said.

"Get mad," I want to see you get mad"

I don't remember getting up, before I knew it I grabbed one of my Japanese swords off the stan on top of the TV and put it to her throat, her feet dangling in the air, I didn't notice I had her at knife point until I felt her tears running down my arm. I released her from my grasp, falling to the floor she immediately started scrambling around the apartment packing her suitcase. She was moving so fast you would've thought she was in Boot Camp. Her friend Pat pulled in front of the apartment parking outside afraid to come inside the apartment, she signal Gina to bring her bags to the car. I continued to watch TV, hardly noticing she left until later that evening when loneliness set in. For the first time I was by myself and had time to think about what I was doing with this women and where was this relationship going. I decided to call it quits, I packed my bags and went home to my wife and kids.

My past experiences from the people around me taught me that repairing our marriage would not be easy, and it will get worse before it got better, but I had to try. I didn't want my children to grow up without my influence. I know what it feels like to be without a father and I made a promise to myself I would not abandon my children like my father did to my siblings and I . He walked away from us and lived Scott free of the responsibility of providing for us. The child support bureaus where not as established in the 60s and 70s as they are today. The government didn't actively seek out and put fathers in jail for not providing support for their children, therefore; my mother was left to her own devices to figure it out. I harvest hate and grew a distaste in my mouth for my father and swore I would never abandon my children. I could be a better man but the question remains, was I mature enough to demonstrate the qualities I knew I possessed.

Cindy scour the newspapers until she founded the perfect two bedroom apartment on the westside of town, west of where we both worked full-time. Cindy found a job as a House keeper in the Indiana teachers Association building. I on the other hand became a special deputy sheriff, a fancy term for security guard with arrest powers. We were doing okay, we took our savings and purchase a new front room and dinette set and a new bedroom set for the girls. We were settling into our new apartment and I thought everything was going okay until three months later I received a call from Gina. She was pregnant.

"I want money for an abortion". She said.

Somehow I gather the money, took it to her apartment but she packed up lock stock and barrel, there wasn't a crumb to be found in the apartment. I didn't know where she was so I made contact with a few of her girlfriends. After three days of searching, one of her girlfriends finally confess that she moved to South Bend Indiana. I was infuriated, I drove down the street going 60 miles an hour searching for the first phone booth within sight.

I spotted a phone booth on the Zaryes parking lot, the phone booth smelled of urine, the receiver was cracked and smelled of whiskey breath. But I didn't care I grabbed the phone frantically dialing her mother's number and she answered.

"What do you want"? She asked.

"Why didn't you tell me you were pregnant?"

"I did know at the time" she said.

"Are you coming back to Indianapolis? I thought you were going to get an abortion"

She angrily replied. "No I'm keeping it because I'm tired of you leaving me".

Then she hung up the phone. I set in my car for an hour that day thinking of what a mess I made of my life, what was Cindy going to think if she found out. I just couldn't take any more of her bipolar episodes but in this instance she would be justified in whatever reaction she choosed. I headed to my mother-in-law's house to pick up my children then to Cindy's job to pick her up before we headed back to our apartment. That became our routine for the next 45 days. All of a sudden Cindy stop talking, I had not yet reveal to her Gina was pregnant, even though Cindy and I were separated for one year during that time of the pregnancy. I knew in Cindy's mind that wouldn't matter.

It wouldn't matter if I left the planet and got an alien pregnant on the moon, it wouldn't change the situation or how she felt about the situation or how she would react.

Over the course of three days, our marriage took a turn for the worse. The atmosphere was ripe with anger, with every breath she took the situation appear to intensify. Cindy started communicating physically rather than orally. One day I work the Graveyard shift at a trucking yard. After working eight hours I decided to stop downtown at the donut shop and treat myself to a cup of coffee and a donut, it was only five in the morning, very few people were up moving around on the snow covered streets. I sat quietly in the coffee shop with my back against the wall, seemingly enjoying my favorite pastime, then I realized I had been satting for 30 minutes so I gather my things and drove home. I walked in the door, I knew it, she was totally predictable. My luggage and clothing bag laid on the front room floor. My luggage was sliced into little pieces, my clothes were sprawled all over the floor, as if they were kicked around. 10 seconds later Cindy comes out of the bedroom steaming mad, yelling.

 "Where the hell you been all morning!" I was too tired to respond I just slumped on the couch and looked at her in disbelief.

She said, "Get your stuff and get out"

I was to tired to argue are fight so I grabbed my bags, collected my clothes and headed toward the door. Cindy jumped in front of the door holding two butcher knives, one in each hand.

She said, "You can go but you can't take the car"

I looked at her with a puzzled look on my face.

"There's snow and ice everywhere, I know you don't expect me to walk out of here carrying this stuff in my hand, walking over ice and snow". I said.

Then I snatched open the window which is ground-level and threw my bags and luggage out the window. Getting through the window was a small obstacle to get around because I was still in peak condition from my military service. I picked my bags up and try to run to the car, by the time I got their she had sliced three of my tires. She looked at me and said.

"Now you can go"

I knew there were gas stations nearby within two blocks, so I jumped in the car and threw the car in reverse trying to make it to the gas station before all the air went out of the tires.

Before I knew it Cindy jumped on the hood of the car like a character from the zombie movie and started stabbing the windshield with the butcher knife. I kept driving as if she wasn't even there. I exit the apartment complex hitting ice, sliding sideways onto 38th Street. I turned left heading towards Lafayette Sq, Mall. I proceeded toward the gas stations two blocks away but I wasn't sure If I was going make it so I increased my speed to about 40 miles an hour. Cindy rode on the hood, clutching each windshield wiper helping her to maintain her balance as I did a U-turn into the parking lot of a tire repair station. Just as I came to a stop three of the tires went flat. Cindy stood outside the car yelling, screaming and stabbing wildly at the drivers door window. I set in the car with my hand placed over the trigger of my 357 magnum. It was 6 o'clock in the morning and I thought to myself.

"It's too early for this shit".

Cindy stood there in her cotton nightgown with no shoes and a scarf wrapped around her head clutching a knife, yelling and screaming, she was so angry I don't even think she knew how cold it was.

She must've stood there for at lease an hour making threats, yelling at me to get out of the car. Suddenly Michaela appeared out of the depths of the snow and began walking down the street. I could see her from a distance so I pointed in her direction. Cindy stopped her rage for the moment to take Michaela back in the house. I sat in the car in disbelief not even noticing seven hours have passed. At 3 PM Cindy came back to the car no longer angry. She offered me money for my tires.

She said, "I will not hurt you, it's okay if you sleep on the couch.

She went back to the apartment and I set in the car for 30 more minutes wondering whether or not I should trust her. I went into the trunk of my car and took out my gun shoulder holster. I shove my magnum into the holster and put it under my jacket, leaving my bags in the car. I reluctantly headed back to the apartment for a sleepless night.

I was willing to do anything to be with my children but she was making it impossible for me to stay. I knew at this point she was bipolar and needed help but she had a real sweetness about her. It was hard for me to walk away from my marriage so I stayed the night. I slept on the couch, eyes wide shut, meaning, my eyes were closed but I was very conscious of any movement around the apartment. I felt like a stranger in my own home, not really welcome but just there to support other people and their agendas. The next morning Cindy walked into the room and toss rolled up bills onto the couch.

"This is for your tires" she said, laughing to herself and walking back into the bedroom.

I pick the money up and counted it. It was only $25.

I said, "What is this? How can I buy three tires with $25?"

She looked at me walking back-and-forth between the bedroom and kitchen, smiling and laughing to herself. She really didn't believe I would be able to repair the tires with only $25 and drive the car off, in her mind she had me beat, but I had other plans. While setting in the car earlier that day I noticed a stack of tires in a bend on the side of the building. I returned to my car and began selectively pulling one tire at a time from the massive stack of hundreds of tires.

The tires seemed to be in pretty good shape, I couldn't understand why someone would discard perfectly good tires, these tires had good rubber and deep threads. As I pulled the tires out from the stack it seemed that one tire was better than the next. It was a gold mine of tires. I stacked three tires beside my car then jacket the car up and remove one tire at a time. Carrying the new tire in one hand, I rolled the flat tire down the street two blocks in the snow and slush to the shell gas station. I was charged five dollars per tire to mount the tires on the rim. It was perfect, I couldn't believe it, finally I was given a break and something was working in my favor.

The snow was so deep I had to walk in the street. I slipped and fell on the wet ground in the ice and slush. I didn't even noticed both legs of my pants were socking wet with snow clinging to the bottom until I was finished replacing the tires. I was over joyed. I gladly drove down the street, my car wobbled its way to my mothers house, feeling as though anytime the tires would just pop off and roll down the street. I couldn't tell at the time all the belts were broken in all three tires, but I was able to make it to my mothers house. I set on the couch holding everything inside. I tried to mentally process what had just happen. I took a deep breath leaning back on the couch sighing in relief, the meditation I learn overseas proved to be very adequate in this time of stress and uncertainty.

I was still wearing my work uniform from the day before, and I had to be at work in three hours. I didn't move, I just sat on the couch trying to forget the day and get two hours of sleep before going to work. I didn't know what the future was going to be, the future of my marriage and more important the future of my children. I went to work that night, socks still wet from earlier in the day, stomach growling because I had not eaten since the night before. I arrived at work 20 minutes early so I could compose myself before going into the restaurant. No matter how hard I try I couldn't be the same happy positive person I always was, so I set in my car on the parking lot of Popeyes chicken until I collected myself, gathering strength from places I never knew I had.

I walked in the restaurant, waved at the employees and position myself in the back corner and half hardly watch the patriots enter and leave with smiles plastered on their face. Carrying bags of pieces of caucus home, so they could sit and devour dead relatives of chickens in front of the TV. I was so tired I was in a daze for 10 hours, I wasn't only tired, I was mentally tired. I watch the clock every second tic by slowly as the night drew to an end. I walked outside to my car and discovered that three of my tires were flat. There was a gas station sign flickering a half a mile away. I tried to drive slow on the side of the road but after a half block three of the tires were totally flat and falling off the rims. I called a tow truck then walked in the snow and slush 4 miles to my mothers house. My sister Sherry grudgingly open the door mumbling something under her breath that only made sense to her. I stomped my feet twice on the porch shaking the snow free from my boots. I sat once again on the couch and let out a sign of relief, trying not to think about tomorrow because it would surely bring its own problems.

I set up listening to the house fall asleep, the floor boards squeaked as my sisters settled in for the night. Everyone had somewhere to sleep except for me, I was in the mist of turbulent times in my life. It had been two days since I had eaten, I didn't care, I was focused on buying new tires and re-establishing my life. There were rumors Gina was back in town, but my life was so out of control I didn't want too add to my problems. I tried to stay as far away from Cindy as possible, but it wasn't long before she called my mother complaining about my abandoning her and the kids, and she didn't have a ride to work. I told her what Cindy had done and I wasn't going to buy new tires again. I made arrangements with Cindy to take her to work and pick her up. I dropped her off every night for a month, the drive began to become taxing, by the time I got back to my mothers house it was 1am. It didn't make sense for me to drive all over the city and I didn't get home until 1 AM. So we alter our arrangements. I began to sleep in the front room on the floor the apartment. I left my clothes in the car, only bringing a small travel bag containing underwear, toothbrush and the change of clothes into the house.

Things seem to be going well for a couple of weeks. Cindy and I managed to sleep in the same bed, even having occasional passionless sexual encounters. I still loved her but I slept with eyes wide shut. Mornings came and went, I could tell over the course of two weeks something was bothering her but I just couldn't put my finger on it. Anytime I tried to ask her what was wrong, she just walked into the other room not saying a word. The one thing we agreed on was church but neither of us was in the mood for being preach too. We needed professional marital counseling but neither of us made more than minimum wage. I was barely able to pay the rent, therefore; paying someone for advice about our life wasn't even an after thought we just couldn't afford it.

The exodus

As usual my days were very predictable, you could set your watch by me. I would get off work, drive by Cindy's job, pick her up, stop by my mother in-laws house, pick the children up then drive to the apartment. I was living an uneventful boring life for a 24-year-old young man. I was beginning to believe this was my permanent place and I didn't foresee any changes in the future. We had been living together for over a month and in the process of rediscovering one another, so I thought. I pick Cindy up from work later that evening, picking up and dropping off everyone, doing my usual route before arriving back at our apartment. Cindy didn't say a word the entire time, although I tried to strike up a conversation but she was non-responsive and just stared out the window, seemingly preoccupied with something else. Once we arrived at the apartment I barely had the car in park before she flung the car door open, grabbing Miya by one arm, snatching her up from the back seat. I took Michaela from the back seat and carried her in the house closing the passenger door before I went inside.

I could tell she wanted to try to start another fight so I walk Michaela inside the apartment and say good night to Cindy but she ask me to stay. I stood there for a moment staring at her.

I ask her. "What's wrong with you, why are you so quiet?"

She looked at me teary-eyed and said,

"I just had a hard day at work that's all".

Once again I felt weak for her and stayed the night. I took off my Gun belt, unloaded my gun and placed it high on the closet shelf. I didn't feel like arguing, instead of going to bed right away I sat on the Front room floor and watched the Benny Hill show. Cindy came in the room several times interrupting the TV program by turning off the TV. I didn't know at the time she wanted attention.

I wasn't educated and I didn't have a clue what she was doing, so I sat on the floor, watched TV and ate my cheeseburger until 5 o'clock in the morning. I heard rustling in the hallway, I looked up Cindy was in the closet fumbling around on the shelf near my gun.

"What are you doing " I asked.

I'm just getting my Bible" E xtending her hand out towards me showing me her Bible "see" she said, before going back into the bedroom.

I got up, I walked over to the closet, my gun was still secured in its holster, so I sat back down to finish watching my TV program. I finally decided to call it a night, my stomach was full for the first time in weeks because I wasn't mentally distracted by constant drama. I walked into the bedroom Cindy was lying very still on her side with a very intense stare, she clutched her Bible in her right-hand occasionally flipping through pages even ripping out three pages and placing them on the dresser. I laid in the bed beside her fully dressed. I tried to watch her but I slowly dozed off. I was soon awaken by sounds of pans rattling in the kitchen. I wasn't disturbed because I figured she was just in the kitchen preparing breakfast for the kids so I slowly begin to doze off once more. Unexpectedly I was awaken by a loud bang, I was so tired I struggle to get my focus. I vaguely her heard Cindy call my name, I sprung to my feet, ran into the front room. I looked at her and said.

"What are you trying to do? Why is it so smoky in here? Turn the stove off."

I rushed into the kitchen, turn the knobs on the stove but the stove wasn't on. I began choking from the smoke so I walk over to the window and tried to open it, I heard Cindy gasp for breath so I turned around and in astonishment there it was my 357 Magnum was lying on the floor. Cindy gasping for air, arching her back. I quickly grabbed her and laid her on the floor, placing pillows under her feet, I knew this much from my first aid training, then I frantically ran around beating on the neighbors doors asking for someone to call an ambulance.

My heart was beating at a thousand minutes per second, the police and ambulance arrived within minutes as well as the news. I was order to sit on the apartments steps while the police detectives conducted gun powder burns on my hands and fingers and halfway up my arm with a cotton swab dipped in a clear resolution. Somewhere between all the chaos I was able to call my mother to come pick up the kids. I was placed in the back of a police car and watch them load Cindy in the back of an ambulance and whisk her off to the hospital. I was taken to the downtown police headquarters and placed in a small 9 x 10 room. Carpet padding on the wall with a small metal table placed squarely in the center of the room. I was left alone in the room for what seemed like an hour before a young white female detective came in the room with the a clip board, and tape recorder in hand. She asked questions in duplicate, writing on a pad, and other times using a tape recorder. I walked in the interviewing booth at nine in the morning and before I know it, it was 4 PM.

One tall gangly police Sgt. walked into the room he looked at me and said.

" Your finger prints were all over the gun".

I squinted my face looking at him in total discuss.

"Of course my fingerprints are all over the gun, it's my gun," I carry it to work every day"
I said.

The detective came back into the room telling me I was free to go. I walked out into the lobby and to my surprise my entire family was their in full support, for the first time in my life I saw my entire family in one place just for me. I was still in a daze and overwhelmed by what just happened, it was as if I was standing outside of my body watching myself go through this horrific ordeal.   I was driven from the police station to my mother's house by my brother in-law and my older brother Denton.   Before I could arrived at my mother's house my sister received three calls from Cindy's family threatening my life.

I didn't bat an eye. I was numb by the process I just went through. I didn't want to speak to anyone or think about anything I didn't even know if I wanted to continue to live. I was hurt right down to my core, crippling pain took over my mind and body. I knew I would have to return to the apartment and go through the distasteful process of packing up all my furniture and moving out.

*O*ut of sight out of mind

I knew it would be impossible for me to live in that apartment again. So with the help of my family I packed up and placed all my furniture into a storage bend. My mother and I packed up the bedroom, while going through Cindy's clothes my mother found a suicide letter written by Cindy, explaining why she killed her self. I didn't know my mother found the letter until several days later. I tried to read it but I was still in a lot of mental pain and had trouble processing the information.

Days later we had to go through the unpleasant experience of making funeral arrangements. My mother continue her support, she escorted me to the funeral home, once inside we were direct to a room filled with endless amounts of caskets lined in rows of 5 stretching from the front to the back of the funeral parlor. My eyes found a beautiful pink and silver casket, I had no clue as to how I was going to pay for the funeral. I gave the funeral director the title to my car without blinking an eye. I didn't care what it cost or how long I would have to pay on it. I wanted her to have it. The next day I took my wives clothes to the funeral home but the director said Cindy's mother purchased her a dress. The dress was a loud pink dress with puffy shoulders and ruffled sleeves. In other words the dress look ridiculous, but I was so emotionally distraught I didn't have it in me to challenge her decision. Before the funeral I gave Cindy's mother Cindy's rabbit fur coat, her new watch I bought her for her birthday and several of her rings. The day of the funeral I sat to the right side of the casket, my friend Billy said my brother Denton ask him to sit with me in his absence, so he sat next to me and provided much-needed tremendous moral support.

My grandmother sat in the front row with my sister Marcia. It was reassuring and made me feel better just having her in the room. As the room began to fill with people my cousin excused himself saying that he had to leave to go and open up his studio. I notice most of the family members were Cindy's relatives, there must have been well over 60 of her relatives in the room. I could hear loud bolstering talking coming toward the front of the room.

I looked up and it was Cindy's brother yelling and loud talking, putting on a show for his friends and family. He turned the corner at the end of the chairs and made his way towards my grandmother. Within seconds he was in my grandmother's face yelling and talking loudly at her. I sprung from my chair tearing across the room, before I could reach him Billy grabbed me and pulled me back down in my chair. I fought and dragged Billy and his 300 pounds closer to the fight. All the sudden the sound of screeching chairs intensify as Cindy's family rushed toward the front of the funeral parlor, pinning me against the wall. I was still trying to make my way toward Robbi, burly grabbing his jacket we tussled occasionally slamming into the casket. The casket began to rock back and forth I thought for sure Cindy would row out onto the floor.

My friend Enron heard the commotion and ran from the back of the funeral home with his gun high in the air, and told everyone.

"Get back you're not going to hurt Mikey today".

I didn't have time in that moment to really appreciate what he done for me but I know I am for ever in his debt. The police swarm the funeral parlor and forced everyone to leave.

My mother was out raged by the incident, she called all my family and told them what happen. Cindy's family continued calling and threatening my life, I wasn't phased the least bit. I was totally focused on putting my wife in the ground and going on with my life. Two days after we destroyed the funeral home I bury my wife, everyone in my family that attended the burial was carrying a weapon except for myself. My mother, step father, and brother in-law had pistols in their coat pockets. All of my sisters had knives and my older brother Rayford had a pump shot gun. Two police officers were assigned to me to insure another fight would not break out. I stood silently surrounded by 50 people and I felt so alone.

The preacher was praying but I couldn't hear a word he uttered. I was numb to everything around me, I felt an incredible weight in my heart, it was as if someone had pulled the plug on my life. I knew I had no time to sit and feel sorry for myself I had to keep moving, feeling sorry for myself wasn't going to take care of my children are put a roof over our heads. I tried to get back on point and focus but there seemed to be a quite storm brewing within my personal space, chaos and order were at odds with one another.

For weeks I sat on the back steps of my mothers patio watching my daughters play with their cousins in the backyard. All of my senses were numb. I could see them yelling and screaming I just couldn't hear them, they were very happy, 'ephemeral' for the time being, temporarily forgetting any thoughts of their mothers death. I waited and waited for them to ask where their mother was and if she was coming home, but the question never came.

Throughout the next several weeks Enron would come by my mothers house trying to encourage me and elevate my spirits, but I was to far gone to respond. It didn't matter how often someone tried to encourage me or say kind words my subconscious would not give my mind permission to hear their kind words. Even Sgt. first class Woods from the ROTC program called and try to lift my spirits but too disconsolate. I was lachrymose from visions of Cindy lying lifeless on the front room floor, tubes coming out of every extremities. I was on the mental journey of mortification, as penance I chose to give up sexual relationships. I no longer gallivanted around looking for easy prey. I accepted it as a form of retribution, my predilection for huge breasts and long brown legs had all but mentally disappeared. I had to travel this road of discontent and despair all by myself, this wasn't a jaunt venture, I was trying to live, a peripatetic life. I had to change because until now every bad decision I made had a female accelerant.

When someone commits suicide not only does it kill that person, it damages everything in its path, it disrupts life by creating unsuspecting battles of blame and fault between the survivors.

Sgt. Watford thought it best that I go right back to work rather than sit around thinking about my wife's death, therefore; three days later I was back at work, carrying a new 38 caliber pistol issued to me by my security agency until I could afford to purchase a new gun. Because I carried a firearm I was placed in some of the most economically de- pressed areas in Indianapolis. I worked in these arrears before, but under my current mental status I was in no mood to arrest or handcuff anyone, in fact I didn't even load my gun. There was a time I would have made three arrest in one day but now I just stood in the food freezer and watched the local kids steal the store blind. I knew I was not doing anyone any good so I requested to work 12 hour shifts on the highway, putting batteries in the yellow blinking lights directing traffic away from the construction zone. I found myself working in a small town on the outskirts of Indianapolis. I didn't know the town exist until I started working in that location.

I carried a six pack of beer on the front seat and a nickel bag of marijuana to help me get the ghost out of my head. It worked for a short while but once the high was gone pain rushed my body like someone had lit a match to my soul. I parked behind the con- struction barriers and chucked rocks at the cows on the other side of the fence. I got lost in space and time watching the cows eat grass while I smoked my grass.

I never liked marijuana, it made my head feel weird, and my eyes burn. I got so hungry I left my post and ran to McDonald's every 15 minutes, but I didn't have a choice, my mind was clogged with thoughts of the morning of March 29, questioning whether I could have done something different that would have prevented this tragedy or was I predestined to travel this road. As they say in the Marine Corps I didn't know whether I was shot, fucked, powder burned or snake bite, I was going down shit creek without a paddle. There were organizations that could have helped me but I wasn't aware of any of those resources. I was a very private person and told my business to no one. I was also too proud to ask for help, I like to handle things on my own with as little interference from the public as possible. My greatest fortune was my mother had the foresight to see that I needed space and time to recover so she stepped in and took charge of my girls which gave me a chance to breath and regroup.

The Bible Lesson

I moved into a shabby run down studio apartment on 38th and Emerson, my two girls lived with my mother, giving me time to collect myself and recuperate. The apartment was small. It couldn't have been more than Ft 200.^{2} in the whole apartment, with just a front room and a bathroom. I didn't care about the condition of the apartment because I was never home for more than an hour at a time if I wasn't sleeping. I worked two jobs to ensure that I was mentally occupied for most of my working hours of the day. I worked two jobs back to back, one job so that I could pay child support and the other job so that I could support myself and my girls. I worked non-stop with a two hour break between jobs, with just enough time to change from one uniform to the other.

Each job required me to be constantly on my feet for 12 hours or more. I walked through the grocery stores on one job and on my other job I walked the hallways of a very ritzy apartment complex. I patrolled the complex half asleep and physically wiped out. Cindy was hunting me from within. I couldn't escape thoughts of her in my head, my mind raced constantly plunging me deeper into depression. I work six days a week mostly 12 hour shifts with one day off each week. I spent most of my free time working on my car ensuring the maintenance was up to date. Occasionally I would see a tall woman walking past my car clutching her Bible to her bosom. Her dress hung slightly pass her knees, she gave me a broken smile, never saying a word as she went up the steps into her apartment. Sunday after Sunday she walked pass, this time she waved, acknowledging my presences, she smiled at me then into the apartment building she went.

One day I was repairing a broken center length on the bottom front end of my car. In an instance a shadow was blocking the sun. I stuck my head from under the car to see what had eclipsed the sun. I stared up and there were two long unshaved legs standing right over my head. I polity turned my head to the right trying not to disrespect her by looking up her dress.

I said, " Can I help you?

She said, " When are you coming to church with me?"

She stood their clutching her Bible, wearing a high collar silk blouse, hair tied to the top of her head as if she was a secretary. She wasn't very attractive but she seemed genuine and religious. I didn't feel threaten by her because I was in no mental position to date anyone. I ignored her and continued to work on my car.

She said. "All right" and back up the stairs she went.

Every Sunday she would stop by and invite me to come to church with her, and every Sunday I refused. I was still angry at God for allowing Cindy to take herself away from her children, so I denied her based on the fact that I worked six days a week and didn't want to spend my only day off work listening to a preacher. After three months of her asking me to attend church, I caved in like a cake in the oven.

 Sunday school began at 8: am I was dead on my feet because I worked the grave yard shift at Morrat apartments until 7: am. After four hours of church I was ready for bed, but she wanted to continue on with the bible lesson. Once we arrived back at the apartment she invited me up stairs for more Bible study. I told her I was tired but she was relentless and insisted I come up stairs.

She said, " Come up in 15 minutes"

So I went into my apartment and changed into sweat pants, grabbed my Bible and a pad of paper then headed up stairs to her apartment. I noticed her apartment door was slightly a jared, so I knocked on the door.

"Come in and have a set I'm in the tub" she said. Yelling from the bathroom.

I step inside and looked to my right, their she was sitting in the bathtub with the door partially opened just enough for me to see that she was in the tub. I thought nothing of it so I sat quietly on her couch until she finished bathing. I could hear her drying off and the water draining from the tub, she yelled from the bathroom.

" Close your eyes I'm coming out.

She wrapped a small white towel around her body, hanging just an eighth of an inch below her pelvic area, then she quickly walked into her closet.

I sat on the couch thumbing through my Bible waiting for the Bible lesson to began, all at once she emerged from the closet wearing a black see through night gown. She strutted back and forth across the room purposely stopping in the light reflecting through the window to feed my sexual appetite. I didn't know what to think. Was she trying to seduce me into sex? I thought. Or did she really not know I could see through her gown when she stood by the window in the light. It really didn't matter because I was brain dead and emotionally drained at the moment. I was damage goods, sex was the farthest thought from my mind, for the first time in my life I didn't recognize a sexually opportunity placed right in my face. I sat quietly turning the pages of my Bible waiting for the Bible lesson that never came. Eventually I headed down stairs leaving her sexually aroused and wanting, as I reached the stair case I heard the door slam behind me in sexual fraustation. I returned to my apartment disappointed because I didn't receive my Bible lesson. I opened the door to my dark cold apartment and fell face down on my sofa bed. I was so tired I was asleep before my head firmly touch the pillow and for the first time in two months Cindy's ghost didn't have room to run free in my head. I woke up six hour later, shower and started to get dressed for work. I sat in the chair next to the window tieing my shoes and that was the last thing I remember. I fell asleep sitting up, tieing my shoes. I was an hour late for work that day, my uniform was neatly pressed, my gun was empty but my mind was full.

The same voice played over and over in my head like a broken record.

"She just check out" "she just checked out" "she just checked out leaving our two girls".

I couldn't get the voices out of my head so for the next several months I worked non-stop day and night until I dropped from exhaustion or had no room in my head for thoughts of Cindy, but it didn't work. So I hit the night clubs in between shifts, trying to find comfort in a bottle of liquor. With two half pints of Windsor Canadian, one in each pocket. That wasn't good enough so I purchased two cans of beer, mixing beer and wine all night until I couldn't walk. The irony of the whole drinking event was, I didn't like alcohol. I couldn't stand the taste of it, but I wasn't drinking for enjoyment, I was drinking to get wasted.

I got so drunk I was carried to the door by a co-worker from the grocery store, he pointed me in the direction of my car then shoved me toward the parking lot. I slowly walked, slipping and sliding my way to my car. Ice crumbling beneath my feet and the wind cut through my suit like razor blades. Ice covering the windows and doors prevented me from entering my car very quickly. First I drunkenly chip the ice from the key hold and forced the door open separating the ice from the door hang. I flopped down lifelessly onto the drivers seat and tossed my keys under the front seat. Within seconds I passed out.

I was awaken four hours later by tapping on my window, someone was asking if I was ok, in that instance my fingers began to burn as if they were frost bitten, for a moment I thought I was back in Korea during Jack Frost training. I frantically began searching for my keys, after several minutes of searching I located my keys and managed to start the car. My fingers were stinging really bad I couldn't even make a fist, but somehow I did get my car started. I jumped on the highway heading for home, going 5 miles per hour the entire way. I barely noticed the other cars blowing their horns and flashing their headlights as I crepe down the highway swaying back and forth crossing several lines before exiting the highway on Emerson. I knew I couldn't continue this pace, my life was flashing before my eyes, it seemed nothing I tried was working. I worked two security jobs, both jobs required that I carry weapons. I made just enough money to pay child support and a few of my bills. I couldn't even make payments on the funeral. Cindy laid in Hill Cemetery in an unmarked grave. I couldn't focus on that for the moment, I had to focus on the living. I had to focus on raising my daughters, everything else is secondary. I needed college but at this time it wasn't an option, I wasn't groomed for college as a child and even if I had been groomed for college I would have failed in the process due to my current mental state.

Armed but not so dangerous

Before the weekend I received my new work schedule and to my surprise someone assigned me to work at the grocery store two blocks from Cindy's brothers house located in a low income part of Indianapolis. It was very typical for an armed guard to be placed in dangerous locations even though I knew how to communicate with people, this location was a double threat, so I had to be really careful and stay out of harms way but I also knew Murphy's law. If something could go wrong it will go wrong. One day Murphy's Law showed up. As usual I was in my depressed mood lost in thought and everyone knew it. They knew I wasn't the same man working in their grocery store two months earlier. I had changed and they could see it was a dramatic change. I no longer felt compelled to arrest anyone. I hardly pay attention to anyone walking in the store.

One day two men walked into the store and position themselves on each side of the door. I automatically knew something was wrong, we staired at each other until the store manager signal me over, he said.

"These two men robbed the store the year before" "the men made us all get undress and lay down on the floor".

After hearing this news my heart began to beat faster, my palms were sweaty. I knew my gun was not loaded so I made my way to the back of the store then slipped behind a two-way mirror in back of the meat department. I loaded my gun then went out the opposite end of the storage room out of the view of the store mirrors. I watched the two men in the mirrors as I slowly walked back to the front of the store. I left the strap to my gun holster unfastened and leaned back against the grocery carts with my right hand slung over the trigger. The two men staired at me very intensely, I believe they thought they could punk me and made me back down, but if they only knew what I had just gone through they would've hastily left the store without a hitch. But that wasn't the case so we staired intensely at one another barley bating an eye. The stair off went on for 5 minutes, we were frozen in time, in dead silence, you could hear a pin hit the floor. The two men began to breathe heavy, looked at each other then quickly stuck their hands down the inside their coats, at that moment I fully gripped my gun with my finger resting along side the trigger guard.

Just as I reclined a little more against the grocery carts, the carts began to roll back causing me to lose my balance and fall toward the ground. The two men seize the opportunity and began to pull their hands out of their coats at the same time as I was falling back on the grocery carts. I drew my gun from its holster, simultaneously cocking the trigger back. The gun began to level in their direction, the two men threw their hands in the air and yelled.

"Ok man were gone" then ran from the store.

That incident was a sobering assessment of reality, I knew I could no longer walk around in a daze and put my life on the line for pennies. I had more to be concerned about than myself or just making a living. I was placing my life and my children's future in jeopardy. I felt overwhelmed with life, I couldn't see a way out, if I didn't know any better I would have thought the moon was in my fifth Solar house. I felt trapped, here I was working in a low income dangerous job with no future prospects, not even health and dental insurance or life insurance. I was making just enough money to survive. This ideal of feeling trapped kept me up for nights pacing the floor and staring out the window, wondering about the future of my children.

By this time Gina was trying to reenter my life. I started out just watching my son while she went to work, then occasionally she would come over with her favorite meal, cold cuts and chips with a 2 ounce bottle of Pepsi to wash it all down. We sat on my sofa bed, ate lunch and talk about nothing, trying to reestablish a relationship that would never come into fruition. Love was lost because I had an anger brewing inside of me for her that burned hotter than fire. I was told by family members a few weeks after Cindy passed away, that Gina was calling her on her job and telling her she was going to make me marry her because he was pregnant with my child. It was hard to believe she did all of those things, I just couldn't see that in her spirit. I was totally disappointed in her and could barely look at her without my eyes watering from rage and disappointment.

I just didn't believe she would do that but I was wrong and I promise myself it will be the last time I would be wrong about a woman's personality. I was to trust no one and feel nothing for anyone. I was just going to go through the motions leaving broken hearts on a tearful path. There was no time for tears I had to make a shift in my life but I didn't know where I was going or how I would get their, but I knew I had to do something even if it was drastic. I needed a third income so I decided to take the exam for the Marine Corps reserves, then a light bulb came on in my head so I returned to Active duty in the Marines and was promptly sent back to Camp Pendleton within a week. Traditionally Marines don't allow single parents with children to serve, but I had an ace in my pocket. May had been after me for sometime to marry her but I wasn't ready at the time, but now I was without a choice. She knew my kids very well and they appear to be emotionally attached to her.

I have known May and her family for most my life, so I decided to married my high school sweet heart. Our first attempt at marriage fell by the waist side. With all the uncertainty around me I wasn't sure if I could go through with it, therefore; I didn't show up the day we were supposed to go to the justice of peace. May was thoroughly pissed off and refused to have sex with me.

She said, "I'm saving that for my husband".

I just couldn't bring myself to do it, it had only been 12 months since my wife passed away and I just wasn't ready for another commitment but every time I looked at my girls I grow weaker. I knew they needed a female presences in their life, someone I could trust, someone that I've known for a long time, someone with some measure of integrity. I decided to move forward with the marriage. The next day May wrapped her arm around my arm then she escorted me downtown to the justice of peace. The court personnel asked.

"When do you want to get married?" "Right now" May said, in an authoritative voice.

She wouldn't let me out of her sight for one-second until the vowels were read and we exchanged rings. I was still feeling the wrath from my first marriage, I wasn't certain if I could consummate our marriage. May went into the bathroom to get ready and I set on the couch trying to remove the tension from around my eyes. After she finished taking a shower I went to the bathroom while she laid on the big orange pillow waiting for our first night of marital bliss.

I stalled in the bathroom taking a long shower than usual, trying to psych myself up for a night of passion and unbridle sex. Little did she know I wasn't in the mood. I was put off by the ideal of her being my latest mistake.

"What did I just do?"

I asked myself over and over trying to find a moment of clarity about the shackles of love I once again signed up for. I was still bleeding inside from the mortal wounds of my first marriage. I knew I couldn't love her fully at the moment because I couldn't love my-self. She laid ready waiting on the large orange pillow in the center of the room for our first attempt at making a child. I was just a shell of the person in bed I once was. I no longer care that she had a perfect set of 36 double D's that made me crumble to my knees just from the excitement of seeing them. I was still mentally traumatized by the events of my first marriage. I stayed awake that night staring out the window as May slept quietly on the large orange pillow. I stayed awake watching the nights walkers come out while all the working stiffs prepared for a night of rest.

Once a Marine

My head was full of excitement and fear, I had just re-enlisted in the Marine Corps, something I never thought I would do again. After my first enlistment I thought I was surely finished with the Corp, with banging my knees up, freezing half to death in 30°

below zero weather, running up mountains and going on 24.3 mile forest Marches with full gear. Reenlisting in the corp was the only choice I had. Four years in the Corp would give me time to clear my head, collect my thoughts, make an effective plan for my kids and myself. I was truly the only parent now and I had no time for tears. I had to think five years ahead because my life had become a chess game, every move I made had to be precise because I was playing for keeps. I had a wife and three kids with one on the way. Every move I made at this point in my life was financially critical. I never thought in my wildest dreams I would be married to someone who didn't want to work or come together as a team to secure our financial independence. But that was the reality, she didn't want to work and it was all left up to me.

I was past my prime for taking orders or putting up with anyones non-since. The Corp was full of people that love to usurp their authority or play head games, such as washing trucks while it's raining, cleaning weapons all day, are performing drill from sunrise to taps. The only good thing about reenlisting was I didn't have to go through boot camp again. If I was aware of other options I would not have reenlisted in the Marine Corps. I was never groomed for college, so the thought of going to college or a trade school never enter into my mind. Jobs were difficult to fine. Most days, lent filled my pockets in places money should've been. Trying to support 3 kids on minimum wage wasn't an easy task. I often found myself short changed, with just a little money to pay bills and buy food, I struggle horribly. I needed a break, I needed to go where I could make a decent income and not worry about where my next meal is coming from. The Marines are a tough outfit and because I was a little older I was uncertain weather I could keep up with the excruciating fast pace the Marines demanded. I had to get my life started again so I requested to be shipped out as soon as possible so that I could get situated before my family arrived.

The first thing I had to do was find an apartment near my base Camp Pendleton which was no an easy task. I needed an apartment less than 10 miles from the base entrance, because my camp was another 10 miles inside the base. Cindy's spirit followed us right into the military, walking around the new apartment, peeking out of closets at our children and occasionally scaring May half to out of head.

This marriage wasn't too bad I thought, she's didn't pull knives out on me and her moments of anger could be defused with an evening out to dinner or a small gift. After five months of marriage I began to open up just a little bit, but I was being sexually deprived, never feeling comfortable enough to express myself sexuality free. We were having sex three times a week and I was beginning to develop some feelings for her but my subconscious was screaming

"No! Don't trust it".

I ignored the voices in my head because I want our marriage to work. I was willing to put every part of myself into it even if it meant I had to put my feelings on hold and bend over backward further than I ever had for anyone. I was willing to do it because I want to stay married. I started off right away practicing what I preached, I stayed home, I didn't talk to or chase other women. I spent most of my recreation time running 5 miles a day or watching the cable less TV.

I was with my family seven days a week, except for the times I would deploy to training. We spent the next five months getting to know one another's faults and the things we enjoy. I enjoyed watching her get out of the tub soaking wet and she enjoyed when I took her places and brought her things. I quickly learned she had two deal breaker faults. The first fault was she didn't know how to cook, I knew it was common for many first-time wives to lack in their ability to cook so I ignored it and pretend to like whatever she prepared, such as the over cooked pork chops, shrink down to the size of a silver dollar, it was like eating leather without seasoning. Ravioli fresh out of the can was the other main course I suffered through weekly.

I didn't even complain about her famous meat loaf which taste like cardboard with ketchup poured over it. Her second and greatest fault, she didn't proform oral sex on me, she loved to have it performed on her but she didn't return the favor. Our sex life was very basic, no experimenting in the bedroom, and there was no element of surprise to our love making. She did nothing to make me want her or want to be around her. I knew the exact date, hour and minute we were going to have sex and it drove me crazy. I was bored out of my mind. I'm a Sagittarius and everyone knows Sagittarius are some of the freakiest lovers on the planet, the one thing we hate more then anything else is boring sex.

Within 6 to 7 months of being married she achieved her ultimate goa,l she was pregnant and I must say her skin was as smooth and healthy looking as I have ever seen it. But her insides were turning into something sadistic and evil, she plotted her escape from our marriage day by day, week by week and month by month, decisively and secretively setting money aside in a separate account unknown to myself. Very often she complained about not having enough money but she set around the house watching TV, constantly refusing to work or offer any help with our financial situation, however I did respect her ability to save money but she wasn't very overt and inclusive with the money she squirreled away. After having our daughter she changed her personality like a burnt out lite bulb, the things she did where no longer hidden they were up close and in my face. She became cold and withdrawn, not wanting to have sex, or sleep in the same bed because she felt I wanted to much sex. She spent every waking hour poisoning my daughter's mind by whispering negative thoughts in her virgin ears.

By the time she was 18 months old she wouldn't come with a foot of me. I believe I lost her, never having a chance to bond with her. I was shut out from having any relationship with my daughter. Her mother carried her around the house continuously in her arms not letting her out of her sight more than a second. I was systematically being removed from my daughters life with hate and lies. During the 36 months we spent in Hawaii, she made my life pure hell, not wanting to cook, and being unaffectionate. She never tried to communicate what was bothering her. Our sexual life was cut down to one day a week, just on Saturdays which meant we had a sexless marriage. I did not understand at first but I quickly learned that controlling sex was her way of having power and having control over something in our marriage. I tried everything to make our marriage work but she became more distance and harder to please.

After being on the island for 18 months my unit was being rotated overseas to Okinawa Japan on a six month deployment. I couldn't help but notice May seemed all to happy that I was going away, I spent most of the day packing my gear, she walked back and forth passed the room smiling every time I packed a jacket or a pair of pants. I was truly hoping we could spend four hours making love before I departed for the bus, but she waited until the last 30 minutes before my departure before offering herself up for sex. As boring as our sexual experience was I couldn't turn it down. I would be without sex for six months, so I obliged her for our usual 10 minutes worth of sex. I tossed my seabag in the back of the car then ran back in the house for one last swallow of Kool-Aid. I couldn't help but notice my half pint of peppermint snaps was three quarters gone.

May lead a very secretive life when I wasn't around, she drank liquor and smoke cigarettes but never in my presence. She was very good at making me believe she was someone other than whom she presented herself to be. We rode quietly to the staging area, I remove my bags from the car and got one last unaffectionate kiss before boarding the bus.

I was on my way to Japan once again where sexual pleasure was $15 for 15 minutes and a five minute cab ride to town, but I was a different person with different desires and needs. I didn't see the geisha girls in the same light as I once did. I no longer cared about the banana shows or having women set on my lap half dressed while I bought them water down drinks with the purpose of securing a night in their bed. During my first three months in Japan I spent most of the time penniless. I wrote letter after letter to May requesting that she send me enough money to maintain my uniforms but there was no reply. I had to borrow money from my friends or work their shift as duty NCO for the night. I charged twenty-five dollars to take their shift while they ran wild in the streets of Japan. Being station in Japan without money was like going to Vegas just to watch everyone else gamble and have fun.

There was so many things I wanted to buy for my children and my wife. Not having money left me restricted to the barracks and the base gym. Lucky for me my roommate rented a television for entertainment so I stayed in my room and watched movies most of the weekend. I didn't need money for food but a special treat once in a while would have helped me get through the six months. I was confined to eating mid Rations handed out at the chow hall at 10 PM. Everyone else was going to town, shopping and having fun. I watched as the honcho's (taxi cab) pulled away from the curb heading to BC Street or Gate Two. Okinawa was not unfamiliar to me because I lived on the island in 1980 during my youth as a young Lance Corporal.

I had experienced the island years before most of the men in my unit had joined the military, however; that didn't stop me from poking my head inside the hotels catching the site of a couple of beautiful Asian women. One thing I didn't have to worry about was fornication because I didn't have much money and the small amount of money I did have I wasn't going to wasted on women. Before I knew it I was boarding a ship on my way to South Korea, a place I thought I would never see again. Orders came down that we were to do a beach assault, it wasn't my first time so I didn't think twice about it, but the other young Marines were apprehensive about riding in a U-boat because of the enormous waves. We set out at 4 AM a.m. in the morning wearing flag jackets and carrying our rifles. I thought it odd that we weren't taking our cannons with us. We rode around aimlessly on the ocean for two hours. Huge waves crashed into the side of U-boats nearly drowning us as we held onto the rails.

"Abandon ship," yelled the U-boat Driver.

I thought he had made a mistake, I looked around the boat for holes but the U-boat appear to be intact.

"Over the side, now," he said with a more forceful voice.

The sides were too high for us to jump over, so one man squatted down while the others stepped on his back to jump over the side. I was the first in the water. Heavy ocean waves slammed against me as I fell head first into the water sinking 5 feet then returning instantly to the surface. It took 10 minutes to empty the six U-boats. My first sergeant stood atop a boat yelling instructions for us to lock arms. The waves were unforgiving, we were being slapped around like a rubber duck in a bathtub. I was one of the strong swimmers, so I was given the task of bring in all the stragglers and connecting them to the rest of the line.

The line lasted about 10 minutes, every time a huge wave came crashing down on top of us taking us under water for more than a second, someone would panic and break free of the chain. We spent three hours in the water that afternoon being slam and swallowed up by huge waves. I thought for sure I would get hypothermia if we stayed in the water much longer. I was shaking so bad from the ice cold water my arms almost let loose several times as I rejoin the group after rounding up stragglers. We played in the water until we successfully broke the chain and reform again and again without breaking the chain due to the massive waves slamming against our platoon. To add insult to injury it took twice as long to get back in the U-boat as it did to get out. We pull back into the whale of the ship five hours after we left, my eyelids were all but frozen to the top of my head.

My ears were red and burning, my fingers were dysfunctional. I couldn't even unbutton my shirt to get undress. Everyone's shook like branches on a tree hurrying to relieve ourselves of the below zero wet clothing. I asked myself the question once again.

"What the hell am I doing here"?

Although I just got my first taste of freezing Korean Ocean waters, Korea was much more pleasant this time, we arrived in the spring. The temperature was around 40° much better than my first time in Korea during Jack frost training. We went straight out to the field, my fingers and ears had yet to return to a normal state from the freezing ocean water.

The country side was beautiful, their were rice patties as far as the eye could see. Captain Head woke us up at four in the morning just for harassment. He made us do jumping jacks, sit ups and push ups on the ice cold rice patties. He stood on top of a hill polluting the air with his stogie cigar, smiling to himself. We were told to get a quick cold shave before going to chow. Everyone saluted the Capt. as they walk past him, but I knew better. You weren't supposed to salute an officer in the field, so I abide by the rule and walked right past the captain not even pretending to like or respect him by giving him a salute. The first sergeant reached over to stop me but the captain said let him go it's okay. I didn't think anything of that incident for the moment but it would come back to haunt me a couple of months later.

I show the young Marines how to negotiate with the Koreans, trading their MRE's for Ramen noodle and a soda. Before pulling out I was told to take my sections and patrol 5 miles out. I was given coordinates on a map and a compass. I was the highest ranking member in my section so I was put in charge of 9 man squad. I put the young man in formation then asked the Korean soldier where the restrooms were, he pointed towards the top of the hill. I sprinted up the hill towards the bathroom snatching open the door I looked around and there was no toilets, it was just a big open empty room. I close the door and ran back down the hill. I ask the Korean soldier.

"Where is the restroom, that's just an empty building"

The soldier said, "lift up the board on the floor".

I ran back up the hill and did as he instructed, there was a bottomless pit of a hole in the floor, the hole was saturated with liquefy feces.

"Not again". I thought to myself, this reminded me of the bathrooms in 1980 during our Jack's frost training.

I got fully undressed pinched a loaf, then went on patrol with my man. We patrol 5 miles out checking the area for high explosives or North Koreans along the DMZ. We came across hundreds of dirt mounds with three course meals on plates at the foot of the mounds, we couldn't read the signs but somehow we knew they were grave sites. Koreans were known for burying their families in upright sitting positions. I found the tradition to be strange but nevertheless I respected their burials and instructed my man to do as well. In the distance I could see a huge bundle of wood going up the side of the mountain. The stack of wood was at least stacked 20 feet high, it seemed to move on his own, but the closer we got we could see there was a little old lady carrying all that wood, she had amazing strength.

We spent our day patrolling through their neighborhoods as occupying forces. I never felt so embarrassed as an American. I knew in my heart the United States would never tolerate an occupying force patrolling their neighborhoods, what we were doing was wrong and I felt the worse for it.

The young Marines were impressed with my map reading skills and my ability to use a compass. I wish my commanders felt the same way. We return to Okinawa six weeks later and I was excited about the possibility of being promoted to Sgt. There was one opening for the rank of Sgt. but I wasn't worried, my only competition was a shit bird Cpl. from Canon number five with a very bad attitude, his uniform was wrinkled, his face was unshaved and his booths were never polished. I knew when they selected one of us for the promotion I would win by a landslide. I stood in formation anticipating to be called forward to have my sergeant stripes pinned on.

The First sergeant called the unit to attention then called Cpl. ving to the front of the formation, as he read the promotion order, I couldn't contain myself. I stepped out of the formation and walk away. No one said a thing not even my Captain, as I walked back to the barracks steam billowing from my ears and total disappointment on my face. I work so hard the last two years trying to prove I was a good leader but they gave my stripes to someone that was unworthy of it just to make a point. I didn't care what they did to me at that point I was done with the Marine Corps. I had approximately 2 years left to serve. And if it weren't for my family I would have gotten myself put in the Brig for disobeying orders. I knew I had to get the captain back for passing me over for promotion. I wanted to frag him but I had no means to carry out the ordeal so I forgot about it for now.

All the sudden Japan got colder, I was no longer performing extra duties for my troops. I laid back and let the new sergeant assume his position, in my mind it was sink or swim. I wasn't going to carry him, he would have to do it on his own. I stop talking to everyone for a while I had nothing else to say at the moment, I set in my barracks and read magazines, occasionally staring out the window watching the honchos lined up below the USO waiting to whisk young Marines to town. I envied the young Marines freedom and single life status, most of the young Marines admired my married life, how I spend time with my family, going to the beach on week ends and walking around the base at night, but they were looking from the outside in. I was living in the corner of perception reality. Every thing they thought they knew about my marriage they were wrong, there were rumors that one of the sergeants saw my wife in the NCO club with another man. I was married to a women that only showed love when she had a pocket full of dead presidents or when everything was perfect for her.

The months passed slowly and no money came from home. I wrote home continuously and still there was no answer. Finally a small envelope arrived with $180.00 dollars wrapped in foil. My base salary was 1700 dollars a month after taxes; my wife was keeping well over 1600 dollars to herself, we lived in base housing , therefore our rent was automatically deducted from my pay.

There was no reason for her not to send me money more often. During the last two months of my tour of duty in Japan I got another letter. I noticed the envelope was stamped with an Indianapolis post mark showing that the envelope was coming from Indianapolis. My emotions shifted I could feel the strings of my heart being tugged across the vast ocean from my hometown Indianapolis. I became very incensed and enraged, there was nothing I could do, it was obvious my wife had left me and returned home, to Indianapolis. I spent my last two months trying not to think of the reason for her exodus, she could had done anything she wanted but she chose to set around the house drinking liquor, smoking cigarettes and complaining about what she didn't have.

The six month tour of duty had run its course, my unit rotated back to Hawaii just in time for tourist season on the Hawaiian Islands. As the bus enter the base gate I noticed wife's of other marine's standing on the side walk waiting for their husbands. I didn't bother to look around for a ride home, I knew my wife wasn't there. I walked six blocks home to an empty house, the grass was over grown, spiders webs cover the front pouch and warning letters from the base housing authority were plastered all over the front and back door. Our new 1987 Mazda 626 was covered with rust and cob webs because the car and the house went unattended for more than a month. I could see the signs that this marriage was not going to work, she blamed me for everything that went wrong in the marriage but little did she know it takes two people willing to move forward in the right direction and build on the relationship. My misfortune of burying my first wife just three years earlier left me tender hearted and sensitive, just the thought of her death made my throat tighten and my eyes water. I couldn't speak often of her before I had to remove myself from the presence of others. I was emotionally invested in this new marriage, but my emotions were mixed between two women, my first marriage and the women I was currently married too.

I hate failure and I wasn't going to see my marriage fail. I believed it was all just a misunderstanding and we could work it out. I made several attempts to reach May over the phone but no answer. After one week of calling she finally answered her phone, I Asked her.

"What are you doing in Indianapolis?" "and are you coming back home"?

She said, "No, I'm not, I'm staying here".

I didn't need to hear anymore I slam the phone down, rip the phone cord out of the wall and tossed the phone on the couch. I couldn't believe her arrogant and unappreciative attitude. She practically begged me to marry her but now that she has a legitimate child through marriage she wants to run off and keep the child all to herself. She had me confused with someone else, I wasn't much for sitting around and crying over spilled milk, besides I was sick of her bullshit, so I took a shower, got dressed and hit the night clubs. One of my friends Sgt. Mallory and I headed for Hickcome Air force base NCO club where Marines were not allowed entry unless they were E-5 or above. Mallory drove that night, as it turned out, it was fortunate for me.

Once in the club I scoped the bar with dishonorable intentions in mind, I took my seat in the stands as far away from the crowd as possible. I couldn't help but noticed a Filipino women with long hair stretching down beyond our waistline seating by herself. With my drink in one hand I approach her and asked if I could set with her, she said that her date was getting her a drink. Several minutes went by and he still hasn't returned with her drinks. I took a detour by the bar to check out the competition, there he was with two young attractive women.

I ran back to the table and pointed at her boyfriend ensuring she saw the two well equipped young girls that he was hoping to replace her with. She moved down by the bar to get a better look then returned to me and asked if could leave with her and show her how to get off the base. I was all to glad to help. I hurry her out of the club to the car so fast she tripped and fell grabbing my crotch on the way down. But I was able to catch her before she hit the pavement. We disappeared off the base like a Fantom in the night before he knew she was gone. We jumped in the car and drove to downtown Honolulu and parked at the tennis courts on Waikiki Blvd. We talked for several minutes holding idol Conversation until my beer went flat. I offered to drive us to the nearest liquor store but she said.

"There's no need".

She popped the trunk of her car open and I found her trunk to be an argosy of several types of liquor, beer nuts, chips and ice. I couldn't believe my eyes, she had everything in her trunk that a local bar would have. We sat in front of the tennis courts until 3 AM in the morning drinking mixed drinks and smoking cigarettes, keeping up idle conversations as the liquor and steal smell of cigarettes brought us closer to what we both wanted. Unbridle sex, and a one night stand. I had no feelings for her, I didn't love her or cared if I ever saw her again. I didn't even remember her name. I just wanted a quickie. I wasn't trying to fall in love, I didn't want her phone number, I just needed quick relief after six months of abstinence. The one night turned into three months.

It seemed like every time I was conscious we were having sex, it didn't matter where or what time of the day she wanted it all the time. We went to a bar just about every night, never entering the bar just sitting on the parking lot and drinking our own liquor from the trunk of her car as she smokes cigarettes and told me about her future plans. After several minutes of downing drinks she climbed to the back seat and disrobe, she was always very demonstrative, stretching spread eagle across the seat with one leg on the back seat head rest and the other between the front seat stroking my side with her foot provoking me into action. I watched her from my rear view mirror taking deep drags from her cigarette while seductively rubbing her hands between her thighs inviting me to climb to the back, for the second time in my life I just wanted to sit and talk, but I thought to myself .

"What the hell"

So I disrobed, jumped into the back seat and rode her hard until the mosquitoes got the best of both of us.

We hanged out just about every night, mostly drinking from the ready-made bar in the trunk of her car, talking about future plans and having unbridle sex. It was a nice break and change of pace from the stalemate marital position I was currently in. I didn't like being unfaithful to my wife but she was forcing me out to the streets, and nightclubs due to her unaffectionate ways and her poor attitude of what she believes a wives roll is supposed to be. I was tired of adjusting myself to fit her attitude, I was tired of coming home to meals that weren't fit for human consumption. I was tired of the sexless nights and sleeping alone. I was just sick and tired of being sick and tired.

For the first time in my life someone had more stamina then I. It wasn't long before she began to fall in love, after every sexual encounter, she placed $40 dollars in my pocket and told me to go have breakfast. I didn't think much of it the first time it happen, but after each time we have sex she put $40 in my pocket. I was beginning to take offense to it so I handed her back the money.

She said, "No, you keep it, go have breakfast".

I said, "Wait a minute I'm beginning to feel like a fucking prostitute. I don't want your money, you don't have to pay me, I like you anyway".

This went on for several weeks and the ideal of taking money for sex was beginning to have a negative mental affect on me. I felt like I was using her but of course I knew I was only using her for sex, money wasn't a part of the deal. The longer we stay together the larger the amounts got. Three months into the relationship I finally got a break. Because of my swimming ability I was selected to go to the Navy seal water survival training in san Diego on the other side of the blue Coronado Bridge. She drove me to the airport that evening, as we stood waiting for the plane she noticed two Hollywood celebrities walking past and pointed them out to me. One was my favorite actor in the world and the other one became famous years later because of his infamous murders.

Before getting on the plane she shoved a wad of hundred dollar bills totaling $500 in my pocket. I quickly took the money out of my pocket and put it back in her hand. She became quite upset and shove the money in my pocket then ran off down the ramp and out to the parking lot. Once I return from the water survival training she picked me up from the airport and drove me to a nightclub parking lot, before the car was in park she stripped down to her panties and grabbed me by the collar dragging me into the backseat. She was on fire but I gave her the right hose to extinguish all her flames of desire.

After three hours of pulsating sex she pulled out her cigarettes and a wod of $100.00 dollar bills from her purse, she stuff the money in my shirt pocket.

I said, "What are you doing, please! Don't give me anymore money."

She looked at me and said.

"Keep it, it's for your birthday"

"My birthday is more than six months away"

"Well just keep it anyway, just keep it for me".

I counted the money and it came to $600. Now I was really beginning to feel like a whore. I tried to turn the money down on several occasions and even asked that she not give it to me anymore, but she was relentless as though she didn't hear a word I said. Every time I saw her she was pulling off her panties jumping in the backseat of the car, we were having sex so much I thought my penis was going to go into a coma.

Three months went by and we were having sex everyday, three or more hours during each sexual encounter, it was beginning to be more than I could bare, the money, the sex and the gifts. It was as if she was buying me and I have no choice in the matter but to be brought. I knew I had to do a disappearing act, so I stop calling and meeting her.

Two weeks went by and I hadn't heard a thing and all the sudden a Young Cpl. came into the office yelling about a crazy lady at the legal office telling one of the attorneys Cpl. Gray Robbed her. I jumped from my chair like a Jack-in-the-Box.

"I'm Cpl. Gray". I exclaimed, "Robbery, who was I supposed to have Robbed?"

"There's a lady at the legal office right now saying you Robbed her". The young Marine said.

I grabbed my cover (Hat) and lit out like a bolt of lightning down the steps and onto the catwalk. Their she was standing in front of my Captains door, I grabbed her by the arm.

I asked her. "What the hell are you trying to do?"

She looked at me then striking me on the shoulder with her fist.

"You're a shit" she said, looking at me out of the corner of her eyes.

"Come on let's go" I said, as I pulled her into her car and off we went across the airstrip and down to the beach.

She appeared upset but I knew exactly what she wanted so I didn't even hesitate are put up a fight. I parked the car in a secluded place climbed into the back seat then let

her have away. She jumped up and down on me for several hours, crying and screaming, professing her love for me. I didn't love her, I never loved her, therefore; I set there
unaffected by her rants and raves about how much she loved me. All I could do was
what I knew how to do, we made love until she relented.

After an 2 hours of pulsating sex we climbed back into the front seat to discuss what
was on her mind. She sat behind the steering wheel of her car, lit her cigarette, reclining her seat back she paused for a minute then turning to me with teary eyes.

She said, "Marry me Mike"

Then reaching into her book bag she pulled out $15,000 dollars cash, still band togeth-
er with paper bank straps, looking as though the money came straight from the bank.
She placed five stacks of money on my lap. I took a deep breath and thought about the
possibilities of a better life. My wife has already left me once and it wouldn't surprise me
if she did it again. I just looked at Luz suggestively as if I might consider taking her offer.

Talking to myself "Only if I wasn't married it would be possible".

My marriage was in ruins but I had to give it another chance. I've known May since the
third grade and beside she's the mother of my child. I had to see my marriage through
to the end. Luz reached across the seat and grab my hand, squeezing it, nervously

looking deep into my eyes, she increased her offer to giving me half of $875,000.00 dollars.

"Where are you going to get that kind of money?" I said, $15,000 is one thing but $875,000 is another.

I didn't believe her of course, so she pulled out a letter from the real estate Company located in Los Angeles. The letter stated the airport wanted to purchase her land located right outside of the fence line. The land was large enough to occupy 14 homes. It wasn't even a second thought, I knew she wasn't a young woman. She was 52 years old, she would need the money to support herself a lot sooner than I. I was only 28 years old and had a full life ahead of me, she was already at the halfway point between life and death. I didn't want to take her money. I didn't even feel comfortable with the $40 she was jamming in my pocket after every sexual encounter.

It reminded me of the time my mother would make me cut my elderly neighbors grass. They could not afford to pay me because they were on a fixed income, and my mother reminded me not to take their money. But the old man refused to let me cut his grass without giving me something, so he shove three dollars in my pocket once I finish cutting his yard. Although the old man paid me, I still learned the lesson my mother was trying to teach me. Help someone who can't pay you back. In other words it doesn't cost anything to be kind. With this life lesson I never used a women or anyone else for that fact and I wasn't about to start with using Luz, so I turned down her offer. We parted ways that evening and I never saw her or heard from her again. I guess she finally got the message that I couldn't be bought. That was a crazy sexual maze I would never forget and all of a sudden I wasn't mad at May for being such a horrible wife anymore. I missed Luz, I often felt the absent of her presences. Most of all, our sex wasn't on a schedule and it lasted far longer than 10 minutes.

I didn't have to pretend I was anything other than my self when I was with Luz, I didn't have to give her handfuls of money, I didn't have to constantly entertain her, I didn't have to beg her to cook a decent meal or have unplanned sex, and most importantly I didn't have to explain to her how to treat her man when he's trying his best. Six months had gone by and I was still living in Hawaii alone, I hung out at the beaches and seemingly had my pic of the foreign tourists but I decided to let it pass me by because I didn't believe I could endure another crazy romance. May refused to return home and I refused to let my marriage end but I wasn't going to kiss her butt or beg her to come back.

Finally May's mother told her she couldn't live with her, she convinced her that she was grown and married and needed to be with her husband. So she returned seven months after she had departed. She looked horrible, her face was broken out with acme from constantly eating french fries and potato chips. I could tell by her attitude she didn't want to be here but she had no choice at this point in her life. As she came out of the terminal I notice she only had my youngest daughter with her. I went to the terminal door and peek down the hallway, I turned around and hunch my shoulders, asking.

"Where is the girls?". I said.

"I didn't bring them" she said.

"Well that's fucking obvious, why not?".

"I didn't have the money."

"I told you to go to the military administrative office on Arlington Road and they would have issued you free tickets for them."

I couldn't believe she had done such an insensitive thing, I was furious. I told her to bring my girls with her when she returned but she purposely ignored me. I needed to see my girls and I wasn't leaving the island until they had a chance to experience it for themselves. I began to pull out all stops, any and everyone I could talk too that had authority. I did just that and two weeks later I flew to Indianapolis and brought my girls to Hawaii. I believe my deceased wife was speaking to me from the grave, I felt compelled too have my girls with me and not 5000 miles across the ocean. Somehow I knew Michaela was struggling with her emotions and she needed to be around her dad.

I arrived at my mothers house two weeks later on Monday afternoon. I walked in the door, my mother was standing in the kitchen ironing my girls clothes and packing their suitcases. My daughters looked up and saw me and both came running with arms wide open. I kneeled down on one knee to huge both my girls. I squeeze them tight as if I hadn't seen them in years. Michaela smiled from ear to ear happy as she could be to see her dad, it made me feel good that I could go get my girls and bring them back to Hawaii with me. I could feel the distance between us and I had to have them with me at all cost.

The plane was so crowded I couldn't get tickets to sit in the same roll with my daughters, but someone was kind enough to switch seats with me so that we could all sit together. The five hour flight was grueling, Miya became very fidgety after two hours in the air, so I let her walk up and down the aisle to stretch her legs, then eventually she fell asleep and didn't awake until we landed in Hawaii. This was probably one of the happiest times of my life.

I was very glad that I could give my girls this experience. Once we landed I was surprised May drove to the airport to picked us up, and for once she even seemed happy with their arrival. I could blame her for being a horrible wife, but she seemed to be a much better mother than she was a wife. I still didn't trust her fully with my children, she was an emotional wreck herself. Confused about what she wanted to do in life and who she wanted to be. Rather than paying her own way through college she blamed the Reagan administration for her failures in college, not being able to finish her training in television production due to financial aid cuts. Blaming would become her trademark in our marriage, blaming everyone for everything around her instead of fixing her life herself. I believe she was internally depressed and wanted me to give her something that I was ill-equipped to provide, 'a sense of purpose'.

Often I would find   May setting on the couch at two in the morning watching TV. I watched her from a distance as she sat quietly eating her bowl of Ramen noodle with a glass of peppermint snaps tucked beside her thigh slightly out of view.

I asked. "Why are you sitting out here at 2 AM in the morning'

She said, "You cry in your sleep over Cindy" and it drives me crazy.

I guess I never got over my wife's passing. I thought about her constantly, I couldn't help it, she was a permanent part of my memory, set deep in my murky subconscious, thoughts of her were automatic, she was forever fermented in my head. I quest May couldn't compete with the thought of another women hanging out in her house, the thought of their mothers sprit watching over her children scared May partly out of her mind.

Months passed and I thought I would have forgotten about Luz by now, but every time I sat on the beach and let the ocean water wash up against my feet thoughts of her come home like truth. I smiled every time I thought about her and her crazy ways. The way she loved me unconditionally and the freedom I felt when I was with her. Those were good memories but when I left the beach and returned to my house and walked through the door all those good memories fade away into thin air returning me to a sobering assessment of reality. I was sick of surviving on a E-4 salary and having a wife that complains about money but never attempted to earn any. I was sick of being depressed, and being in a dysfunctional marriage. I was sick of not being able to make love to my wife anytime I wanted too. I was sick of not having a good home cooked meal. However; I did get some joy out of life, Sgt. ving got his comeuppance that year. A young Lance Cpl. was standing fire watch, he got bored in the middle of the night and decided to take a hit of acid.

The acid had very little effect on him, he lost his patiences, so he decided to take another hit. Within seconds of the second hit of acid the Young Lance Cpl. begin to flip out. He called the officer of the day requesting to go to the hospital. The officer of the day asked him what did he take, the young marine refused to answer the officers question. The officer told the young marine.

 "I'm not going to transport you to the hospital until you tell me what you took and who you got it from".

The Young Lance Cpl. Inform the officer that Sgt. ving sold him the drugs. The next morning Sgt. King was arrested and escorted to the Brig. After his trial he received five years in Leavenworth prison in Kansas City. I wasn't jumping for joy over another man's misery but I couldn't help but smile when I walk pass my Captains desk. I gave him the stink eye and a smirky look, with a broken smile.

I said to myself," how do you like those green eggs and ham, asshole."

I couldn't believe they gave that shit Bird my Sgt. Stripes, but it all worked out in the end for the better good. Before I knew it we were shipped back to 29 Palms Desert for 12 weeks of training. I couldn't wait to get this trip over with because it will be my last trip to Twentynine Palms and when I return to the base I would have at exactly 12 months left in the corp.

Once again we reached Twentynine Palms base and drove all night into the desert until we were far from the main base, as soon as the trucks stopped I jumped out the back and dust a pound of sand off my uniform. Sgt. Tubman called out my name while simultaneously tossing me a round ball. I reached up and caught the ball with my hand. The ball turned out to be a small cactus covered with thorny pin pricking needles. I shaked my hand violently trying to get the cactus off my skin, the harder I shook my hand the more the cactus crawl up my arm. I stopped flinging my arm around long enough to take out my K bar knife and cut the cactus off my arm. I looked at Sgt. Tubman with a look that could kill, but all of a sudden I had an idea. I began walking around picking up the small cactus with a pair of wire cutters, placing them in my cover and storing them under my cot for later that evening.

I patiently waited all night until everyone was asleep. I walked off a hundred meters from the Canon and fired up a heat tap to make my cup of mocha. I left my stove burning, making the fire watch believe I was 100 m away cooking. To distract the fire watch I tossed a can in the opposite direction of their position, like idiots they follow the noise, then I crept up the hill to the Captains tent. I stood outside the tent for several minutes to ensure he was asleep. I could here low tone snoring coming from inside the tent so I put on my night vision goggles and stepped inside the tent quickly as though I was reporting in. I shine my flashlight with the red lens around the room and "bingo" there he was lying on his side with his back towards the door. It couldn't have been a more perfect situation. I creeped over step-by-step, using my wire cutters I sat each cactus from head to toe down inside of the sleeping bag, then I crapped out of the tent and back to cooking my coffee and cocoa.

I lay on my cot and nibble on a chocolate bar from my C rations. I stare up into the emptiness of the night watching the stars race across the sky. I love the twilight hours, it was my favorite time in the universe, the entire world was dead to me, everything was standing still. It was as if I was the only survivor after an apocalypse.

At 4 AM I could hear my first Sargent and Captain talking in a very low voice and all of a sudden the Captain came bursting out of the tent yelling and screaming as he ran out into the Baron desert clawing and ripping at his back trying to remove the cactus that rolled all over his body as he shake vigorously trying to remove the cactus balls. Two Marines tackle him while a third tried to extract the cactus balls a with pair of pliers. I sat quietly in front of my Canon heating a cup of coffee while I watch the spectacle unfold. I didn't even pretend like I was going to help him or cared. I laughed so hard I almost spilled a very good cup of mocha. Fragging him almost made me feel better about not being promoted to Sgt. I was able to move on with my Marine Corp career that I knew would end in a few short months, I was no longer angry at the Capt. are the Marine Corps for the fact. I was done with the ideal of serving my country and I no longer wanted to play Marine. My new life and the civilian road I was about to face, would challenge me, emotionally, physically, and financially to the limits of stress I had yet to encounter.

Our time being stationed in Hawaii and my military service has come to an end. I sent my family back to Indianapolis while I looked for work and a place to live in Los Angeles California. I left the base with $640.00 dollars to my name and a bus ticket to Los Angeles. I stayed in a rundown hotel in the center of downtown Los Angeles that had a community bathroom I shared with six other families and roaches the size of my thumb.

It was my first time staying in downtown LA and I wasn't taking any chances so I hide the remainder of my fortune behind the roach patrolled mirror in my room and ventured out onto the streets of Los Angeles. The sidewalks were smother with the dispossessed living in card board boxes and panhandling for money. I had little money but felt come pelt to share what I had with those less fortune than myself, little did I know it was faith come calling. I was riding the city bus looking for work but not making much progress, so I decided to walk around the city and take in the sights. At last I saw a big party at a small park across the street,

"This looks like fun I thought"

So I made my way toward the park. Just as I stepped off the side walk a huge city bus came to a screeching halt right in front of me, the doors fling wildly open.

"Get on the bus' the bus said.

I looked at him with a puzzled look on my face,

"What," I said.

"Get on the bus!" Adamantly he saids this time.

"I don't have any bus money" I said.

"That's ok I will take you a few blocks".

We traveled about a mile, before the bus driver explain the reason for picking me up. He said the park I was head toward was a gang members park, where the Southern Mexican gangs hungout. I thought for sure at the moment my guardian angels were truly watching over me. Later that evening I stayed close to the hotel, not walking more than two blocks in any given direction. I peeked in the windows and to my surprise I was able to watch a television soap opera being filmed.

 I walked the streets and rode the bus lines for two days looking for work. Everywhere I went it seemed as though they were shooting a movie. Extras for the movie were lined up on the street, the motion picture cameras were on high lifts, other personnel were carrying boom microphones. I thought it was cool to see a movie made up close and personal but I had more pressing issues to think about, my money was dwindling fast due to hotel and food expenses.

I had to make a decision due to my shortage of funds and the lack of resources, I was forced to return to my enclave in Indianapolis. The bus ride was 2 1/2 days long. Sitting in an upright position with an empty stomach made the trip extra difficult. The bus to stopped to pick people up from the middle no where, alone side the road and near corn fields, some of the bus stations were just local bus stops with a sign sticking out of the ground attached to a metal pole in the middle of no where. I felt very vulnerable and in-secure as I stood in total darkness three hours waiting alone in some desolate spot for the bus to arrive.

The bus trip home cost $180.00 using up all the money I had left. I didn't even have money for food. I rode the bus for 2 1/2 days, with an uneasy feeling settling in my stomach. I was starving until one kind gentle man struck up an idle conversation about the military. I politely listened as he spoke. I passively shake my head in agreement while my stomach grout loudly. He stop talking long enough to reach into his sandwich bag and offered me a vegetarian lettuce and cheese sandwich, normally I wouldn't accept food from strangers but under these circumstances I grabbed the sandwich without hesitation and gormandize the sandwich to nothing but crumbs in my hand.

I arrived in Indianapolis on Monday evening about four pm. It was a much different feeling than living in Hawaii, the Air even smelled different, it felt heavier and wet. I took my seabag out of the bottom of the bus storage and walked from the bus station to my mothers house. It was about a 3 mile walk, I couldn't help but reminisce about the time I walked home from downtown Indianapolis after spending all my money on a new pair of converses tennis shoes.

Everything seemed so different and new. A new wave of Hispanics migrated into the area making the city polychromatic as well as multicultural. It was a far cry from when I was a child, the city was primarily occupied by blacks and whites, with a very small population of Asians. I had never seen a Hispanic person until 1978 when I enter Marine Corps.

The city had changed drastically, I was so amazed by the new features in the city and the scenic view I was getting, I didn't even notice how far it was from the bus station to my mothers house. It was a strange feeling as I walked down Meridian Street. The street seemed different but very familiar, and before I knew it I was turning the corner at Saul Subway. I couldn't help but smile as I look at the empty parking lot full of memories the younger generation will never know about. I stood on the rendezvous part of the sidewall where I met Cindy for the first time. I paused to consume the essence of her memory and allow my mind to capture the moment that change my life forever. I was uncertain about a lot of things in my life but I wasn't uncertain about Cindy's menacing presences.

www.ingramcontent.com/pod-product-compliance
Lightning Source LLC
Chambersburg PA
CBHW070830310526
45788CB00017B/17